All You Need is

HELP!

Rory Hoy

NEW HAVEN PUBLISHING LTD

Published 2023
First Edition
NEW HAVEN PUBLISHING LTD
www.newhavenpublishingltd.com
newhavenpublishing@gmail.com

All Rights Reserved
The rights of Rory Hoy, as the author of this work, have been asserted in accordance with the Copyrights, Designs and Patents Act 1988.
No part of this book may be re-printed or reproduced or utilized in any form or by any electronic, mechanical or other means, now unknown or hereafter invented, including photocopying, and recording, or in any information storage or retrieval system, without the written permission of the
Author and Publisher.

Cover Image © Shutterstock Vector
Cover Design © Pete Cunliffe

new haven

Copyright © 2023 Rory Hoy
All rights reserved
ISBN: 978-1-912587-90-2

CONTENTS

Introduction	5
CHAPTER ONE - JOHN	7
CHAPTER TWO – PAUL	21
CHAPTER THREE – GEORGE	84
CHAPTER FOUR – RINGO	123
CHAPTER FIVE - OTHER MEMBERS	154
CHAPTER SIX - JOHN AND PAUL	159
CHAPTER SEVEN - JOHN AND GEORGE	171
CHAPTER EIGHT - JOHN AND RINGO	174
CHAPTER NINE - JOHN, PAUL AND GEORGE	179
CHAPTER TEN - JOHN, GEORGE AND RINGO	180
CHAPTER ELEVEN - PAUL AND GEORGE	182
CHAPTER TWELVE - PAUL AND RINGO	183
CHAPTER THIRTEEN - GEORGE AND RINGO	193
CHAPTER FOURTEEN - PAUL, GEORGE AND RINGO	206
CHAPTER FIFTEEN - JOHN, PAUL, GEORGE AND PETE	209
CHAPTER SIXTEEN - JOHN, PAUL, GEORGE AND RINGO	214
CHAPTER SEVENTEEN - PEOPLE WHO HAVE WORKED WITH THE BEATLES	217
CHAPTER EIGHTEEN - WHERE ARE THEY NOW?	234
References	241
About The Author	242

INTRODUCTION

The Beatles are, arguably, the most successful band in musical history. They have sold around 800 million records worldwide and have pioneered the way popular music is today. Chances are, you will know at least one of their songs, and if you don't, you are probably living under one very hard rock!

The four canonical members of of the band - John Winston Ono Lennon, Sir James Paul McCartney, George Harrison and Sir Richard Starkey AKA Ringo Starr - were very prolific musicians before, during, and after they were in The Beatles, and they were never idle, always doing something in the music and film industry throughout the decades. In my previous book chronicling our fabulous foursome, *The Beatles - Acting Naturally*, I talked about their work in film and television, and how they remained in the public eye through acting and performing in various television and film appearances, as well as performing on stage. Of course, they never quit their day jobs, and they all had successful solo careers. As well as their own individual musical adventures, they also helped out on other people's records and projects. On someone else's recording, you may catch George playing slide guitar, Ringo might be on drums, and John or Paul could be singing backing vocals. Throughout the years, you may have been listening to something by someone else, which has some sort of Beatle magic, without you realising it!

As you will have gathered by now, this book chronicles The Beatles' collaborations with other artists, both individually and collectively. For instance, did you know…

-There are numerous Beatles/Rolling Stones crossover records?
-Ringo Starr once collaborated with Vera Lynn?
-The Beatles were secret pioneers of hip-hop?
-Paul McCartney had a drunken collaboration with an obscure band from Portugal?
-There are many numerous Beatles "reunion" records?

If not, read on!

To quote our boy Ringo - Peace and Love, Peace and Love!

Rory x

CHAPTER ONE - JOHN

Some people say he was a dreamer, but he wasn't the only one. John Winston Ono Lennon was the reason why The Beatles existed. He originally formed a skiffle group called The Quarrymen in the summer of 1956, which in 1960 became the band we know and love as The Beatles. As well as being a very talented musician and songwriter, he was a peace activist, an artist, and a poet, and he had a wicked (but sometimes cruel) sense of humour. He was also known for lending a helping hand on a few of his friend's tunes (especially during his "lost weekend" period, when he separated from Yoko Ono for 18 months and made headlines with his wild, alcohol-fuelled behaviour). Here is a selection.

    Artist - Darren Young (AKA Johnny Gentle)
    Title - I've Just Fallen For Someone
    Year - 1960 (released in 1961 and 1962)
    Label - Parlophone

Johnny Gentle (real name John Askew) was born on the 8th December 1936 and, like The Beatles, he grew up in Liverpool. His connection with The Beatles was a very important one, as he was partly responsible for the Fab Four's very first professional engagements (when they were The Silver Beatles), backing Gentle during a May 1960 tour of Scotland. It was during this time that Gentle wrote the song 'I've Just Fallen For Someone'. Assisting him was none other than John Lennon, who, to this day, remains uncredited. The very first professional recording of this song was by the famous British teen idol, Adam Faith, in 1961; it appeared on his self-titled album on Parlophone Records, making it the very first composition co-composed by a Beatle to be put on wax officially. It was arranged by the famous John Barry, who was best known for composing the theme music to the James Bond movies.

Gentle himself recorded his own version under the alias of Darren Young, also on Parlophone Records, in 1962, as the B-side to his single 'My Tears Will Turn To Laughter'. Despite selling well, with 30,000 copies sold, the song failed to chart.

Artist - The Jimi Hendrix Experience
Title - Day Tripper
Year - 1967
Label - Unreleased

NOTE – This is actually mislabeled as having involvement from a Beatle, so it is here to set the record straight.

Jimi Hendrix, in a nutshell, was a guitar god. This afro-haired virtuoso was revered by all guitarists at the time, and still is to this day. He also covered the opening title track from *Sgt. Pepper's Lonely Hearts Club Band* in his live gigs, learning it almost immediately after the song came out, something which, to this day, still amazes Paul McCartney.

Apparently, John Lennon reportedly provided backing vocals on Jimi's cover version of The Beatles' classic 'Day Tripper'. Sadly, this wasn't the case: this was misinformation provided by bootleg albums. In reality, this was a recording of a studio session of Hendrix's band, The Jimi Hendrix Experience, for BBC Radio 1, and the man actually providing backing vocals was Experience member and bassist, Noel Redding.

Artist - Grapefruit
Title - C'mon Marianne
Year - 1968

Label - RCA Victor

Grapefruit were a British psychedelic rock band who were formed in 1967 and disbanded in 1969, then briefly reformed in 1971. They were one of the first bands to openly use the vocoder, preceding many of the famous acts to use it by several years. The band were named by John Lennon, using the same name as his future wife, Yoko Ono's, book, which was published in 1964, before she and Lennon met.

The song 'C'mon Marianne' was originally written by L. Russell Brown and Raymond Bloodworth, and was popularised by The Four Seasons; it would later be covered by Donny Osmond in 1976.

Grapefruit's version was recorded in 1968 at Trident Studios in London, and the brass section was arranged by an uncredited John Lennon. Despite the song having lots of commercial potential, it was only a modest success, reaching No.31 in the UK Singles Chart. 'C'mon Marianne' would later be covered by The Beatles themselves, as they played it during the *Get Back/Let It Be* sessions of 1969.

Artist - The Rolling Stones
Title - Salt Of The Earth
Year - 1968 (released in 1996)
Label - ABKO

That other massively successful group from the 1960s, still massive today, The Rolling Stones (or just simply, The Stones) are pretty much the greatest rock band of all time not named The Beatles. They were set up by their manager, Andrew Loog Oldham, as the "bad boys" of rock 'n 'roll and the antithesis to the clean image of The Beatles. Their classic line-up included Mick Jagger, Brian Jones (1942-1969), Keith Richards, Bill Wyman and Charlie Watts (1941-2021) and their story is for another book! The Stones and The Beatles were friends, and respected each other; in fact, The Stones' first major hit in 1963, reaching No.12 in the UK charts, was their version of the Fabs' 'I Wanna Be Your Man'.

1968 saw them release the album *Beggars Banquet*, and its finale song was a little number entitled 'Salt Of The Earth'. This was also the year of their TV concert special *Rock and Roll Circus* (which actually didn't get shown in public until 1996) and, as with the album, the concert ended with 'Salt Of The Earth'. For this rousing finale, a supergroup was formed called Dirty Mac, featuring John Lennon on guitar and vocals, Eric Clapton on guitar, Keith Richards on bass, Mitch Michell of the Jimi Hendrix Experience on drums, Ivry Gitlis (who had performed with the world's top orchestras) on violin and Yoko Ono providing "vocals".

It was the closest thing to a supergroup with both The Beatles and The Rolling Stones, and a classic tune in the deeper cuts of The Stones 'extensive back catalogue.

> Artist - The Rolling Stones
> Title - Is Winter Here To Stay?
> Year - 1968 (released in 1996)
> Label - ABKO

'Is Winter Here to Stay? 'is a lesser-known tune from The Rolling Stones' discography. It was also played by the Dirty Mac supergroup in the *Rock and Roll Circus* TV special.

This blues-inspired song would later be revisited in 1973 as a Yoko Ono solo tune from her album *Approximately Infinite Universe*, which coincidentally features Mick Jagger on guitar.

> Artist - Bill Elliot and The Elastic Oz Band
> Title - God Save Us
> Year - 1971
> Label - Apple Records

The late Bill Elliot (July 28th 1950 - June 6th 2021) was a member of the musical duo Splinter, who worked with George Harrison for his Dark Horse label. They were musically compared to The Beatles. In 1971, Elliot released a solo single in collaboration with The Elastic Oz Band, which was a pseudonym for John's Plastic Ono Band, entitled 'God Save Us '(initially titled 'God Save Oz 'in a shout-out to the radical left-wing magazine *Oz*, which was then facing an obscenity trial). Lyrically, it's very similar to Lennon's protest songs of the time, and John also played electric guitar on it. Initially, this was going to be a Lennon solo single, but for contractual reasons, the vocal was given to Elliot. Lennon's version was released in the 1998 box set *John Lennon Anthology*.

The B-side actually didn't feature Elliot, and was a strange Lennon/Ono piece called 'Do The Oz', which was designed to promote a dance craze that didn't catch on. This track (as well as 'God Save Us') was produced by the infamous Phil Spector.

Despite the Lennon connection and commercial sound, the song failed to chart. As far as the magazine *Oz* was concerned, in both Australia (its country of origin) and the UK, the creators were prosecuted on charges of obscenity. They were later both acquitted (after initially being found guilty) in two separate trials, one in Australia in 1964 and the other in the UK in 1971.

More on Splinter later in the book...

Artist - Tibetan Chants
Title - Tantric Llamas Parts 1 and 2
Year - 1971
Label - Apple Records (unreleased)

A very mysterious recording, which is said to have stemmed from the sessions of the David Peel album *The Pope Smokes Dope* (read on later in the book for more info on this). According to David Peel himself, he brought 30 people off the streets of New York City to record some Tibetan Chants. This session was recorded on the 16th December 1971 at the Record Plant (East) studios, and the producer for the session was John Lennon, but according to John's ex from the "lost weekend" era, May Pang, Lennon and Ono stamped their names onto many random things that they didn't actually have hands-on involvement in producing, meaning that Lennon's involvement may have only been superficial.

Artist - Elephant's Memory
Album - Elephant's Memory
Titles - Crying Blacksheep Blues/Gypsy Wolf/Wind Ridge/Power Boogie/Local Plastic Ono Band
Year - 1972
Label - Apple Records

Elephant's Memory were a New York-based American rock band which lasted from 1967 to around 1976, probably best known for backing John and Yoko Ono from late 1971-1973; in fact they were sometimes billed as The Plastic Ono Elephant's Memory Band. Their sound is a tribute to 1950s rock 'n' roll, but with a harder, contemporary edge. They got their initial start when two of their songs ('Jungle Gym at the Zoo 'and 'Old Man Willow') were used in the soundtrack to the 1969 John Schlesinger drama *Midnight Cowboy*, starring Dustin Hoffman and Jon Voigt (father of Angelina Jolie).

Naturally, they were signed to Apple Records, where they released their self-titled album in 1972 (in an act of confusion, they had also released another album with the same name in 1969 on Buddah Records). The 1972 Apple Records incarnation of this album was produced by John and his wife, Yoko Ono.

On the Kansas City-esque sounding song 'Crying Blacksheep Blues', John provides backing vocals and also plays guitar. John also sings backing vocals on the song 'Gypsy Wolf' and so does Yoko (whose backing vox are quite drowned out in the mix). Lennon also plays electric piano on 'Wind Ridge ' and both he and Yoko sing backing vocals on 'Power Boogie ' (which features some guitar work from John). The album closes with the song 'Local Plastic Ono Band', which has backing vocals from both John and Yoko.

Elephant's Memory would later team up with Ono on the 1973 album *Approximately Infinite Universe*, notable for containing the song 'Death of Samantha', which would inspire the name of an American punk rock band.

Artist - David Peel & The Lower East Side
Album - The Pope Smokes Dope
Titles - The Ballad Of New York City/The Pope Smokes Dope
Year - 1972
Label - Apple

David Peel (1942-2017, real name David Rosario) was a New York-based "street rock" artist, who was a hippie and stoner icon, and liked to sing about 'Mary Jane' and 'Pigs'. He was also infamous for discovering the controversial shock rocker GG Allin. The best way to describe his music is that it's basically folk, but with almost punk-like vocals.

On April 17th 1972, Peel (backed by Manhattan group The Lower East Side) released the album *The Pope Smokes Dope* on Apple Records. It was produced by John Lennon and Yoko Ono. On the song 'The Ballad Of New York', John and Yoko provide backing vocals, and to promote the release, Peel, Lennon and Ono appeared on the BBC TV series *The David Frost Show*, performing it live, with John playing tea-chest bass, skiffle style.

John and Yoko also provide backing vocals on the album's title track 'The Pope Smokes Dope '- it's a good rhyme! The song also features a sample of a John Lennon interview.

The album was a commercial flop, reaching only No.191 in the US *Billboard* album chart.

Artist - Phil Ochs
Title - Chords Of Fame
Year - 1972
Label - Unreleased

Phil Ochs was a transgressive poet, singer/songwriter and peace activist from the USA, who was active throughout the 1960s and 70s, until his tragic suicide in April 1976 aged only 35. He was known for his sharp wit and political activism, and he took part in many protests and rallies of the time. He unfortunately suffered from mental health issues, including bipolar disorder, and a nasty bout of alcoholism.

A recording of him jamming with John Lennon singing his Dylan-esque ditty 'Chords Of Fame' has surfaced on bootlegs. The original song was released in 1970 on Ochs 'album *Greatest Hits* (ironically an album of new material). It would later be covered by Melanie, Teenage Fanclub, Daniel Johnston, Marianne Faithful and Krysia Kocjan, who sang with my dad's band, the Natural Acoustic Band, who played it in their live sets.

This version was originally recorded from an audiotape from around 1972 which was personally owned by Lennon himself. While Lennon doesn't contribute to anything vocally, the recording begins with a fascinating conversation between the two musical legends. *Chords of Fame* was also the name of a 1984 documentary about Ochs.

Artist - Frank Zappa
Titles - Scumbag/Well (Baby Please Don't Go)/Jamraa/Au
Year - 1972
Label - Apple Records

Frank Zappa was a one-off eccentric, as well as being an awesome guitarist, producer, songwriter, singer and film director, who recorded 75 albums, and covered pretty much every genre known to man and woman before his death in 1993. He also named one of his children Moon Unit (nowadays Moon Zappa)!

On the 6th June 1971, Frank Zappa and his band, The Mothers Of Invention, held a concert at the Fillmore East venue in New York, and for a four-song encore, John and Yoko joined them on stage for an improvised jam, which included 'Scumbag', 'Well (Baby Please Don't Go)', 'Jamraa' and 'Au'.

This was later included on Lennon's *Sometime In New York City* compilation album in 1972, as well as Zappa's 1992 compilation *Playground Psychotics*

Artist - Crowbar
Title - Rocky Mountain Tragedy
Year - 1973
Label - Epic
NOTE - It is unknown if Lennon actually played on this record.

Crowbar were a 1970s Canadian rock band from Hamilton, Ontario, best known for their 1971 hit single 'Oh What A Feeling'. They were Ronnie Hawkins 'backup band during the 70s, and still perform today, doing the odd sporadic concert appearance.

1973 saw the band release their self-titled album containing the song 'Rocky Mountain Tragedy'. Apparently [32], John and Yoko contributed some vocal work alongside Lennon's "lost weekend" flame, May Pang, and Lou Reed. It was recorded at the Record Plant (East) Studio A in New York City circa July or August 1973. It was produced by Jack Douglas, who would later produce Lennon's final solo album *Double Fantasy* in 1980, as well as the song 'Move On Fast 'for Yoko Ono for her 2016 LP *Yes, I'm A Witch Too*, giving the rumours of Lennon and Ono's contribution to this song a little more credibility.

Artist - Mick Jagger
Title - Too Many Cooks (Spoil The Soup)
Year - 1973 or 1974 (not released till 2007)
Label - WEA/Rhino

The king of the chicken dance, Sir Mick Jagger, is of course the charismatic front man for The Rolling Stones. He is known for his incredible voice and stage presence, and is still a cool guy, even though he's nearly 80!

In 1973, during John Lennon's infamous "lost weekend" period, Lennon produced a very funky tune for Jagger - a cover version of Willie Dixon's 'Too Many Cooks (Spoil The Soup)'. It was recorded in LA around the time of Harry Nilsson's *Pussy Cats* album, and a lot of Lennon's solo band appeared on this tune (and others) including Jack Bruce (of Cream fame) on bass, Al Kooper on keyboards, Jim Keltner on drums, Jesse Ed Davis on guitar, Bobby Keys on sax and Nilsson himself on backing vocals.

The song didn't see a commercial release until the 1st October 2007, when it appeared on the compilation album *The Very Best of Mick Jagger*.

Artist - Elton John Featuring John Lennon And The Muscle Shoals Horns

Title - I Saw Her Standing There
Year - 1974 (released 1975)
Label - MCA Records

Sir Elton John, better known to his mother as Reginald Dwight, is a legendary British singer/songwriter and pianist who has sold over 200 million records worldwide, and to this day he holds the record for the best selling song in UK singles history with his 1997 remake of his tune 'Candle in The Wind (Goodbye English Rose)', which he performed in tribute at the funeral of the late Princess Diana. It sold over 4 million copies in the UK and 33 million copies worldwide. In 1992, he established the Elton John AIDS Foundation, which has raised over $600 million, with programmes in 55 countries. On a lighter note, he is also known for his eccentric and flamboyant dress sense, which would sometimes even make Lady Gaga blush - that Donald Duck outfit springs to mind!

On the 28th November 1974, John Lennon would join Elton John for Lennon's final live concert appearance before his tragic assassination in 1980. Elton had previously helped Lennon out with his single 'Whatever Gets You Thru The Night', and in return, Lennon appeared in this show, which took place at the gigantic Madison Square Gardens in New York City. One of the songs they performed together was 'I Saw Her Standing There', which, of course, was the opening song to The Beatles 'debut LP *Please Please Me* in 1963. Lennon announced the track as one he had originally performed "with an old estranged fiancé of mine called Paul". They also sang 'Lucy In The Sky With Diamonds 'from *Sgt. Pepper*, and the aforementioned 'Whatever Gets You Thru The Night'.

This recording was released as the B-side to Elton's 'Philadelphia Freedom 'single, which came out in 1975, and this live recording (as well as the two live songs mentioned above) was released as a single in March 1981 on DJM Records (Dick James Music) to capitalise on renewed interest in Lennon after his death. It reached the lowly heights of No.40 in the UK Singles Chart. It was the first time this tune made it into the aforementioned chart.

Yoko Ono was in the audience for the concert in 1974, and had sent the orchids that Lennon and Elton John sported on stage. She was backstage afterwards, but it was a little later when she and John eventually reconciled again after John's infamous "lost weekend" period.

After this show, John Lennon would never perform on stage again. When he came off stage, he said to journalists who were waiting," It was good fun, but I wouldn't like to do it for a living."

Artist - Elton John Featuring John Lennon And The Muscle Shoals Horns
Title - Whatever Gets You Thru The Night
Year - 1974 (released 1981)
Label - DJM Records

See' I Saw Her Standing There'.

Artist - Elton John Featuring John Lennon And The Muscle Shoals Horns
Title - Lucy In The Sky With Diamonds
Year - 1974 (released 1981)
Label - DJM Records

See' I Saw Her Standing There'.

Artist - Maschine Nr.9
Title - Maschine Nr.9
Year - 1974
Label - Phillips

Maschine Nr.9 was a German one-off sound-theatre project headed by Wolf Wondratschek, Bernd Brummbär and Georg Deuter. It is similar to the experimental records John made with Yoko Ono with their infamous 'Unfinished Music 'series, featuring spoken word, weird electronic sound effects, and heavy sampling. One of the samples used was the Beatles (ahem, Lennon solo) experimental piece 'Revolution 9 'and the *White Album* closer 'Good Night', and Lennon even receives an acknowledgement in the record's liner notes, suggesting that the sample was officially cleared by him, making it one of the few very rare instances of The Beatles being legally sampled. It also contains samples of Ted Kennedy, Pink Floyd, Timothy Leary, Donald Duck, and what sounds like an early use of turntable scratching, preceding hip-hop pioneer Grand Wizzard Theodore's claim of inventing it by a couple of years.

If you like Lennon and Ono's weird experimental tunes, then you may enjoy this. Also, the name Maschine Nr.9 is very similar to Revolution No.9.

Artist - Harry Nilsson
Album - Pussy Cats
Titles - Many Rivers To Cross/Don't Forget Me/Old Forgotten Soldier/Save The Last Dance For Me/Rock Around The Clock
Year - 1974
Label - RCA

Harry Edward Nilsson III, mostly just simply known as Nilsson, was a singer/songwriter legend who was a good friend of The Beatles, especially John Lennon. He was best known for his hits 'Everybody's Talkin '(from the hit movie *Midnight Cowboy*) and 'Without You '(originally written and recorded by Badfinger, famously covered by Mariah Carey), and he was also known for his eclectic back catalogue, covering everything from pop to rock and, with his amazing effortless vocal range, even crooner music.

1974 saw the release of his album *Pussy Cats* and it was produced by John Lennon during his infamous "lost weekend" era - an 18-month period in which Lennon was accompanied by Nilsson, May Pang (following his temporary split from Yoko Ono) and various others. These months seemed to consist of drinking, drinking and more drinking - and some rather controversial behaviour from our Beatle hero.

The opening track of the *Pussy Cats* album was a cover of a song by reggae legend Jimmy Cliff entitled 'Many Rivers To Cross'. Lots of artists have covered this song over the years including Joe Cocker, Percy Sledge, Cher, Desmond Decker, The Animals, The Brand New Heavies, Linda Ronstadt, Annie Lennox, Bryan Adams and many more.

Another notable tune on the album was 'Don't Forget Me', which is a beautiful ballad with Nilsson's trademark crooning. Seriously, Nilsson should have been as big as Frank Sinatra or Bing Crosby, his voice is that good (but perhaps his stage presence wasn't?)! Another stand-out song was 'Old Forgotten Soldier', featuring Nilsson doing some more beautiful crooning. Why haven't more people heard of him outside of hardcore Beatle nuts like myself and 1970s music aficionados? Maybe it was his wild hedonistic lifestyle that didn't get him that next level up?

There were also some more great cover songs on the album including 'Save The Last Dance For Me', a cover of a classic song written by Doc Pomus and Mort Shuman and popularised by The Drifters with Ben E. King on vocals, and a reworking of the classic song 'Rock Around The Clock', made popular by Bill Hailey and The Comets, which has the so-called distinction of being the first rock 'n' roll song.

Speaking of first rock 'n 'roll songs, just for fun, check out Virginia O'Brien's 'Rock-A-Bye Baby 'from the Marx Brothers film *The Big Store* in 1941!

Artist - David Bowie
Title - Fame
Year - 1975
Label - RCA Records

The late, great David Bowie (real name David Jones) was one of classic rock's finest. He was one of the most acclaimed stars of the second half the 20th century. This theatrical character performed under many pseudonyms, and had a very eclectic (not to mention very good) discography, and detailing his colourful career would take a book in itself to cover. He also did 'The Laughing Gnome', which he preferred to forget!

In 1975, he teamed up with none other than John Lennon for the very funky ode to dissatisfaction at being at the top - 'Fame'. Bowie and Lennon met in 1974 during the infamous "lost weekend" period at a party thrown by actress Elizabeth Taylor. The two of them became good friends, and they jammed together in early 1975 at the Electric Lady Studios in New York City, and during this jam session, sowed the seeds of what would become the single 'Fame'.

The main track was recorded at the Sigma Sound Studios in Philadelphia, where many great soul records of the 1970s were recorded. While John's lyrical contributions were minimal, he would provide backing vocals as well as playing acoustic guitar with Bowie's guitarist, Carlos Alomar, coming up with the song's iconic guitar riff.

Despite only reaching a somewhat modest No.17 in the UK Singles Chart, it was a massive hit in America, reaching No.1 in the US *Billboard* Chart, and two remixed versions were released in 1990 - a house music version and a hip-hop version with guest vocals from US rapper, Queen Latifah. These new versions were a moderate success in European countries. The original track is still loved by the fashion industry, along with other Bowie hits.

Artist - Lori Burton
Title - Answer Me, My Love
Year - 1975
Label - Collector's Guide Publishing

Lori Burton was an American singer, songwriter and producer who wrote songs for Lulu among others, and she also contributed backing vocals for Lennon's solo hit '#9 Dream'. Born and raised in Connecticut, Burton came from a musical family, with her brother, James Anthony, being a fill-in drummer for Karen Carpenter of The Carpenters, and her father was a singer and saxophonist who had a 15-piece band called the Jimmy Nichols Orchestra (not to be confused with the temporary Beatles drummer, Jimmie Nichol, from 1964). In January 1975, in the midst of his "lost weekend" period, John was assisting engineer Roy Cicala at his Record Plant East studio in New York City. One of the songs that Lennon produced during this session was a disco cover of Nat King Cole's hit 'Answer Me My Love'.

It sadly never saw a commercial release until 1998, when it was featured on the supplemental CD that came with the book *Beatles Undercover* by Kristofer K. Englehardt [32]. Another upbeat version of the same song was a hit for Scottish singer Barbara Dickson in 1976, reaching No.9 in the UK Singles Chart. Coincidentally, Dickson performed the music for the 1974 successful Willy Russell West End musical *John, Paul, George, Ringo and Bert*.

Artist - Lori Burton & Patrick Judd
Title - Let's Spend The Night Together
Year - 1975
Label - Collector's Guide Publishing

The second of the songs Lennon produced for Lori Burton, this time a cover of The Rolling Stones 'classic 'Let's Spend The Night Together', which was met by some controversy when it came out, due to its risqué lyrics. In 1973, the song would also be covered by David Bowie.

This was also a collaboration with a musician named Patrick Judd.

Artist - Lori Burton
Title - The Big Hurt
Year - 1975
Label - Unreleased

Another tune from the same sessions as 'Answer Me My Love 'and 'Let's Spend The Night Together'. This is a cover version of the 1959 pop song 'The Big Hurt 'written by Wayne Shanklin, which was a hit for Toni Fisher when it reached No.3 in the *Billboard* Top 100 in the US and No.30 in the UK Singles Chart. Other versions of this song have been performed by Del Shannon, Wes Montgomery, Scott Walker, Vikki Carr, Nick Cave and others.

Artist - Dog Soldier
Title - Incantation
Year - 1975
Label - White Label

Dog Soldier (not the hardcore punk band of the same name) were a rock collective who were signed to United Artists Records in 1975 and only had two records released - a self-titled album, and a single entitled 'Pillar To Post'. They consisted of Derek Griffiths, Keef Hartley, Mel Simpson, Miller Anderson and Paul Bliss. Their song 'Thieves and Robbers 'would later become a popular 'breakbeat 'tune with hip-hop producers, thanks to the open drum break at the beginning of the track. Interestingly, their name was originally going to be Community Apple, though this was probably changed so that it wouldn't get confused with a certain record label.

On the 22nd January 1975, they recorded a session at the Record Plant East in New York City, performing three cuts - 'Incantation', 'April Rainbow 'and 'Everyday Living'. These sessions were produced, alongside Roy Cicala, by none other than John Lennon during his "lost weekend" period. According to Lori Burton, who was also present at the recording sessions, the tune was originally going to be called 'Jubilation', but it was Lennon who rewrote the lyrics and gave it its name of 'Incantation'.

Artist - Dog Soldier
Title - April Rainbow
Year - 1975
Label - White Label

See' Incantation'.

Artist - Dog Soldier
Title - Everyday Living
Year - 1975
Label - White Label

See' Incantation'.

CHAPTER TWO – PAUL

Sir James Paul McCartney is a really nice bloke, not to mention "the cute one". Having had the privilege of bring invited to meet this legend backstage in 2018 (see my previous Beatles book, *Acting Naturally*), I can confirm the above! Paul has music running through his veins, and is probably the most eclectic of the Fab Four. He arguably doesn't get the recognition he deserves for his wide ranging musical talents and collaborations; he was the first one to explore the avant-garde scene, and experimental music. Not many people can do both classical and hip-hop and succeed in both!

Artist - Johnny Devlin & The Devils
Title - Won't You Be My Baby
Year - 1965
Label - RCA

Johnny Devlin & The Devils were a rock and roll band of the 1950s and early 1960s, based in New Zealand, featuring their aforementioned lead singer and guitarist, who, at the time, was hailed as New Zealand's answer to Elvis Presley (his haircut didn't help!). According to Johnny Devlin himself, he has sold over 200,000 singles and he still performs in New Zealand and Australia today. He is probably best known for his 1958 cover version of Lloyd Price's 'Lawdy Miss Clawdy', which was an iconic local one-hit-wonder at the time.

His 1965 single 'Won't You Be My Baby' was written in 1964 and, according to Devlin, Paul McCartney helped with the writing process. This claim has some credibility, as Johnny Devlin & The Devils were one of the support acts on The Beatles' 1964 tour of Australia and New Zealand. The tune was recorded at AWA Studios in Sydney, Australia, circa January 1965, and it was released later that year. The song would be reissued again in 1979.

Artist - Cliff Bennett & The Rebel Rousers
Title - Got To Get You Into My Life
Year - 1966
Label - Parlophone

Straight outta Slough (you may remember it from the hit UK TV sitcom *The Office*), Cliff Bennett & The Rebel Rousers are an R&B group who were established in 1957 and had two top ten hits - 'One Way Love' in 1964 and the tune we are covering in this book, 'Got To Get You Into My Life', which reached No.6 in the UK Singles Chart in 1966. Brian Epstein became their manager back in 1964, and they were also signed to Parlophone Records, as were The Beatles.

As you would expect from the title, it's a cover of the Beatles track from the *Revolver* LP, and this is one excellent, critically acclaimed cover version. The track was actually produced by none other than Macca himself! They would later cover the *White Album* cut 'Back In The USSR' in 1968, but sadly it didn't chart.

Interestingly, a recording of them performing The Olympics' track 'Hully Gully' is often mistaken in bootlegs as a recording of The Beatles performing at The Star Club in Hamburg.

The Rebel Rousers are still touring today, minus Cliff Bennett.

Artist - The Escorts
Title - From Head To Toe
Year - 1966
Label - Columbia

Not to be mistaken for the US group from the 1970s and 80s, The Escorts were a fellow Merseybeat group, lasting from 1962-1966. Members included John Kinrade, Mike Gregory, Peter Clarke, and Terry Sylvester, who would later join The Swinging Blue Jeans and The Hollies after leaving the band. They were, in 1963, the 9th most popular group in Liverpool voted by readers of *Mersey Beat* magazine (have a wild guess who No.1 was?) from a competitive field of several dozen popular Liverpool groups from the period. Looking at their publicity photographs, with their hairstyle and dress code, they were obviously emulating a certain Beatles.

1966 saw them release their final single 'From Head To Toe' on Columbia Records (they were previously signed to Fontana) and playing uncredited tambourine is none other than Paul McCartney who, according to others, helped the band in the recording process. Not much documentation exists about this session, other than that it was featured in an article for *Mersey Beat* magazine by Bill Harry. It was recorded on a late afternoon at Maximum Sound Studios on Old Kent Road in London, which was used by the likes of Manfred Mann, Ian Dury, The Damned, Marmalade, The Heat, and Motorhead, and it was where Musical Youth's No.1 hit 'Pass The Dutchie' was recorded. The studio subsequently burnt down, and was later converted into an Asda supermarket in 2004.

Artist - Peter and Gordon
Title - Woman
Year - 1966
Label - Columbia

Peter Asher and Gordon Waller were a British pop duo who were pretty popular during the "British Invasion" of the mid-1960s. Peter was, in fact, the brother of the beautiful actress Jane Asher, who was dating Paul McCartney at the time, making the Beatle connection rather apt. Their debut single 'A World Without Love' was a massive hit, and it was written by the songwriting team of Lennon/McCartney (more on that later in the book!).

Not to be confused with John Lennon's 1980 hit single of the same name, 'Woman' was written by Bernard Webb, which is a pseudonym for our good friend, Sir Paul McCartney. The reason for Macca not being credited under his real name was to see if Peter and Gordon could have a hit record without the crutch of a Beatle (the publishing credit of Northern Songs was something of a giveaway, though!).

It did pay off, however, reaching No.1 in Canada and No.7 in New Zealand, though it did more modestly in the US and UK, reaching No.14 and No.28 in those countries respectively.

Artist - Chris Barber & His Band
Title - Catcall
Year - 1967
Label - Marmalade

The late Chris Barber was a British trad jazz icon whose career spanned seven decades. He was a pioneer of the skiffle movement, which sowed the seeds for acts like The Quarrymen (the proto-Beatles). He played the trombone and the double bass, and in 1959, he had a hit record with the single 'Petite Fleur', which reached No.3 in the UK Singles Chart. He and his band had previously covered Beatles hits 'Can't Buy Me Love', 'From Me To You', 'I Saw Her Standing There 'and 'She Loves You 'in 1966 for French label Disques Vogue for the EP 'Joue Les Beatles'.

1967 saw Barber release the single 'Catcall', which started life as a Lennon/McCartney instrumental piece called 'Catswalk'. It was conceived around the end of 1958, and was a staple in the early live shows of The Beatles.

McCartney gave the song to Chris Barber, and Barber's version was recorded in late July 1967, and was eventually released as a single on the 20th October of that year. Paul also provided uncredited backing vocals, and it was also published by The Beatles 'regular publishers, Northern Songs. It would reappear in 1969 on Barber's album *Battersea Rain Dance*. The song sadly failed to chart.

The Beatles 'own version of the song has surfaced on bootleg recordings which are said to be rehearsals from the Cavern Club sessions around late 1962. Another bootleg version exists, this time from the *Get Back/Let It Be* sessions, said to have been recorded circa 24th January 1969.

Artist - The Beach Boys
Title - Vegetables
Year - 1967
Label - Capitol

NOTE - There is no confirmation of this, but evidence suggests that McCartney's involvement is very likely.

The brothers Wilson (and cousin Mike Love and school friend Al Jardine) were America's de-facto rock band in the 1960s and are often regarded as the US's own rivals to our beloved foursome. Their most famous member would have to be the incredibly talented (and incredibly eccentric) Brian Wilson, and he pretty much became the unofficial leader of the group by the mid-1960s. Like The Beatles, they were pushing musical boundaries at the time, must to the distaste of member Mike Love, who supposedly wanted Brian not to "f**k with the formula." 1967 saw the band record their acclaimed album *Smile*, which was scrapped because of Brian's mental breakdown, and didn't get released officially until 2011.

The *Smile* project wasn't completely abandoned, and a watered-down version entitled *Smiley Smile* came out in 1967, and one of the tunes featured was a song entitled 'Vegetables '(alternately titled 'Vega-Tables'), which was about Brian's obsession with physical fitness. The song features the sound of chomping celery, and rumoured to have contributed to the chomping sounds is none other than Paul McCartney. There is still debate on whether this is true or not, but one thing that is confirmed is that Paul did indeed visit The Beach Boys during a vocal session in April 1967. During that time, he played 'She's Leaving Home 'from the then-upcoming *Sgt. Pepper* album to Brian and his wife, and they both cried, as they thought it was so beautiful.

Artist - Donovan
Title - Mellow Yellow
Year - 1967
Label - Epic

Donovan is a legendary singer-songwriter from Scotland who was popular in the mid-late 1960s with hits such as 'Catch The Wind '(his debut single), 'Sunshine Superman', 'Atlantis 'and 'Jenifer Jupiter'. He was an icon of the flower power generation, and was known for his eclectic genre splicing, as well as for being a guy who could imitate many voices, as proven on his track 'The Walrus and the Carpenter'. He was often referred to as the UK's answer to Bob Dylan.

He also infamously contributed to the critically panned *Sgt. Pepper* movie with The Bee Gees, and appeared in an episode of the famous futuristic sci-fi cartoon series *Futurama*, appearing in an informercial about the lost city of Atlanta (spoofing his song 'Atlantis').

His most well-known tune would have to be 'Mellow Yellow '(quite rightly), which young people today may know best as the song that plays during the closing credits to the 2015 animated film *Minions*. Donovan was a Beatle buddy, being part of the inner circle in the Maharishi days in India, and he made a small contribution to the lyrics of the Fab's 1966 classic 'Yellow Submarine'. In return, Paul was one of the background revellers in 'Mellow Yellow'. Paul also did some uncredited bass work on the album of the same name.

Lyrically, the song is rumoured to be about smoking dried banana skins, but according to Donovan himself, this wasn't the case. It was also rumoured that Macca contributed to the song 'Atlantis 'by singing backing vocals, but Donnie responded to the rumour by saying "No. [chuckles] Paul did the 'Mellow Yellow 'session and added the clap and the giggle. The only thing we ever got close to doing was that Mary Hopkin album." [33]

'Mellow Yellow 'was a hit, reaching No.2 in America and Canada and No.8 in the UK.

On another note, Donovan's hit tune 'Hurdy Gurdy Man 'was written in Rishikesh on a tamburg given to him by George Harrison.

Artist - The Bonzo Dog Doo Dah Band
Title - I'm The Urban Spaceman
Year - 1968
Label - Liberty Records

Me with the late Neil Innes at The Frazer Theatre in my hometown of Knaresborough after a show of his circa November 2009. What a nice chap!

The Bonzo Dog Doo Dah Band were a surrealistic and comedic group who first came to prominence on the Monty Python prototype show *Do Not Adjust Your Set*. They also appeared in The Beatles 'infamous *Magical Mystery Tour* film in 1967, and member Neil Innes played the John Lennon role (Ron Nasty) in the wonderful Beatles parody film *The Rutles - All You Need Is Cash* (see my previous book *Acting Naturally*).

Probably their most famous song would be 'I'm The Urban Spaceman' released on Liberty Records - a delightful number written by Innes. The track even won an Ivor Novello Award in 1968. Producing it was a bloke named Apollo C. Vermouth, better known to you and me as Paul McCartney (with help from Gus Dudgeon). The song would be featured on the children's sketch series *Do Not Adjust Your Set* as well as *Rutland Weekend Television* and even in Monty Python's live shows. It reached No.5 in the UK Singles Chart.

"He [Vivian Stanshall of the Bonzos] asked me to produce their next single 'I'm The Urban Spaceman', which I did at Chappell Studios," recalls McCartney." I went down there, met the guys, and Viv had a length of brightly-coloured plastic piping which made a noise when he swirled it around his head. That was to be his contribution. We chatted a while and then I produced the record. He suggested that I be credited as Apollo C Vermouth, which indeed I am, still, to this day. It turned out to be the Bonzos' only hit, although hit singles is not what they were about anyway. I'll always remember Viv and Keith Moon being a sort of double act, the two of them playing very, very posh English gentleman. They did have their crazy side, of course, but whenever I saw them together they were perfect gentlemen. Over the following years Viv and I would see each other, on and off, at functions, but I gradually lost touch with him, so it was with particular sadness that I heard he had died. He was a wonderful man and he'll be much missed." [17]

When the Bonzos (and later Innes with Monty Python) performed the song live, a female tap dancer appeared to perform an enthusiastic but under-rehearsed routine around member Neil Innes. This role was sometimes performed by the legendary Carol Cleveland, who, like Innes, was an honorary member of the Monty Python team (she appeared in almost every Python project). Sadly, Viv Stanshall died in 1995, and Neil Innes passed away in 2019. I had the very good fortune to meet Neil Innes in 2009, when he performed in my home town, and he was a really lovely chap.

Artist - Mary Hopkin
Title - Those Were The Days
Year - 1968

Label - Apple Records

Mary Hopkin was one of the first artists to be signed to The Beatles' very own record label, Apple Records. She was born and raised in Pontadawe in Wales, and joined the Beatle camp when the model, Twiggy, saw her winning the ITV talent series *Opportunity Knocks* and recommended her to Paul McCartney. She would end up selling millions of records, and in 1970 achieved second place in the Eurovision Song Contest with the song 'Knock, Knock, Who's There '(written by John Carter and Geoff Stevens), which became a worldwide hit.

Her debut single, and her biggest hit, was 'Those Were The Days', which was the second single to be released on Apple Records (the first being 'Hey Jude'). It's an English reworking of the romantic Russian composition, 'Dorogoi Dinnoyu (By The Long Road)', and it was produced by Paul McCartney. The earliest recordings were made circa 1925 and 1926 by Tamara Tesereteli and Alexander Vertinsky. Another version was performed in the 1953 Gordon Perry movie *Innocents in Paris*, sung by Ludmila Lopato.

The recording of Hopkin's version was made circa late July 1968 at the famous EMI (Abbey Road) studios, and it is said that McCartney played acoustic guitar as well. The Beatles 'regular studio engineer, Geoff Emerick, was the engineer for the session, and also included were Richard Newson as orchestra arranger, Gilbert Webster on cymbals, and on backing vocals, the Aida Foster Children's Choir.

Hopkin's version was a huge commercial success, reaching No.1 in various charts around the world, and selling an outstanding 8 million copies worldwide, making it one of the biggest selling singles of all time. Hopkin even rerecorded the tune in different languages, including Spanish, German, Italian and French.

Artist - Paul Jones
Title - And The Sun Will Shine
Year - 1968
Label - Columbia

And The Sun Will Shine 'was originally a single by the brothers Gibb AKA The Bee Gees, back when they were singer/songwriter types with beautiful harmonies, rather than the falsetto voiced disco superstars they would be best known as, when they performed the music for the film *Saturday Night Fever* in 1977. Despite The Bee Gees 'original song only charting modestly in France, reaching a paltry No.66, it would inspire a cover version by Paul

Jones, a member of the popular 60s group Manfred Mann, who are still performing live shows today.

The musical line-up of Jones' version could be considered something of a mini-supergroup, as we have Jeff Beck on guitar, Paul Samwell-Smith of The Yardbirds on guitar, Nicky Hopkins on piano, and Paul McCartney on drums! It was recorded at Abbey Road Studios' Studio 2, and was produced by Peter Asher of Peter and Gordon fame.

Jones' version failed to chart, but third time's a charm, as it would end up becoming a hit a year later for Puerto Rican singer Jose Feliciano, reaching No.25 in the UK Singles Chart.

Artist - Paul Jones
Title - The Dog Presides
Year - 1968
Label - Columbia

The B-side to the single 'And The Sun Will Shine' with Paul McCartney on drums. A funky little number, which would have fitted in well on *The White Album*.

Artist - McGough & McGear
Album - McGough & McGear
Titles - So Much/Little Bit Of Heaven/Basement Flat/From "Frank, A Life In The Day Of" And "Summer With Monika" - Prologue/From "Frank, A Life In The Day Of" And "Summer With Monika" - Epilogue/Come Close And Sleep Now/Yellow Book/House In My Head/Mr. Tickle/Living Room/Do You Remember/Please Don't Run Too Fast/Ex-Art Student
Year - 1968
Label - Parlophone

McGough and McGear was a collaboration project between Liverpool poet and playwright Roger McGough and Paul McCartney's younger brother, Peter McCartney, who went by the alias of Mike McGear. They were both members of the novelty trio Scaffold (the other member being John Gorman) who were best known for the hit songs 'Lily The Pink' and 'Thank U Very Much'.

During the summer of 1967, McGough and McGear cut their only album as a duo, entitled *McGough and McGear*, which came out on May 17th 1968. The whole album was produced by none other than McGear's brother, Macca! It's a delightful melting pot of pop, rock, comedy and poetry, with a late 1960s psychedelic touch, comparable to artists like the Bonzo Dog Doo-Dah Band, and spawned a modest hit with the song 'Do You Remember 'reaching No.34 in the UK hit parade.

Recorded at De Lane Lea Music Recording Studios in London (and possibly other studios), a lot of famous stars of the time helped out on this release including Graham Nash of The Hollies and later CSN and CSNY, Dave Mason of Traffic, Gary Leeds of The Walker Brothers, Viv Prince of Pretty Things, Paul Samwell-Smith of Yardbirds, Jane Asher, and even Jimi Hendrix helped lend a hand!

Despite the baggage behind this release, it didn't sell like hotcakes, but today is remembered as a cult classic in the late 1960s psychedelic pop canon.

Artist - Badfinger
Title - Come And Get It
Year - 1969
Label - Apple Records

Badfinger (formally known as The Iveys) were an underrated rock band from Swansea in Wales, who sold an impressive 14 million albums, considering their relative obscurity today. They sounded very similar to later era Beatles, and were signed to their Apple Records label, and their song 'Without You 'would later see success being covered by Harry Nilsson and Mariah Carey. Interestingly, Badfinger was the working title for the *Sgt. Pepper* track 'With A Little Help From My Friends', and that's how they got their name.

'Come And Get It 'initially started out as a Beatles tune made during the *Abbey Road* sessions, and it was written by Paul. He later gave the song to Apple's new signees, Badfinger, and Paul helped contribute by producing it and playing tambourine. It was recorded on the 2nd August 1969 at EMI (Abbey Road) studios and Tony Clark was the engineer for the session.

It was released on the 5th December 1969, reaching No.4 in the UK and No.7 in the US. It was also used in the Ringo Starr acting platform *The Magic Christian* as the film's opening theme (more about that in my other Beatles book *Acting Naturally*).

The Beatles 'own version of 'Come And Get It 'was recorded on the 24th July at EMI (Abbey Road) studios, but ended up on the cutting room floor. It was eventually featured 27 years later in the 1996 compilation release *Anthology 3* and again in the 2019 reissue of *Abbey Road*. Acclaimed

Beatles author, the late Ian MacDonald, praised The Beatles version by saying it's "by far the best unreleased Beatles song" (this was written before its eventual release, as, at the time, it only appeared on bootlegs).

Regarding Badfinger themselves, the band's ending wasn't a pleasant one, as they suffered an array of legal, managerial and financial hardships. Pete Ham took his own life in 1975, aged 27; Tom Evans hanged himself in 1983, reportedly over a dispute with former bandmate, Joey Molland, over royalties for the song 'Without You'; Mike Gibbons unfortunately suffered from a brain aneurysm and died in 2005 leaving Joey Molland the only surviving founding member. The band does survive today as a series of splinter groups, with Molland forming a band called Joey Molland's Badfinger, and short-lived keyboardist and guitarist Bob Jackson forming his own splinter band.

Artist - Badfinger
Title - Rock Of All Ages
Year - 1969
Label - Apple Records

The B-side to 'Come And Get It'. It was a co-production between McCartney and Beatles friend, roadie and professional autograph forger Mal Evans, who also had an uncredited hand in writing the song. He also played piano parts, and Paul provided the guide vocal, alongside Badfinger's Tom Evans, though Macca's vocals were replaced with a second vocal line by Tom.

Artist - The Fourmost
Title - Rosetta
Year - 1969
Label - CBS

Rosetta 'was a single by fellow Liverpudlian group, The Fourmost, which was released on CBS Records in 1969. Recorded in early February 1969 and coming out on the 21st of that month, this cover version of the old jazz standard was produced by Paul McCartney, and Macca also produced the B-side 'Just Like Before'. Ironically, Paul was going out with a lady named Rosetta at the time! John and Paul mention her in an aside in the album version of 'Get Back 'from the *Let It Be* album.

The single unfortunately failed to chart.

Artist - The Fourmost
Title - Just Like Before
Year - 1969
Label - CBS

See 'Rosetta'.

Artist - Jotta Herre
Title - Penina
Year - 1969
Label - Phillips

Jotta Herre were a little-known band from Portugal who only released one EP before completely fading to obscurity. The members of the band included Jaime Joalo, Anibal Cunha, Carlos Pinto and Rui Pereira.

"I went to Portugal on holiday and returned to the hotel one night slightly the worse for a few drinks," recalls Paul for an interview for *Club Sandwich* in 1994." There was a band playing and I ended up on the drums. The hotel was called Penina, I made up a song with that name, someone made enquiries about it and I gave it to them. And, no, I shouldn't think I'd ever record it myself!" [3]

To help promote the single, the band were sometimes billed as Paul McCartney's Jotta Herre, though even that didn't help make the song successful, and the band unfortunately remained in the depths of musical obscurity until 2022, when Carlos Pinto from the band (who would later end up becoming president of Sony Music, Portugal) told the tale of this song on the YouTube Channel 'Almost Beatles Songs '(the video is called 'THE BEAUTIFUL STORY OF PAUL McCARTNEY'S 'PIENNA''). It's amazing viewing, and highly recommended to anybody who loves a heartwarming Beatles story. [36]

Artist - Mary Hopkin
Album - Post Card
Title - Lord Of The Reedy River/Happiness Runs (Pebble And The Man)/Love Is The Sweetest Thing/Y Blodyn Gwyn/The Honeymoon Song/The Puppy Song/Inchworm/Voyage of The Moon/Lullaby Of The Leaves/Young Love/Someone To Watch Over Me/Prince En Avignon/The Game/There's No Business Like Show Business
Year - 1969
Label - Apple Records

In 1969, Mary Hopkin would release her debut album *Post Card*. It was a commercial success, reaching No.3 in the UK Albums Chart and No.28 in the US *Billboard* Chart. It also fared well critically, though there were some criticisms that the album was full of covers of pre-rock 'n 'roll standards, rather than the simplistic folk songs that Hopkin would be best known for.

The opening number,' Lord Of The Reedy River', was written by Beatle buddy, Donovan. Donovan's own version of the song wouldn't come out until 1971, when it was featured on his ninth studio album, *HMS Donovan*. 'The Honeymoon Song 'is a cover of a track from the 1959 Michael Powell movie *Honeymoon*. The Beatles themselves covered the song in 1963, as the theme tune for their BBC radio series *Pop Go The Beatles*.

Another highlight would have to be 'The Puppy Song'. It was written by a good friend of our fabs, Harry Nilsson. 'The Puppy Song 'would later end up being a hit for David Cassidy, where it would reach No.1 in the UK Singles Chart and No.10 in Australia.

The song 'Inchworm 'is a cover of a track by Danny Kaye, originally featured in the 1952 film *Hans Christian Anderson*. Paul would later record his own version of the song in 2012 for his album *Kisses on the Bottom*. 'Lullaby Of The Leaves 'is a cover of a 1932 Tin Pan Alley song, which has been performed by the likes of Benny Goodman, The Ventures and Ella Fitzgerald. 'Young Love 'is a popular country song written by Ric Cartley and Carole Joyner, first performed by Cartley himself with his band, the Jiva-Tones. The tune would later find success in 1973 via Donny Osmond, when it would reach No.1 in the UK Singles Chart (not to be confused with his similarly titled 1972 hit 'Puppy Love').

'Someone To Watch Over Me 'is a cover of the George Gershwin classic jazz standard, written for the 1926 musical *Oh, Kay!* Other notable cover versions included Frank Sinatra, Ella Fitzgerald, Ray Charles, Barbra Streisand, Willie Nelson, Elton John and Amy Winehouse. 'Prince En Avignon', however, is a French canton about a would-be-monarch without a castle, originally written by Jean-Michel Rivat. A very classy tune. The song 'The Game' was actually written by the fifth member of The Beatles, George Martin (he was!). He also plays piano, while 'There's No Business Like Show Business' is a cover of the 1946 Irving Berlin song, from the musical *Annie Get Your Gun*, often associated with the 1954 movie of the same name.

Artist - Steve Miller Band
Title - Celebration Song
Year - 1969
Label - Capitol

The Steve Miller Band are an American rock group based in San Francisco, formed in 1966 and still performing today. If there isn't a big clue in the band's name, they are led by guitarist and vocalist Steve Miller. They are probably best known for their string of hit songs including 'Abracadabra', 'The Joker 'and the amazing 'Fly Like An Eagle'. Like the Sugababes, they are known for having a high turnover rate of band members.

1969 saw Steve and his band release their third album *Brave New World*, which contained the song 'Celebration Song '(not the very well-known hit by Kool & The Gang or the classical piece McCartney recorded for his 1997 *Standing Stone* LP). Contributing to backing vocals was a guy named Paul Ramon AKA Paul McCartney. The Paul Ramon name was previously used in 1960 when The Beatles (then the Silver Beatles) did their first official tour, backing a guy named Johnny Gentle (as mentioned previously in this book).

Artist - Steve Miller Band
Title - My Dark Hour
Year - 1969
Label - Capitol

The second Ramon/Miller collaboration from their *Brave New World* album. This was recorded during a late-night session on the 9th May 1969 after Paul and his Beatle buddies were having a "beef" over signing a contract appointing Allen Klein as The Beatles 'new financial manager. The rest of the Fabs walked out, while Macca remained at the Olympic Studios in London, and Steve Miller's band happened to be in the studio at the time; this song emerged from him and Paul jamming.

Also, on an interesting note, the song 'Space Cowboy '(nothing to do with the hit song by Jamiroquai), from the same album, uses the same riff as 'Lady Madonna 'and was surprisingly spared by the Beatle lawyers.

Artist - Timon
Title - Something New Everyday
Year - 1969 (released in 2010)
Label - Rev-Ola

Timon was a pseudonym for multi-instrumentalist Stephen John Murray, better known as Tymon Dogg (maybe that's where Snoop got his name?). Dogg is probably best known for being a member of the short-lived band

The Mescarleros, led by Joe Strummer of The Clash fame, as well as working with Lily Allen before she became famous. Timon may or may not have a friend called Pumbaa!

In the early stages of his career, he was signed to Pye Records in 1967, where he recorded the single 'The Bitter Thoughts Of Little Jane', which featured future Led Zeppelin members Jimmy Page and John Paul Jones. In 1969, he migrated to Apple Records, where he had a few songs produced by Peter Asher. One of these songs recorded was a tune entitled 'Something New Everyday', which featured Paul McCartney on piano, as well as James Taylor on guitar. Unfortunately, the tune was never released on Apple Records, as it got the veto from George Harrison, who wasn't impressed, which resulted in Timon never being officially signed to Apple. Contrary to what Harrison thought, it's actually a really nice piece of late 1960s flower-power pop.

The tune wouldn't see a commercial release until 2010, when it surfaced on the compilation album *The Irrepressible Tymon Dogg: A Collection 1968-2009*, which was released on reissues and rarities label Rev-Ola.

Artist - Karen Young
Title - Que Sera, Sera
Year - 1970
Label - Major Minor

Not the American disco vocalist of the same name, Karen Young is a singer from Sheffield, UK, best known for her version of 'Nobody's Child', which reached No.23 in Australia in 1969. In 1970, she recorded her own version of the old standard 'Que Sera, Sera '(as previously covered by Mary Hopkin - see the Paul and Ringo chapter later in the book). This version was arranged by McCartney, but sadly, very little information about the recording session has surfaced. It was produced by Glaswegian singer/songwriter Tommy Scott, who produced hits for Them (Van Morrison's early group), The Troggs, Lena Zavaroni, Sydney Devine, and he even had a No.1 with the first two albums by Irish folk band The Dubliners.

Young retired from the music industry in 1974, and there is no information on what she is doing today.

Artist - John Christie
Title - 4th July
Year - 1974
Label - Capitol

John Christie is a singer/songwriter, and while having some impressive credentials, is somewhat overlooked nowadays, despite having a minor hit in 1976 with 'Here's To Love'. He has sold over a million records, and has written and composed with the greatest, including Stevie Wonder, Freddie Mercury, Sir Laurence Olivier, Cliff Richard, Ashford & Simpson, John Lennon's son, Julian… and The Wurzels!

Written by Paul and Linda McCartney, '4th July' is a nice number about feeling blue on American Independence Day. Paul's original demo version would later be featured in the 2014 remastered edition of the 1975 Wings album *Venus and Mars*.

Artist - Adam Faith
Album - I Survive
Titles - Change/Never Say Goodbye/Star Song
Year - 1974
Label - Warner Bros. Records

Adam Faith (real name Terence Nelhams Wright) was a British teen idol who went from being a pop icon/actor in the 1960s-1980s to later being a financial analyst/journalist for the *Daily Mail* among others - we are not making this up! He was one of the most charted acts of the 1960s, and his first seven hit singles all reached the top five, not to mention being one the first acts to record original compositions (in partnership with songwriters Les Vandyke and John Barry), instead of covers, on a regular basis. Faith had previously sung the song 'I'd Just Fallen For Someone', which had an uncredited writing contribution from John Lennon, and was the first record to have professional involvement from a Beatle (see the John Lennon chapter).

Back in the tumultuous year of 1974, Faith (now an adult idol) released his album *I Survive*. On the songs 'Change 'and 'Never Say Goodbye', Paul McCartney provides some synthesiser work, and they are musically comparable to a John Lennon solo-era ballad, with 'Change 'containing light orchestral production; while on the cut 'Star Song 'both Paul and Linda McCartney provide backing vocals. It's a fun, upbeat number, which has a vibe similar to that of a Wings track.

Faith would later have a very successful acting career in a number of television series including *Budgie* and *Love Hurts*. During the 70s, he went into music management, managing Leo Sayer among others. He also co-produced Roger Daltry's first solo album, which included the hit single 'Giving It All Away '(penned by Leo Sayer). Sadly, he passed away of a heart attack in 2003.

Artist - Peggy Lee
Title - Let's Love
Year - 1974
Label - Atlantic

Peggy Lee was a jazz music legend who recorded over 1,100 masters and composed over 270 songs in her expansive career. Her repertoire included massive hits, such as 'Fever', 'Big Spender' 'Is That All There Is 'and 'Why Don't You Do Right?', known by film buffs today as the Jessica Rabbit song from the classic film *Who Framed Roger Rabbit*. She was also an actress, most notably providing the speaking and singing voices for several characters in the classic 1955 Disney animated film T*he Lady and The Tramp*, and she co-wrote all the songs for the movie with Sonny Burke.

In 1974, she recorded the album *Let's Love* and the LP's title track was written, arranged and produced by none other than Macca! How this all came about was when Peggy was doing a show at the Royal Albert Hall in London, she invited Paul and his wife, Linda, to dinner at the famous Dorchester Hotel, and as a gift for her, Paul gave her a song that he had written with Linda entitled 'Let's Love'. It was recorded in June 1974 at the Record Plant in LA.

Artist - Mike McGear
Album - McGear
Titles - Sea Breezes/What Do We Really Know?/Norton/Leave It/Have You Got Problems/The Casket/Rainbow Lady/Simply Love You/Givin' Grease a Ride/The Man Who Found God On the Moon
Year - 1974
Label - Warner Bros. Records

McGear was the second and final (to date) album by Mike McGear (McCartney's younger brother), and was released on Warner Bros. Records in 1974. It was a collaboration between McGear and Wings, who were, of course, Paul McCartney's other very successful band - it is surprisingly not called a McGear/Wings album in the publicity, as I think the album could have sold like hotcakes if that was the case! Recorded at Strawberry Studios in Stockport, Greater Manchester, the LP contained the lead single 'Leave It', which reached a modest No.36 in the UK Singles Chart. The album featured contributions from Linda McCartney, who played Moog keyboards, percussion and backing vocals, and fellow Wings members, Denny Laine on electric guitars and backing vocals, Jimmy McCulloch on electric guitars and Denny Sewell on drums, not to mention Paul on bass, guitar, keyboards, piano, synthesiser and both co-lead and backing vocals.

Also on this album were Gerry Conway, Tony Coe, Paddy Moloney (The Chieftains), The Halle Orchestra, former Beatles press agent Derek Taylor speaking on the song 'Norton', Brian Jones (the guy from The Undertakers, not the guy from The Rolling Stones) on saxophone, and Mike's daughters, Benna and Theran McCartney, singing backing vocals on the final song on the album,' The Man Who Found God On the Moon'.

Despite not having commercial success, the album was well received critically, and it has been reissued several times: firstly in 1991 on Rykodisc in the US, featuring an alternate version of the song 'Dance The Do'; in 1992 in the UK on See For Miles Records, featuring another mix of 'Dance The Do 'and the B-side to 'Leave It 'entitled 'Sweet Baby', which, according to the liner notes, was originally going to be called 'All My Lovin'', but "some other group had already done one with that name" - both reissues are out of print. It would finally get a 2-disc remastered special edition in 2019 on Esoteric Records, a sub-label of Cherry Red Records.

Artist - The Scaffold
Title - Liverpool Lou
Year - 1974
Label - Warner Bros. Records

As previously mentioned in this book, Scaffold were a comedic trio that featured Paul's brother, Mike McGear, Roger McCough and John Gorman. In 1974, they released the single 'Liverpool Lou', which was produced by Paul McCartney. It was a commercial success, and it reached No.7 in the UK Singles Chart, and was recorded around the time of McGear's 1974 studio album *McGear*.

'Liverpool Lou 'is a Liverpudlian ditty originally written and performed by Irish songwriter and playwright Dominic Behnan (1928-1989). It was was originally released in 1964. The song has been covered many times over the years, with notable versions coming from artists such as Max Boyce and The Dubliners. The Liverpool Football Team even recorded a version in 1977.

'Liverpool Lou 'is a delightful little number, which has a similar vibe to McCartney's 1977 megahit 'Mull of Kintyre'.

It would later be featured on The Scaffold's 1975 album *Sold Out*, released on Warner Bros. Records. It would end up being their final LP.

Artist - The Scaffold
Title - Ten Years On After Strawberry Jam
Year - 1974
Label - Warner Bros. Records

The B-side to 'Liverpool Lou'. As well as being produced by Paul under the name of McCartney Productions, it was written by Paul and his wife, Linda.

Artist - Carly Simon
Title - Night Owl
Year - 1974
Label - Elektra

Carly Simon is a New York-born American singer/songwriter legend with a deep sensuous voice, the ex-wife of another singer/songwriter legend, James Taylor, and one of the most popular singer/songwriters of her time, with thirteen top 40 US hits. She sang the theme song to the James Bond movie *The Spy Who Loved Me* ('Nobody Does It Better'), and sang on two Winnie The Pooh films, but her most famous song would probably have to be 'You're So Vain '(rumoured to be about the actor Warren Beatty and featuring Mick Jagger on backing vocals). If you're a fan of 1970s singer/songwriter types, then it's pretty much guaranteed you will have at least one of her songs in your collection.

1972 saw her release the album *No Secrets*, which was a massive commercial hit, reaching No.1 in the US *Billboard* Albums Chart and remaining in that position for five weeks. The song on the LP 'Night Owl 'was written by her husband, James Taylor, and on backing vocals is none other than our Beatle friend, Paul. Linda was also present at the sessions, but didn't participate, but Klaus Voormann, who appeared on many Beatle solo projects in the 1970s, played bass.

Artist - Rod Stewart
Title - Mine For Me
Year - 1974
Label - Mercury

Sir Roderick David Stewart is a very popular UK pop star, who has been in bands such as The Faces and the Jeff Beck Group, as well as being an ultra-successful solo artist. He has a distinctive raspy singing voice and a flair for some great lyrical storytelling, and is still selling records and selling out arenas today. If you ever get to meet him, he will ask you if you think he's sexy, and if he does - your answer must be yes!

In 1974, Paul and Linda McCartney wrote a song for him entitled 'Mine For Me', which was featured on his 1974 album *Smiler*. It unfortunately didn't sell particularly well, reaching a modest No.91 in the US *Billboard* Top100, which is a shame, as it's a really lovely tune.

Artist - James Taylor
Title - Let It Fall Down
Year - 1974
Label - Warner Bros. Records

Singer, songwriter and (according to Homer Simpson) former US President James Taylor is awesome! His laidback bittersweet tones have been delighting audiences since the late 1960s, and he was one of the first signees to Apple Records back in 1968. He's still extremely popular today, and he still sells out arenas, plus Taylor Swift was named in tribute to him - his legacy will be around for some time.

1974 saw the release of his single 'Let It Fall Down', which was on his album *Walking Man*, featuring the fan-favourite title track of the same name. Providing backing vocals on this tune were none other than Paul and his late wife, Linda Eastman McCartney. It's about the infamous Watergate scandal and the downfall of President Richard Nixon. It was, unusually for Taylor, a commercial flop, considering the very topical nature of the tune at the time, as Nixon had just resigned when this track was released.

Artist - James Taylor
Title - Rock 'n' Roll Is Music Now
Year - 1974
Label - Warner Bros. Records

Another lovely song with the beautiful vocal stylings of James Taylor. As on 'Let It Fall Down', Paul and Linda provide backing vocals, and it was featured on Taylor's *Walking Man* album.

Artist - Thornton, Fradkin & Unger And The Big Band
Title - God Bless California
Year - 1974

Label - ESP Disk

Thornton, Fradkin & Unger And The Big Band were a collective consisting of Bob Unger, Leslie Fradkin, and Paul Thornton. In 1974, they released their one-and-only album *Pass On This Side*, which contained the single 'God Bless California'. Providing backing vocals are Paul and Linda McCartney. Also playing are Danny Seiwell on drums and Randy Edelman on piano and vocals.

The tune would later be reissued on the 2000 compilation album *Godzology*, which features a really dreadful cover (which makes it look like a cut-price CD by a local covers band), despite the high quality of the music contained within.

Artist - Roger Daltrey
Title - Giddy
Year - 1977
Label - Polydor

Roger Daltrey CBE is the lead singer and co-founder member of The Who - one of the greatest bands of the 1960s (and still going). They were, like our Fabs, one of the biggest bands of the "British Invasion", and were known for their rock operas (which were surprisingly unpretentious) and for that infamous "art" known as instrument destruction. Despite half of their original line-up having gone, they are still performing today to huge crowds (I've seen them with Zak Starkey - Ringo's son - on drums, and they are very, very good!).

1977 saw Roger Daltrey release the solo album *One Of The Boys* (nothing to do with the Katy Perry album of the same name, which came out a LOT later!) and the song 'Giddy 'was written by Paul McCartney. It's a number that starts off slow, and then goes into a really funky almost-disco sound (after all, it was 1977), before going back to being slow, and then going disco again! This song tempo progression was quite typical of McCartney and Wings in the 1970s, and I think it's a shame that most pop songs today stick to a rigid tempo, and don't experiment more with time changes and genre shift (unless you're LF System, that is!).

Artist - Roy Harper
Title - One Of These Days In England (Part 1)
Year - 1977
Label - Harvest

Roy Harper is a famous Mancunian singer/songwriter who has released 32 albums, and has fans including people like Jimmy Page, Robert Plant, Pete Townshend, Kate Bush, Pink Floyd and Jethro Tull.

1977 saw him release his ninth album *Bullinamingvase* (Bull In A Ming Vase - possibly a reference to the phrase 'bull in a china shop'), and on the album's opening song 'One Of Those Days In England (Part 1) 'Paul and Linda McCartney provide backing vocals.

    Artist - Denny Laine
    Album - Holly Days
    Title - Heartbeat/Moondreams/Rave On!/I'm Gonna Love You Too/Fools Paradise/Lonesome Tears/Medley: It's So Easy/Listen To Me/Look At Me/Take Your Time/I'm Looking For Someone To Love
    Year - 1978
    Label - Capitol

Denny Laine is a guitarist originally from the famous classic rock band The Moody Blues, who was in Paul McCartney's 1970s group, Wings, which saw enormous success in that decade; in fact Norwich's legendary DJ Alan Partridge (AKA British comedian, Steve Coogan) sees Wings as "the band The Beatles could have been"! Laine also had a successful solo career, and in 2018 he was inducted into the Rock and Roll Hall of Fame as a member of The Moody Blues.

In 1978, he released an album of Buddy Holly covers with the rather "puntastic" title of *Holly Days*. If you don't know who Buddy Holly is, shame on you! He was an early rock and roll pioneer whose career was tragically cut short in 1959, when he, Richie Valens and The Big Bopper (Jiles Perry Richardson Jr.) were horrifically killed in a dreadful plane crash. He was only 21. He was a massive influence on The Beatles, and all musicians of the 1960s onwards, and still is influential today. In fact the name of his band, The Crickets, was possibly the inspiration behind The Beatles' name.

The first cover on this LP was one of Holly's classic songs, 'Heartbeat', which is also remembered for being the theme song to the UK 1990s ITV police drama of the same name, set in the 1960s. The tune 'I'm Gonna Love You Too 'would also see another cover version the same year, this time from Blondie, which was featured on their famous album *Parallel Lines*. These are some very tasteful versions of these timeless songs, with Laine doing a pretty decent pastiche of Buddy's distinctive vocals.

Both Paul and Linda McCartney were involved in the album's creation. Paul would provide background vocals, as well as providing some of the instrumentation, all done on a four-track recorder. It was recorded in the summer of 1976 at Rude Studio in Campbeltown, Scotland, which was a wood-lined, tin-roofed shack, where McCartney would record some of his solo projects in the 1970s. To keep the music sounding authentic to Holly's 1950s sound, it was recorded in mono, with an artificial stereo effect using electronic reprocessing.

Artist - Kate Robbins
Title - Tomorrow
Year - 1978
Label - Anchor

Kate Robbins is the daughter of Mike and Elizabeth Robbins, and is the first cousin of Paul McCartney on his father's side. Apparently, Kate's dad helped teach Paul how to play the guitar. Kate is a singer, as well as being an actress and an impressionist, who is probably best known in the UK for being many famous voices on the iconic satirical puppet sketch show *Spitting Image* from 1986-1996, including the voice of the late Queen Elizabeth II, despite the show ironically ribbing her cousin once or twice.

On the 30th June 1978, Robbins released her debut single 'Tomorrow', which was produced by Del Newman, and recorded at Abbey Road studios. Paul helped out with the song, having an 'executive producer' role, though this was in the loosest of terms, as Macca simply chose the final mixdown, which was used for the single's release. Kate would later sing backing vocals on several of Paul McCartney's other recordings.

Her brother is the famous entertainment personality Ted Robbins, who is probably best known for being the villain, Den Perry, in the Peter Kay sitcom *Phoenix Nights*. Like Ringo Starr, Ted Robbins would also narrate the *Thomas The Tank Engine* audio books.

Artist - Freddie Starr
Title - You've Lost That Loving Feeling
Year - 1978
Label - PVK Records

The controversial late Freddie Starr (no relation to Ringo) was a singer, actor, stand-up comedian, Elvis impersonator and former member of the Merseybeat group The Midniters, who were managed by Brian Epstein. They also performed in the same nightclubs in Hamburg around the same time as our Fabs. He may or may not have had an appetite for hamsters (see UK tabloid newspapers in the 1980s!).

Paul provided backing vocals on the song 'You've Lost That Loving Feeling '(a cover of The Righteous Brothers' classic), which was featured on his 1978 self-titled album released on PVK Records (which was also partially an Elvis covers album), and later featured again on Starr's 1990 album *The Wanderer* released on Dover Records. Interestingly, Starr was also allegedly in the horn section of Wings during their 1975-1976 world tour and again during their 1979 world tour.

> Artist - Godley & Creme
> Title - Get Well Soon
> Year - 1979
> Label - Polydor

Godley and Creme are Kevin Godley and Lol Creme, former members of the intellectual pop-rockers 10cc, who lasted from 1977-1988. As well as being musicians, they directed several music videos for artists such as Status Quo, The Police, Culture Club, Duran Duran, Peter Gabriel, Herbie Hancock, Frankie Goes To Hollywood, Lou Reed and most notably for Beatle fans, George Harrison ('When We Was Fab', which we will cover later in the book). Godley also directed the video for The Beatles '1996 "reunion" single, 'Real Love'.

In 1979, they released their third album, *Freeze Frame* (which featured a rather risqué cover designed by the famed London-based art design group, Hipgnosis). On the album's closing tune,' Get Well Soon', Paul sings backing vocals. This is an excellent number, which sounds very trippy and spaced out, if you like that sort of vibe!

> Artist - Denny Laine
> Album - Japanese Tears
> Title - Send Me The Heart/I Would Only Smile/Weep For Love
> Year - 1980
> Label - Scratch

In 1980, Laine released his third studio album, *Japanese Tears*, which was shortly before Wings 'disbandment a year later. McCartney contributed to three of the album's fourteen songs, which includes playing bass on the songs 'Send Me The Heart 'and 'I Would Only Smile '(which was actually recorded in March 1972), and he provided backing vocals on 'Weep For Love'.

>Artist - Chris Moffa And The Competition
>Title - You Know How Hot (It's Been Getting Around Here)
>Year - 1981
>Label - Change Records
>NOTE - It is unlikely that Paul McCartney had any involvement in this track, but it is here to set the record straight.

Chris Moffa And The Competition were an obscure American punk rock group featuring Chris Moffa (who was also in the group Soul Attack) on guitar, Frank Roselli on bass and Jim Ohm on drums.

According to some sources, the 1981 single 'You Know How Hot (It's Been Getting Around Here)', which is quite similar sounding to mod rockers The Jam, was produced by Apollo Vermouth, which is, of course, a pseudonym for Paul McCartney, though there is no evidence to back this up, other than a credit when the song appeared on the 1983 compilation release *Trouser Press Presents The Best of America Underground*. It could be another producer who shared the same name or alias (although McCartney's pseudonym was always Apollo C. Vermouth).

>Artist - Rockestra
>Album - Concerts For The People Of Kampuchea
>Titles - Lucille/Let It Be/Rockestra Theme
>Year - 1981
>Label - Atlantic

Rockestra were a supergroup formed for the Concerts For The People Of Kampuchea, which took place from December 26th-29th 1979 at London's famous Hammersmith Odeon, now known under the commercialised name Eventim Apollo (to be renamed the Disney-McDonald's Apollo in 2033!?). The concerts were a collaborative effort between Paul and Secretary General of the United Nations at the time, Kurt Waldheim, and featured an all-star line-up, which included Queen, The Who, The Clash, Elvis Costello, Ian Dury, and Matumbi. It was rumoured at the time that the finale of these concerts would be a fully-fledged Beatles reunion, but (somewhat) anticlimactically, we had this new supergroup, which consisted of:

Paul McCartney (Wings)
Linda McCartney (Wings)
Denny Laine (Wings)
Laurence Juber (Wings)
Steve Holley (Wings)
David Gilmour (Pink Floyd)
Pete Townshend (The Who)
Hank Marvin (The Shadows)
Tony Ashton (Ashton, Gardner & Dyke)
Gary Brooker (Procol Harum)
Bruce Thomas (Elvis Costello & The Attractions)
Ronnie Laine (The Small Faces)
John Paul Jones (Led Zeppelin)
John Bonham (Led Zeppelin)
Kenny Jones (The Small Faces)
Ray Cooper (famous percussionist, who has worked with everybody)
Tony Carr (jazz drummer and percussionist)
Morris Pert (session drummer)
Howie Casey (saxophonist who had worked with Tony Sheridan from the Hamburg days)
Tony Dorsey (horn player, who had worked with Wings)
Steve Howard (trumpeter)
Thaddeus Richard (multi-instrumentalist friend of Paul McCartney)
Speedy Acquaye (percussionist)

This amazing dream-team line-up more than made up for all those Beatle reunion rumours, though to be fair, a reunion of our beloved Fabs would have been a fantastic surprise for everybody!

Enough of my side-tracking; as you guessed from the title,' Lucille 'is a cover version of the 1957 rock 'n' roll hit from Little Richard, and a rather rockin 'one I might add. 'Let It Be 'meanwhile is a cover of... have a guess! The track 'Rockestra Theme 'would later be remade for Wings 'final studio album *Back To The Egg*, which sadly didn't get great reviews, and performed modestly commercially.

Artist - Michael Jackson
Title - The Girl Is Mine
Year - 1982
Label - Epic

Originator of the word "shamone", the late Michael Jackson was one of the most successful acts in musical history, whose popularity was comparable to that of The Beatles themselves. Despite some very worrying controversy surrounding his private life, let's just remember him for the amazing music he made in his five decade career. Jackson had previously covered the Wings song 'Girlfriend 'on his brilliant *Off The Wall* album, which was co-incidentally a song McCartney wrote with M.J. in mind.

'The Girl Is Mine 'was the debut single from Jackson's fantastic sixth solo album, *Thriller* (supposedly the best selling album of all time, and not a bad one to have that moniker, may I add). The writing of the song occurred when M.J. and Macca were watching cartoons. The producer - the legendary Quincy Jones, who is said to not be a Beatles fan - also suggested to Jackson about adding a rap verse, which ultimately didn't happen (instead, we have a spoken word segment). "One of my favourite songs to record, of all my recordings as a solo artist, is probably 'The Girl Is Mine', because working with Paul McCartney was pretty exciting and we just literally had fun," remembers M.J. "It was like lots of kibitzing and playing, and throwing stuff at each other, and making jokes. We actually recorded the (instrumental) track and the vocals pretty much live at the same time, and we do have footage of it, but it's never been shown." [19]

Despite the concept of the two of them doing a duet together sounding awesome on paper, it is arguably the weakest track on the whole album, a very soppy middle-of-the-road ballad featuring the very "naff" aforementioned spoken-word bit at the end. Despite the song being mediocre, it was a massive hit, reaching the top 10 worldwide, and was even No.1 in Spain and on various US *Billboard* charts.

A remix was released by Jackson in 2008, featuring Black Eyed Peas member Will.I.Am, with Will replacing Paul's sections. This new version was not well-received by critics. Jackson and McCartney would duet again in 1983 for the really funky single 'Say Say Say 'for Macca's album *Pipes Of Peace* and also on the tune 'The Man 'on the same album. Both these tracks, I feel, are far superior to 'The Girl Is Mine', and interestingly, both were actually recorded before that song.

Artist - Laurence Juber
Title - Maisie
Year - 1982
Label - Breaking Records

Laurence Juber was a member of Paul McCartney's very successful post-Beatles band, Wings, which lasted from 1971-1981. He is a guitarist who was raised in Stepney in North London and has collaborated with the likes of Rosemary Clooney (aunt of Hollywood actor, George Clooney), Belinda Carlisle, Barry Manilow, Beach Boys member Mike Love, One Direction's Harry Styles and, most notably, Ringo Starr.

In 1982, he released his debut solo album, *Standard Time*. Some of these songs were recorded when he was still in Wings. The song we are covering, 'Maisie', for instance, was actually recorded in July 1978 at McCartney's farm near Campbeltown, Scotland, around the time of the recording of Wings' final album, *Back To The Egg*, and the song features Paul McCartney on bass and his fellow Wingmen - Denny Laine on harmonica and drummer Steve Holley. It is an instrumental composition, and it was Juber's first tune where he played fingerstyle guitar.

Artist - John Williams
Title - Paul McCartney's Theme From *The Honorary Consul*
Year - 1983
Label - Island Records

John Williams (NOT the famous movie soundtrack composer of the same name) is an Australian classical guitar guru, who guitar historian Graham Wade says is "perhaps the most technically accomplished guitarist the world has seen." He has been performing since the 1950s and is still performing today, despite his age. As well as being a focal figure in the classical circles, he has even dabbled in pop and rock once in a while, most memorably jamming with Pete Townshend himself at the 1979 Secret Policeman's Ball on The Who's 'Won't Get Fooled Again', which gave him more kudos in the world of rock. Perhaps he's most famous for his 1979 hit record 'Cavatina', theme from the film *The Deer Hunter*.

In the early 1980s he ended up crossing paths with Paul McCartney when he performed the instrumental title theme to the 1983 drama film *The Honorary Consul*, directed by John Mackenzie, and starring screen legends such as Michael Caine, Richard Gere, Bob Hoskins and Elpidia Carrillo. It was based on the 1973 novel of the same name, and received mixed reviews from film critics.

The instrumental was produced by Stanley Myers, Richard Harvey and Paul himself, and it was recorded at the Olympic Studios in London circa 1983. A really beautiful tune.

Williams would later cover 'Here Comes The Sun' in 1998 as part of George Martin's Beatles covers album *In My Life*.

Artist - Band Aid
Title - Feed The World
Year - 1984
Label - Phonogram

Do They Know It's Christmas ' is a very well-known all-star charity single, which was the best selling single in UK history, selling 3.8 million copies, until Elton John gazumped them with 'Candle In The Wind (Goodbye English Rose) ' in 1997. The song was written by Boomtown Rats member Bob Geldof and former Ultravox member Midge Ure, as a response to the awful famine crisis which was happening in Ethiopia at the time. It was recorded on a single day, the 15th November 1984, with its release being on the 3rd December of that year. It naturally reached No.1 in the UK Singles Chart, where it stayed for five weeks, dethroning McCartney's own 'Mull of Kintyre ' as the best selling single of all time in the UK at that time. The single's cover was designed by none other than Peter Blake, who, of course, designed the super-famous cover for *Sgt. Pepper's Lonely Hearts Club Band*.

Inspiration for the song came from BBC news reports by newscaster Michael Buerk about the ongoing famine that was happening in Ethiopia. Geldof and his wife at the time, the late Paula Yates, were deeply saddened by what they saw. As a response to this tragedy, Geldof teamed up with Scottish musician Midge Ure for the ultimate ensemble charity musical event with the one-off supergroup, Band Aid. Unfortunately, Paul McCartney wasn't available to take part, due to other commitments, so he contributed to a spoken-word segment on the B-side, entitled 'Feed The World ' (which is also the name of part of the hook to 'Christmas'). Other musicians contributing to spoken word parts for the B-side included David Bowie, The Thompson Twins, Big Country and Holly Johnson from the band Frankie Goes To Hollywood.

Artist - The Everly Brothers
Title - On The Wings of A Nightingale
Year - 1984
Label - Mercury

Don and Phil Everly were a legendary classic rock 'n' roll duo, known for their beautiful harmonies and acoustic guitars. They were inspirational to many of the groups that followed, including The Beatles. The Everlys were massively popular in the late 1950s and early 1960s, known for hit records such as 'Bye Bye Love', 'Wake Up Little Susie', 'All I Have To Do Is

Dream 'and 'Cathy's Clown'. 'On The Wings Of A Nightingale 'was produced by Welsh singer, guitarist and record producer, Dave Edmunds (of Love Sculpture and 'I Hear You Knocking 'fame), who worked with McCartney on his *Give My Regards to Broad Street* album and was a former member of Ringo's All Starr Band. He also produced Status Quo's comeback single 'I'm In The Army Now 'and Shakin' Stevens' 'Merry Christmas Everyone'.

In 1984, the Everlys released their album *EB 84*, which contained the song 'On The Wings Of A Nightingale', which was written by Paul McCartney. The song sold modestly in the US, reaching No.50 in the *Billboard* Hot 100, but it was a big hit in The Netherlands, where it reached No.3, and it also reached No.6. in South Africa.

Artist - The Crowd
Title - Messages
Year - 1985
Label - Spartan Records

The Crowd was a one-off supergroup which produced a charity record in aid of a terrible fire that happened at Bradford City football stadium on the 11th May 1985, which claimed the lives of 56 people. A huge array of popular artists took part in this project, including Gerry Marsden of Pacemakers fame, John Entwistle from The Who, light entertainment icons Keith Chegwin and Bruce Forsyth, singer Tony Christie, Colin Blunstone of The Zombies, singer/guitarist/entertainer John Otway and many more including Ringo Starr's son, Zak Starkey.

As with Band Aid, Macca didn't contribute to the single's A-side, (a cover of Gerry & The Pacemakers 'hit single 'You'll Never Walk Alone', which in itself was a cover of the same song featured in the musical *Carousel* and which has become a standard football anthem for Liverpool and Celtic). McCartney contributes some words to the B-side, which was entitled 'Messages'. The single reached No.1 in the UK Singles Chart.

Artist - Ferry Aid
Title - Let It Be
Year - 1987
Label - CBS

An all-star ensemble group covering the Beatles classic, performed in memory of the victims of the Zeebrugge ferry disaster on the 6th March

1987, which killed 193 passengers and crew. Produced by Stock, Aiken and Waterman, and featuring Paul himself, he was joined by the likes of Boy George, Mel and Kim, Edwin Starr, Bananarama, Bucks Fizz, Hazell Dean, The Drifters, Frankie Goes To Hollywood, Go West, The Nolans, Hazel O'Connor, Su Pollard, Suzi Quatro, Alvin Stardust, Bonnie Tyler and popular singer, who became a future internet meme, Rick Astley.

The single was a commercial success, reaching No.1 in the UK, Norway and Swiss charts and reaching top five in many other countries.

Artist - Duane Eddy
Title - Rockestra Theme
Year - 1987
Label - CBS

Duane Eddy is an American guitar legend noted for his "twangy" sound, and he has influenced guitar players around the world. His most well-known song would have to be his cover of the theme tune to the television series *Peter Gunn*, which would later be sampled by artists such as The Art of Noise.

1987 saw Duane release his self-titled solo album. Track two on the LP was entitled 'Rockestra Theme' and featured McCartney on backing vocals and bass. The tune was also produced by Paul, and it was recorded on the 4th February 1987 at McCartney's Hog Hill Studios in Rye. The mixing for the track would be followed a day later. As suggested by the title, it is a cover version of 'Rockestra Theme 'originally performed by McCartney's charity supergroup, Rockestra.

Artist - Johnny Cash
Title - New Room Over Jamaica
Year - 1988
Label - Mercury

"The Man in Black", Johnny Cash (1932-2003), was a country music legend, who was one of the biggest icons of 20th century music. He had a deep, calm bass-baritone voice, and has sold over 90 million records worldwide. He would later be portrayed by The Joker himself, Joaquin Phoenix, in a biopic entitled *Walk The Line* in 2005, featuring Reese Witherspoon as his wife, June Carter.

His 1988 album *Water From The Wells of Home* contained the song 'New Moon Over Jamaica', which was produced by Paul McCartney. It was recorded on the 9th May 1988 at Hog Hill Studios in Rye, and Paul also played bass and sang backing vocals. Linda McCartney also assisted on vocals, and Beatles-era veteran Geoff Emerick was the sound engineer for the recording session.

> Artist - The Crickets
> Title - T-Shirt
> Year - 1988
> Label - CBS

The Crickets were a legendary classic rock 'n' roll band, formed in 1956 in Lubbock, Texas, USA, and their most well-known member would have to be the late, great Buddy Holly, who was a huge influence on our Fab Four. It wasn't just their music that was influential, but allegedly their name too - Crickets, Beetles ahem Beatles, get it?

With the line-up of Jerry Allison on vocals and drums, Joe Mauldin on vocals and bass, and Gordon Payne on vocals and guitar, 1988 saw them release the single 'T-Shirt', and it was produced by Paul McCartney. He also played piano and provided backing vocals, and it was recorded at Paul's own recording studio in England. This came about as The Crickets made an appearance at Paul's annual Buddy Holly Week celebration (London, 1976-1999), and Macca was interested in working with the legendary band. The song would later be featured on the 1988 album of the same name.

> Artist - Spirit Of Play
> Title - Children in Need
> Year - 1988
> Label - Release Records

One-off charity project featuring Craig Mathieson on vocals, Woody Woodmansey on drums, and Nicky Hopkins on piano and keyboards. This was produced by Paul McCartney, and was made for the famous Children In Need charity which is still running today.

Paul also plays bass and provides backing vocals. It was recorded circa September 1987 at Hog Hill Studios in Rye. The engineers for the session were Matt Butler and Peter Henderson and other musicians on the single included Ken Wilson, Paul Frank, Andrew Skirrow, and a string section from the London String Quartet. Mixing the tune were Stuart Breed and Paul Mortimer.

Artist - Elvis Costello
Album - Spike
Titles - This Town/Veronica/Pads, Paws And Claws
Year - 1989
Label - Warner Bros. Records

Elvis Costello is possibly the second most successful person in the world who shares the name of Elvis, though his real name is Declan McManus, technically making Canadian skating champion Elvis Stojko the second most successful Elvis of all time! One interesting fact you may not know about this musical marvel is that he actually supported my dad's former group, The Natural Acoustic Band, at a gig at Quarrybank High School (John Lennon's old high school) in Liverpool in the early 1970s (see Elvis Costello's autobiography, *Unfaithful Music and Disappearing Ink*)!

In 1989, he released the album *Spike* (featuring a rather creepy cover, where Elvis resembles the Batman villain, Two-Face). The LP is known for featuring collaborations with Paul McCartney, and was a critical and commercial success, reaching No.5 in the UK Album Chart.

On the song 'This Town', Paul McCartney plays a Rickenbacker bass. When it was played on the radio, the moderately profane word "bastard" was replaced with "sweetheart" in the chorus (ironically, the clean version is called the "bastard mix").

The song 'Veronica', meanwhile, is a 1960s style pastiche about an old lady named Veronica who is unfortunately suffering from dementia. It's a surprisingly upbeat track considering the depressing subject matter. Paul plays bass on his iconic Hofner, and he also co-wrote the song. While charting at the modest No.31 in the UK when released as a single, the tune was a big commercial success in the States, reaching No.1 in the *Billboard* Alternative Airplay charts.

The third McCartney/Costello collaboration on the album, 'Pads, Paws And Claws', is a rockabilly throwback number, co-written by Macca. All three of these songs were recorded at the famous Ocean Way Studios in Los Angeles and AIR Studios in London circa 1988.

Artist - The Christians, Holly Johnston, Paul McCartney, Gerry Marsden, Stock Aitken Waterman
Title - Ferry Cross The Mersey
Year - 1989
Label - PWL Records

The Hillsborough disaster was a multiple human crush that happened on the 15th April 1989 during a football (soccer) match between Liverpool FC and Nottingham Forest at Hillsborough stadium in Sheffield, which left 96 people killed, and 766 people injured. Less than a month later, on the 8th May, a charity single was released featuring an all-star cast of Liverpudlian talent including The Christians, Holly Johnson from Frankie Goes To Hollywood, Gerry Marsden (of Pacemakers fame) and of course Paul McCartney. It was a cover version of the Gerry and The Pacemakers hit 'Ferry Cross The Mersey 'and it was produced by the trio of Mike Stock, Matt Aitken and Pete Waterman, who opened the doors for the likes of Kylie Minogue, Jason Donovan and Rick Astley.

The song was a commercial success, reaching No.1 in the UK and Ireland, and reached the top 40 in many countries around the world.

Artist - Elvis Costello
Album - Mighty Like A Rose
Titles - So Like Candy/Playboy To A Man
Year - 1991
Label - Warner Bros. Records

Mighty A Rose is the 13th studio album by rock music legend Elvis Costello. As it was made during the time of the first Gulf War, the record has a bit of an angry tone to it. It received mixed-positive reviews from music critics, and was a commercial success, reaching No.5 in the UK Albums Chart.

'So Like Candy 'was written by McCartney, and originally recorded in 1987 during the time of Paul's solo album *Flowers In The Dirt*; it eventually saw the light of day in 1991, when it was featured on Costello's aforementioned album. Macca's original version was recorded on the 3rd September 1987 at McCartney's Hog Hill Mill Studios, with a subsequent version recorded on the 26th January 1988.

The final version was recorded around late 1990/early 1991 at Ocean Way Studios in Hollywood and Westside Studios in London, and came out on the 10th May 1991 on Costello's studio album *Mighty Like A Rose*. The line-up on this version included Jim Keltner, Mitchell Froom, Marc Ribot, Larry Knechtel, Jerry Scheff and T-Bone (Tom) Wolk. McCartney's original demo versions were eventually released in 2017 on a reissued version of McCartney's *Flowers In The Dirt* LP.

Like 'So Like Candy', 'Playboy To A Man 'had its origins in the *Flowers In The Dirt* sessions. The line-up for the final version of the song was the same as 'So Like Candy 'with the exception of T-Bone Wolk. McCartney's original version of this song was released in 2017 on the reissued version of his *Flowers In The Dirt* album.

Artist - Kiri Te Kanawa
Title - The World You're Coming Into
Year - 1991
Label - EMI Classics

Kiri Te Kanawa is an operatic soprano hailing from New Zealand, and is of European and Maori heritage. Despite retiring in 2017, she has won many accolades, and her voice has been described as "mellow yet vibrant, warm, ample and unforced". She is probably best known for singing at future King Charles and Princess Diana's wedding back in 1981.

1991 was the year Paul McCartney released his classical *Oratorio* in Liverpool with the Liverpool Philharmonic Orchestra. For the segment entitled 'The World You're Coming Into (From Movement VII: Crises)', we are treated to the wonderful vocal stylings of Kiri Te Kanawa. The single was, in fact, a live recording of the *Oratorio*, recorded on the 28th June 1991.

This is a beautiful piece, which shows the diversity of McCartney's repertoire.

Artist - Eddie Murphy
Title - Yeah
Year - 1993
Label - EMI Classics

What can I say about Eddie Murphy? He's one of Hollywood's biggest stars, and is a hilarious stand-up comedian, not to mention an actor, film director, producer, singer... and of course the voice of Donkey in the *Shrek* movies! His stand up film *Delirious* is probably one of the funniest comedy shows ever put onto tape, and his impressions of stars of the day such as Michael Jackson and James Brown are spot on. His character of Donkey (other than possibly Puss-In-Boots) is easily, in my opinion, the highlight of the *Shrek* films... and that's only scratching the surface of his five decade career! He (well, his character on *Saturday Night Live*, Clarence Walker) also has the rather dubious claim of being the fifth member of The Beatles.

1993 saw him release a record entitled *Love's Alright*, and the album opens with a single called 'Yeah '(not be confused with the song by Usher or the song I did... ahem, shameless plug!) which featured more people than a charity ensemble single. Performing on this song included Aaron Hall, Amy Grant, Babyface, Barry White, Jon Bon Jovi, Elton John, Emmanuel Lewis, En Vogue, Garth Brooks, Heavy D, Howard Hewlett, Johnny Gill, Julio Iglesias, Luther Vandross, MC Hammer, Michael and Janet Jackson, Patti LaBelle, Richie Sambora, Stevie Wonder, Teddie Pendergrass, Stanley Clarke, Herbie Hancock and of course, our Paul - talk about a lineup!

The song was a critical and commercial failure, though in all honesty, it's not bad at all, as we have some amazing musicians on the one record, even if the lyrical content is rather limited, featuring the word 'Yeah 'repeated the same amount of times Paul has said "You know" or Ringo has said "Peace and Love" in their lifetimes.

Artist - 10cc
Album - Mirror Mirror
Titles - Code Of Silence/Yvonne's The One
Year - 1995
Label - Avex UK

10cc are a very well respected classic rock group from the 1970s, probably best known for the hit single 'I'm Not In Love'. Eric Stewart from the group has worked with Macca quite a few times, including on his albums *Tug Of War* and *Pipes Of Peace*, and he even co-wrote songs for Paul's album *Press To Play*. Kevin Godley and Lol Creme would later have careers directing music videos, including videos for George Harrison's solo hit 'When We Was Fab 'and (well, Godley on his own) 'Real Love 'from The Beatles' *Anthology* project.

In 1995, 10cc released their eleventh and final studio album, *Mirror Mirror*, and sadly, it was a commercial dud. However, it was a big success in Japan, which reminds you of an old rock cliche. On the song 'Code Of Silence 'Paul plays the electric piano, percussion, strings and sound effect loops, plus he co-wrote it with member Eric Stewart. Also, on the track 'Yvonne's The One 'Paul plays rhythm guitar. Two pretty decent tunes in my opinion, even if they don't match the brilliance of 'I'm Not In Love'.

Artist - Yoko Ono
Title - Hiroshima Sky Is Always Blue
Year - 1995
Label - Unreleased

I think most people who know their Beatles know who Yoko Ono is. She was John Lennon's second wife and is one of the more controversial figures in the Beatles story. Regardless of what you think of her, Yoko's impact in the world of The Beatles was a massive one.

In 1995, Yoko teamed up with Paul McCartney for the song 'Hiroshima Sky Is Always Blue', which was broadcast on Japanese television for the 50th anniversary of America's bombing of Hiroshima. The song was recorded with both John and Paul's children, and was recorded in secret on January 28th 1995 when Yoko and Sean Lennon spent a weekend at Paul's house outside London. Macca showed them into his private recording studio, and suggested they did a track together. Yoko told him about a song she had written about her traumatic memories of living in Japan during the Second World War, when she saw the victims suffering. Yoko sang and Sean played the harpsichord his dad used on the song 'Julia' from the Beatles '1968 *White Album*. Linda McCartney, Paul's late wife, played organ, James McCartney (Paul's son) played guitar and the McCartney daughters, Stella and Mary, were on percussion. Paul played an upright bass, which was originally played by Bill Black, one of Elvis Presley's bassists.

The song contains Yoko doing a spoken word introduction dedicated to her husband, John, and gives a shout out to The Beatles 'hit single 'Strawberry Fields Forever', and Ono sings in a vocal style inspired by Japanese kabuki theatre. While it's possibly not most people's cup of tea, it's admirable that Yoko paid tribute to victims of one of humanity's most despicable man-made disasters.

Artist - The Smoking Mojo Filters
Title - Come Together
Year - 1995
Label - Go! Discs

The Smoking Mojo Filters was a one-off supergroup formed in 1995 consisting of Paul McCartney, Paul Weller from The Jam, Noel Gallagher from Oasis, Steve Cradock from Ocean Colour Scene, Steve White and Carleen Anderson from The Young Disciples (seriously, hear her version of 'Don't Look Back In Anger 'by Oasis - it's amazing!).

They came together in 1995 for the charity War Child, to raise funds for war-torn areas such as Bosnia and Herzegovina. For their single, they opted to cover the old Beatles classic 'Come Together 'and like John when he recorded 'Instant Karma! 'back in 1970, it was released as soon as it was recorded. It reached the healthy No.19 in the UK Singles Chart.

With the awesome Paul Weller on lead vocals, this is a great cover version of a great tune for a great cause, and it's probably the closest thing to having The Beatles and Oasis doing a tune together (ironically, Oasis have worked with the famed tribute band, The Bootleg Beatles!).

    Artist - Elvis Costello
    Title - Shallow Grave
    Year - 1996
    Label - Warner Bros. Records

Another collaborative effort between Macca and Costello. From Costello's seventeenth studio album, *All This Useless Beauty*, this, like many of the McCartney/Costello collaborations, had its origins in the 1987 *Flowers In the Dirt* recording sessions. The finalised version was recorded in the summer of 1995 at Windmill Lane Studios in Dublin. "It was mostly his doing," reflects Elvis Costello in an interview for *The Guardian* in 1996." He wrote more of the words than I did. Even the title. It isn't very typical for him, supposedly Mr Comfortable. It's this slightly frightening idea with this pop melody." [11]
    A great number, which has a vibe that combines blues with the contemporary 'Britpop' sounds of the time.

    Artist - Allen Ginsberg & Paul McCartney, Phillip Glass, Lenny Kaye
    Title - The Ballad Of The Skeletons
    Year - 1996
    Label - Mouth Almighty Records

An unusual collaborative effort with the famous poet extraordinaire, Buddhist and LGBTQ+ activist, Allen Ginsberg, keyboardist Phillip Glass and producer/bassist Lenny Kaye. The original poem 'The Ballad Of The Skeletons 'was published in 1995, and the musical adaptation was recorded in October 1995 at the Hog Hill Studios in Rye. Paul plays drums, guitar, Hammond organ and maracas. "I had a gig at Albert Hall in London. A reading," recalled Ginsberg." I had been talking quite a bit to McCartney, visiting him and bringing him poetry and haiku. So, McCartney liked it and filmed me doing '(The Ballad of The) Skeletons 'in a little 8 millimetre home thing. And then I had this reading at (the) Albert Hall, and I asked (him) if he could recommend a young guitarist who was a quick study. So he gave me a few names but (then) he said, 'If you're not fixed up with a guitarist, why don't you try me? I love the poem.' So I said, 'It's a date.'

"We went to Paul's house and spent an afternoon rehearsing. He came to the sound check and we did a little rehearsal there, again. And then he went up to his box with his family. It was a benefit for literary things. We didn't tell anybody that McCartney was going to play. And we (had) developed that riff really nicely. In fact, Linda (McCartney) (had) made a little tape of our rehearsal. So then, we went on stage and knocked it out. There's a photo of us on the CD. It was very lively and he was into it." [12]

The track wasn't a commercial success, but to this day remains a cult classic.

Artist - Peter Kirtley Band
Title - Little Children
Year - 1998
Label - Jubilee Action

In 1998, McCartney teamed up with The Peter Kirtley Band to produce a charity single entitled 'Little Children '(not a cover of the song by Billy J. Kramer) to help Brazilian street children, who live a very sad and difficult life.

The line-up for this release included Liane Carroll on piano and vocals, Colin Gibson on bass and percussion, Nana Tsiboe playing cabasa, Liam Genockey on drums and percussion, Peter Kirtley on guitar and vocals, Kenny Craddock on accordion, mandolin and organ and spoken-word vocals from Paul.

Appropriately, the song has a beautiful Brazilian vibe to it, even if the lyrics are very harrowing, which makes you think about the horrors that these poor children have to go through.

All proceeds went to Jubilee Action in aid of Brazilian street children.

Artist - Heather Mills feat. Paul McCartney
Title - Vo!ce
Year - 1999
Label - Coda Records

1999 wasn't a particularly great year for mainstream music - the end of the 20th century was something of an anticlimax, as the charts at the time were dominated by endless manufactured pop, but on a positive note, it was a golden age for electronic dance music with the likes of The Chemical Brothers, Daft Punk and Fatboy Slim ripping up the clubs and festivals worldwide.

It was during this time that Paul was in a relationship with a former model and activist named Heather Mills. Unfortunately, Heather had a leg amputated because of a traffic accident, and this single was a spoken-word tune, where Heather spoke out about disability rights over a groovy house beat. Paul provided backing vocals and guitar, and it was produced by Greek dance music legend Nikko Patrelakis.

The tune failed to chart, and McCartney and Mills would eventually split up and divorce in 2008.

Artist - Lindsay Pagano
Title - So Bad
Year - 2001
Label - Warner Bros. Records

Lindsay Pagano is an American teen idol singer, best known for the 2001 song 'Everything U R'. On her debut album *Love, Faith & Inspiration* (released in 2001), she managed to get hold of the Beatle legend, Paul McCartney, to collaborate with her. This all came about because Lindsay was recording her album at Henson Recording Studios in Los Angeles, where Macca was recording his *Driving Rain* LP. Paul introduced himself and asked to hear some of her tunes. Pagano remembers:

"I played him some, and he was dancing all around the studio, Everyone was freaking out that it was Paul McCartney, and I would be like, 'Oh, I just saw Paul. Whatever. 'He just became a regular person. He asked how the album was doing one day, and I said, 'Well, I'm just looking for a really simple acoustic song for the end of the album, just to end it. 'And he said, 'Well, I wrote this song called 'So Bad, 'which I think would go really good with your voice. 'I laid down a rough track, and when I came back to work on it again, I hear this vocal in the back, and it's Paul's vocal. He was singing on it as kind of a surprise. So it became a duet." [9]

As some may have guessed from the title,' So Bad 'is actually a reimagining of a song from Paul's 1983 album *Pipes Of Peace*.

Artist - Super Furry Animals
Title - Respectable For The Respectable
Year - 2001
Label - Epic

2001 was a dark time in our history - 9/11, the foot and mouth crisis, the death of our beloved Beatle George, not to mention the rise of reality TV, but on a positive note, music was still going strong, and in that year, Macca teamed up with the Welsh Britpop band, The Super Furry Animals. Their sound is fairly psychedelic, and they blend every other genre with it, and their lyrical content fluctuates from being nonsensical to being deeply profound and philosophical.

On their 2001 album *Rings Around The World*, the Super Furries were inspired by Paul's talent for eating celery (see The Beach Boys' 'Vegetables') and on this track, Macca provided a carrots and celery rhythm track. In fact, in 2021, the band released a "Maccapella" of Paul's celery track, which makes a great beat for any upcoming hip-hop MC wanting to compete in a battle rap (as long as you have enough money to clear it!).

    Artist - Lulu
    Title - Inside Thing (Let 'Em In)
    Year - 2002
    Label - Mercury

Lulu is a legendary Scottish musical icon. She is noted for her amazing singing abilities (hear her hit, 'Shout!'- total classic) and she also won the Eurovision Song Contest in 1969 (alongside Spain, Netherlands and France in a four way tie) with 'Boom Bang-A-Bang'; plus she sang the title song for the James Bond film *The Man With The Golden Gun* in 1974. She also starred in the film *To Sir With Love* alongside Sidney Poitier in 1967 and she sang the theme tune.

In 2002, she released her collaborations album *Together*, in which she worked with contemporary artists such as Ronan Keating, Sting, Westlife, Take That and Atomic Kitten, as well as a few legends such as Elton John and Cliff Richard, and including a really great Fatboy Slim-esque remix of 'Stop Fooling Around' by Kerphunk.

Paul McCartney collaborated with the great Scottish songstress on the track 'Inside Thing (Let 'Em In)'- it's a remake of the hit song 'Let 'Em In' by Paul's band, Wings, from the 1976 album *Wings At The Speed Of Sound* and the tune is reinterpreted with a late 1990s/early 2000s R&B style twist. It was previously covered by singer Billy Paul, and this version is also used in the UK Postcode Lottery adverts. Lulu is still performing and releasing records today.

    Artist - Rusty Anderson
    Title - Hurt Myself
    Year - 2003

Label - Oxide Records

Rusty Anderson is a guitarist from California, and is the owner of several record labels. He has been a member of Paul McCartney's backing band since 2001, and in 2003, he released his album, the rather provocatively titled *Undressing Underwater*. Paul plays on the first tune of the album, 'Hurt Myself'.

"Well, I can say the recording process was pretty cool," recalls Rusty. "Paul said: 'Let's plan something', and I realised we had only three days to do it so I quickly booked a session, everybody came on board and David (Kahne) said: 'Sure I'll produce it', and because it had to be organised so quickly because we were just about to go to Mexico City and then Japan and then everyone would disperse, so we quickly found ourselves in the studio, I was singing the song, Paul was playing bass and then made a mistake and he goes: 'S**t!' and I felt it was me, mad at myself for not learning exactly how I thought it should, it just made me realise how human we all are." [20]

It's a really nice track, which has a bit of a late 1960s psychedelic vibe to it. He is still playing lead guitar in Paul's backing band today.

Artist - Band Aid 20
Title - Do They Know It's Christmas
Year - 2004
Label - Mercury

The year was 2004 - Geldof and Ure were back with their pop music friends to inform the world about the horrors of the troubles of the Darfur region of Sudan. Unlike the last time, McCartney actually appears on the A-side, where he plays bass. Also joining him in Band Aid 20 are Thom Yorke and Jonny Greenwood from Radiohead on piano and guitar, Justin and Dan Hawkins from The Darkness on guitar and on drums, and Phil Collins from Genesis and Danny Goffey from Supergrass also playing drums.

Vocal wise, we have people as diverse as Damon Albarn (Blur, Gorillaz), Chris Martin (Coldplay), rapper Dizzee Rascal, Neil Hannon (The Divine Comedy), Bono (U2), Joss Stone, Robbie Williams (Take That), Rachel Stevens (S Club 7) and even presenter Cat Deeley. While not as famous as its 1984 namesake, the single was still a commercial success, and sold 72,000 copies in its first 24 hours. It went straight to No.1 in the UK Singles Chart, selling over a million copies in the UK alone, the last single physically to do so.

Artist - Brian Wilson
Title - A Friend Like You
Year - 2004
Label - Rhino Records

Would you like a friend like Brian Wilson? I would (but after all, I am a little eccentric)!

Brian and Macca crossed paths again in 2004 for Brian's album *Gettin' In Over My Head*, which was released on Rhino Records. The album received mixed reviews, and commercially it wasn't very successful, probably because it was overshadowed by Wilson's remake of the then-lost 1967 Beach Boys album *Smile*, which garnered all the publicity and love, and came out only three months later.

Paul's contribution was with the song 'A Friend Like You '- unlike the last time, this was more than just chewing celery! He actually played acoustic guitar and sang vocals with Wilson. Also appearing on the album are Elton John, Eric Clapton and a posthumous appearance from Brian's brother, the late Carl Wilson.

The song would later be recorded in 2011 by Steve Wrigley and Glen Richardson for the Beach Boys tribute album *California Feeling*, and a Spanish version would also be recorded by Beach Boys drummer, Bobby Figuero, but never released.

Artist - Stevie Wonder
Title - A Time to Love
Year - 2005
Label - Motown Records

Stevie Wonder is one of the few people who could be considered a musical genius (alongside our Macca!). He is one of the funkiest people that has ever lived on Planet Earth and he can play any musical instrument and sing pretty much anything, making it sound awesome, plus he can do all this despite being totally blind.

It wasn't the first time Stevie and The Beatles crossed paths. In 1966 he covered 'We Can Work It Out', and in 1982, Stevie did two duets with Paul McCartney for Paul's *Tug Of War* album - the middle of the road mega-hit 'Ebony and Ivory 'and the outstanding 'What's That You're Doing'.

In 2005, Stevie released the album *A Time to Love* which featured guest appearances from the likes of Kim Burrell, Hubert Laws, Kirk Franklin, En Vogue and Prince on the track 'So What The Fuss'. The title track 'A Time to Love ' featured vocals from neo-soul singer, India.Arie, and playing guitar was none other than our old buddy Macca. A great tune, which harks back to classic 1970s era Stevie.

Artist - George Benson & Al Jarreau
Title - Bring It On Home To Me
Year - 2006
Label - Concord Records

George Benson is a legendary jazz guitarist, who is probably best known for his album *Breezin'* and hit songs such as 'The Greatest Love Of All' from the Muhammad Ali film *The Greatest*, and tracks like the incredibly funky 'Give Me The Night'. His partner in crime, the late Al Jarreau, was another jazz-funk legend, who is probably best remembered for singing the theme to the 1980s TV show *Moonlighting*. In 2006, the two of them teamed up on the album *Givin 'It Up*.

The album closes with a cover of the Sam Cooke classic 'Bring It On Home To Me ' featuring a great vocal from Sir Paul McCartney. Macca had previously covered the song in 1988 on the album *Choba B CCCP*, which was an album made exclusively for the Russian market.

Artist - Linkin Park, Jay-Z and Paul McCartney
Title - Numb/Encore/Yesterday
Year - 2006
Label - Unreleased

"I've got 99 problems but a Macca ain't one, hit me!"
Linkin Park are a very successful American rock collective, who were one of the biggest bands in the rather divisive nu-metal sub-genre of the 1990s and 2000s. They have sold over 50 million records worldwide, and are probably best known outside of the music world for their association with the soundtrack to Michael Bay's *Transformers* movies, and their music being used in Anime fan videos of the early 2000s.

Jay-Z on the other hand is a very popular hip-hop icon, who is one of the most successful and revered in the game. He is, of course, married to Beyoncé Knowles, and they have three children together.

In 2004, Linkin Park teamed up with Jigga for their collabo EP 'Collision Course', which spawned the very successful single 'Numb/Encore', which sold over 2 million copies in the US, despite only reaching No.20.

In 2006, the song won Best Rap/Sung Collaboration at the Grammy Awards. Linkin and Jay performed the track onstage, and after Jay's rap verse (Jigga was wearing a John Lennon T-shirt), Chester Bennington (Linkin Park's late vocalist) sang the first few lines of 'Yesterday', which was then succeeded by a surprise appearance from Paul McCartney joining them on stage! I may not be much of a nu-metal person myself, but even I had to admit, this collaboration is pretty epic!

Artist - George Michael
Title - Heal The Pain 2006
Year - 2006
Label - Epic

George Michael (1963-2016) was a pop music icon of the 1980s and 1990s and was one half of the boy-band Wham! He was a massive solo star, who, despite attracting some controversy with the tabloids, was revealed to be a pretty decent bloke, donating to charitable causes and giving a free concert to nurses to thank them for looking after his dying mum.

In 2006, he re-recorded, with Paul McCartney, his lesser-known 1991 single 'Heal The Pain', which had originally reached a modest No.31 in the UK Singles Chart at the time. Despite the extra kudos of having the song reinterpreted as a duet between Michael and an ex-Beatle, the 2006 re-re-cording failed to chart, but it was included on Michael's greatest hits compilation *Twenty Five*, also released in 2006, which actually sold really well.

George Michael, in the documentary film *Freedom*, recalls making this legendary collaboration: "I was big into *Abbey Road* and *Revolver*. I made one record to show how much I loved Lennon ['Praying for Time'], I made another record to show how much I loved McCartney ['Heal the Pain']. I didn't dream McCartney would ever sing it. And actually when he sings it, it sounds like a Paul McCartney record!" [21]

A beautiful song, and definitely a recommended track.

Artist - Kylie Minogue and Paul McCartney
Title - Dance Tonight
Year - 2007
Label - Not Released

Kylie Minogue is an Australian pop music legend/sex symbol/gay icon. She has had hits spanning five different decades (my favourite being 2001's 'Can't Get You Out Of My Head '- awesome tune) and has had excellent longevity in the fickle world of the music business. She remains popular with all age groups and all genres, which is something of a feat for a recording artist and performer.

In 2007, the pop princess from down under teamed up with our Macca for a duet version of Paul's 2007 hit 'Dance Tonight 'from his *Memory Almost Full* album, which was played on Jools Holland's 2007 BBC New Years Eve TV special *Hootenanny*, performed just before midnight came along.

The McCartney hit became a duet between the Beatle legend and the Aussie pop princess with Minogue adding a slightly country-esque twist to her vocals (which is funny, as Kylie would later do a country album in 2018!). Jools Holland joined in playing piano, and for *Doctor Who* fans, look out for the tenth and fourteenth Doctor himself, David Tennant, clapping along; also watch out for Dawn French and Seasick Steve.

Artist - Nitin Sawhney
Title - My Soul
Year - 2008
Label - Cooking Vinyl

Nitin Sawhney is an Indian-British Ivor Novello award winning musician, who combines jazz with electronic music. In 2008, he released the album *London Undersound*, which featured the song 'My Soul', written by Paul McCartney. Paul also sang, and played bass, acoustic and electric guitars.

"I've known Paul McCartney for a long time, and he came over the first time back in the 90s, to the shared flat I was in with Sanjeev Bhaskar (famous British actor and comedian) actually. It was amazing because he called me up in the morning and said, I'm thinking of coming over and watching what you're doing," remembered Sawhney." He was the easiest person I've ever worked with. He had no ego. He was really chilled." [22]

A really lovely number, and definitely one for your record collection!

Artist - Yusuf
Title - Boots and Sand
Year - 2009
Label - Island Records

Cat Stevens (nowadays Yusuf Islam) is a singer/songwriter legend with a lovely singing voice, who has produced and written some fantastic songs over the years, which have become standards, such as 'Moon Shadow', 'Father and Son', 'Peace Train 'and 'Wild World', and he even had a brief foray into Krautrock with 'Was Dog A Doughnut'. He is also a humanitarian, who donates more than half his income to charity.

In 2009, Yusuf teamed up with Paul McCartney and Dolly Parton on the song 'Boots and Sand'. It was written after Yusuf was denied entry into America in 2004 because he shared the same name with a known terrorist, along with thousands of others (this was during the height of the 'war on terror'). This song combined influences of The Beatles, as well as Dolly Parton's country music style. It was recorded in the summer of 2008, and was released as a single on July 20th 2009. It was also featured on Yusuf's album *Roadsinger*.

The song is classic Cat Stevens/Yusuf Islam, and having both Paul McCartney and Dolly Parton into the mix just adds to the musical awesomeness.

Artist - Glen Aitken
Title - Ordinary People
Year - 2010
Label - Right Recordings

Glenn Aiken is a singer, songwriter and multi-instrumentalist from New Zealand, who was discovered by Paul McCartney circa early 2000s during his holiday in the Maldives, where he witnessed him playing. Aitken then moved to England, and had his music published by Paul's MPL Communications, and in 2010, he released his debut album *Extraordinary Lives*. The LP contained the single 'Ordinary People 'and playing bass is none other than Macca himself!

It's a beautiful tune, and it's a shame that so few people have heard it. Luckily, Aitken is still singing and performing today, so check him out live, or buy one of his records if you have the chance.

Artist - Fran Healy
Title - As It Comes
Year - 2010
Label - Wreckord Label

Fran Healy is the lead singer and main songwriter of the successful Scottish Britpop collective, Travis. They always get rained on, because Healy lied when he was 17, but despite this, they are still performing today, selling out records and music venues.

In 2010, Fran released his one-and-only solo album, *Wreckorder*, and on his ode to vegetarianism on the song 'As It Comes', Paul plays bass guitar. "I wrote this song called 'As It Comes', and the refrain reminded me of The Beatles," recalls Healy in *Spin* magazine." I thought, 'Why don't I get in touch with him? 'I know Paul. We met in 2000 on holiday - we were staying in the same place. Anyway, I thought I should ask, because if I didn't, I'd always wonder if he would have done it. So I sent it to him last July and he did it. People always ask him to sing on their albums, but I don't think he's ever played bass on anyone else's album before." [8]

As this book informs you, Healy was mistaken in this belief that McCartney hadn't played bass on anyone else's records before. It's a lovely little number, which wouldn't feel out of place on a Travis album, and the track coincidentally has a Beatle-esque vibe to the backing.

    Artist - Billy Joel
    Album - The Last To Play At Shea
    Title - Magic In Music (I Saw Her Standing There)/Finale (Piano Man/Let It Be)
    Year - 2010
    Label - Lionsgate

Hailing from the birthplace of hip-hop culture, the Bronx, Billy Joel is a very popular singer/songwriter, who is nowadays known as the face of middle-of-the-road daytime radio, and he has a residency at New York's legendary Madison Square Gardens, where he performs once a month (except in most of 2020 and the first half of 2021 for obvious reasons!). He has sold over 160 million records worldwide, making him the seventh best selling recording artist of all time (the best selling artists of all time are, of course, our Fabs!). He was inducted into the Songwriters Hall Of Fame in 1992 and into the Rock And Roll Hall Of Fame in 1999.

This CD/DVD is a recording of a performance of Joel's at Shea Stadium in 2008. As stated in the title *The Last To Play At Shea*, Joel was the last person to play at the legendary baseball stadium, which, of course, hosted arguably the most famous Beatles gig of them all, back in 1965, and what better way to close Billy's show than have old Macca come on for the encore. For the number 'Magic In Music', Joel mashes it up with the old Beatles standard 'I Saw Her Standing There', and the final number 'Piano Man' is mashed together with 'Let It Be'. Say what you want about Billy Joel, but this collaboration between two rock legends is a must for both McCartney and Joel fans.

Artist - Victoria Villalobos
Title - You Won't See Me
Year - 2010
Label - The Beatles Complete On Ukulele

Victoria Villalobos is a lady who hails from San Salvador, who has been singing since she was the tender age of seven. She was signed to MCA Universal back in the day, when she was in the band Big Bang Theory (nothing to do with the comedy show of the same name). Her biggest claim to fame would have to be her very prolific career in music for advertising, and her work as a producer. In 2010, she covered the 1965 Beatles song 'You Won't See Me', originally from their 1965 album *Rubber Soul*. Her version is notable as it actually features a sample of the real Paul McCartney taken from an answerphone message.

This was part of a project by Roger Greeenawalt and David Barratt called 'The Beatles Complete On Ukulele', which was a musical effort done between 2009-2012 to prove that if every citizen spent a little bit of a time playing the ukulele, the world would be nicer place (George Formby would be proud!). Notable people who took part in this project included Wang Chung, Nicki Richards, Victoria Rox, Gerard Ross, Jim Boggia, Elena Hayden, page three girl Sam Fox (!) and John's ex-wife, Cynthia Lennon.

The project even sent ukuleles to ten of the most important people in the world at the time, and they even got a thank you message from the first lady of the United States at the time, Michelle Obama. Unfortunately, finding copies of this, and other recordings for this project, is scarce, as the site was a target for hackers.

Artist - Steve Martin
Title - Best Love
Year - 2011
Label - Rounder Records

Well excuuuusseee me! Steve Martin is a very funny man and despite what people might say, he was never an official cast member of *Saturday Night Live* in spite of his predominance in the show. He has starred in many films including the infamous 1978 *Sgt Pepper* film, *All Of Me*, *Three Amigos*,

The Jerk, The Man With Two Brains and *Planes, Trains And Automobiles* among many other hits.

He is also a successful musician, and even had a hit record with 'King Tut ' in 1978. In 2011, he released a bluegrass album entitled *Rare Bird Alert*, which, according to Martin himself "I wrote all the songs on this record - and by the way they're all terrible". [14] Contrary to what Martin says, listening to the album for research for this book, I would have to disagree.

The highlight of the album would have to be the rather unexpected collaboration between a comedic legend and a Beatles legend. "[*Saturday Night* producer] Lorne Michaels came to me a year ago and he says 'You know Steve, you don't impose on your friends' and I thought, I don't, I'm very shy about asking people to do something - and I thought I had this song," recalled Martin. "It's sort of a light hearted love song, and Tony Trischka - the producer of the record - his son who's 15 suggested - we were trying to think who could sing this - and he said Paul McCartney - and I thought gee, that's absolutely right.

"So I met Paul McCartney maybe three times in my life so I can't really call him a friend but Paul doesn't know that - he might think we're friends as he meets so many people he can't remember who his friends are. So I managed to get an email of Paul's assistant. First I recorded the song in my iPhone and played it on the banjo and I sang it myself so it's a little modest recording and I emailed to his assistant and I waited about a month, I heard nothing. But I knew Paul was on tour so it was gonna take some time.

"So about a month later I got an email back from Paul. It said 'I'm on tour, haven't had a chance to listen to the song yet but don't worry I will' and another like three weeks went by and then finally he said 'I'll do it' and I thought 'Wow this is fantastic' so we went to Asheville - where we recorded the whole album - and we laid down the dummy track. I sang it again and then we sent that off to Paul.

"And now it's time to schedule Paul, so I wrote him, and we get an email from his assistant, 'Paul wants to know what part you want him to sing' and I said 'Well, we thought the whole thing.' 'Paul thought he was going to back you up' - I said 'Okay but I'm a terrible singer' so then I got an email back from Paul and he said 'Well as a little-known band from Liverpool once said, we can work it out.'

"So I went in, and now I record the song again with me singing doing my best efforts - and Paul arrives and he said 'You know, when you said you were a terrible singer, I thought you were being humble, but you weren't' and he ended up singing the entire song, the most charming guy in the world, friendly to everyone - I learned a lot - so nice and finally we recorded it for a couple of hours, and we said 'Okay I think we got it.' He said 'Oh let me do it a couple more times' - he was that energetic and enthusiastic." [14]

Artist - Jimmy Fallon feat. Paul McCartney
Title - Scrambled Eggs
Year - 2012
Label - Warner Bros. Records

James Thomas Fallon is a New York-based television host, comedian, actor, singer, musician and producer. He is best known for presenting the long running comedic chat show *The Tonight Show with Jimmy Fallon*, which has been running since 2014, and is still going today. In 2012, he released his second album, *Blow Your Pants Off*, which features Fallon exposing his bare bottom on the cover, much to the disgrace of grannies everywhere!

The album contained not-so-family-friendly numbers such as 'My Upstairs Neighbours Are Having Sex (And Listening To The Black Eyed Peas) 'and 'Balls In Your Mouth', as well as pastiches of the theme tune to *The Fresh Prince Of Bel-Air* and *Charles In Charge* done in the styles of Neil Young and Bob Dylan respectively.

The LP also contained the song 'Scrambled Eggs', which, as hardcore Beatle fans may already be aware, was the working title of 'Yesterday'. In 2010, as a joke, McCartney sang the original 'Scrambled Eggs 'version on *Late Night With Jimmy Fallon*, and this is a recorded version put onto wax. Great to see that Paul has such a good sense of humour.

Artist - The Justice Collective
Title - He Ain't Heavy, He's My Brother
Year - 2012
Label - Metropolis Recordings

An all-star musical ensemble covering The Hollies 'hit single in memory of the victims of the 1989 Hillsborough disaster. The mastermind behind this release was Keith Mullen of the indie rock band The Farm, and it was produced by Guy Chambers, who is probably best known for his work with Robbie Williams.

Playing on this recording were Gerry Marsden (of Pacemakers fame), Paul Heaton (from The Housemartins and The Beautiful South), Robbie Williams (Take That), Mel C (The Spice Girls), Holly Johnson (Frankie Goes To Hollywood), Paloma Faith, Beverley Knight, Eliza Doolittle,

Bobby Elliot (The Hollies), Tony Hicks (The Hollies), Mick Jones (The Clash), Elton John and many more… and of course, Paul McCartney.

The tune proved to be a commercial success, reaching the Christmas No.1 spot in December 2012, with the proceeds of the single's sales going towards the Hillsborough families' legal costs in their fight for justice, which in 2021 they finally got.

McCartney, as stated previously, had also taken part in another Hillsborough charity single in 1989 with 'Ferry Cross The Mersey'.

Artist - Bruce Springsteen
Title - I Saw Her Standing There
Year - 2012
Label - Eagle Vision

Jersey Shore resident Bruce Springsteen is an extremely popular and iconic rock star, and close friend of former president Barack Obama, who was 'Born in the USA'. He started getting recognition in the 1980s, selling out stadiums everywhere, and even in 2023 is still selling out stadiums. He is also nicknamed 'the Boss' and was inducted into both the Rock And Roll and Songwriters Hall Of Fame in 1999. He has sold over 150 million records worldwide, making him one of the best selling pop stars of all time.

In 2012, he did a massive show at Hyde Park in London, and for the encore, he brought out the Beatle legend Paul McCartney to join him on stage, and to do a cover of that old Beatles standard, which was the opener to their 1963 debut album *Please Please Me*,' I Saw Her Standing There'. This please pleased everybody in the audience, until the "jobsworths" at the council pulled the plug on it, as they went over the curfew time. Even the Mayor of London at the time (and future Prime Minister) Boris Johnson was furious! Macca returned the compliment at Glastonbury 2022, when he brought out Bruce Springsteen for an encore to sing with him for the songs 'Glory Days 'and 'I Wanna Be Your Man'.

This was all documented on the 2013 DVD/Blu-Ray *Springsteen & I* released through Eagle Vision.

Artist - Etienne Charry
Album - L'ecume Des Jours
Titles - Mais, Aime La - Loane/Courses Cloches/Fleuiste
Year - 2013
Label - Mercury

Etienne Charry is a French singer who hails from Toulouse in the South of France and sometimes goes by the name of Trinidad. In 2013, Charry composed the soundtrack to the surrealist romantic comedy film *L'ecume Des Jours* (known in English speaking countries as *Mood Indigo*), which was directed by Michael Gondry - it received mixed reviews from critics. Gondry had previously directed the music video for McCartney's 2007 hit single 'Dance Tonight'.

Paul plays bass on three of the songs in the film's score, 'Mais, Aime La - Loane', 'Courses Cloches 'and 'Fleuiste'. Paul's sections were recorded circa January-March 2013 at Avatar Studios in New York, with Brian Montgomery being the recording engineer for the session, and French singer Loane sings vocals on the song 'Mais, Aime La'.

Artist - Eric Clapton
Title - All Of Me
Year - 2013
Label - Surfdog

Eric Clapton CBE is a very popular blues-rock guitarist extraordinaire, plus he was married to George's former wife, Pattie Boyd. He was a good friend to all four Beatles, especially George Harrison, as they would collaborate on many projects together (as recorded in this book), plus he played guitar on the *White Album* track 'While My Guitar Gently Weeps'. He was a member of iconic and legendary bands such as Derek & The Dominoes and Cream, and is a very famous and revered solo artist. While his views on certain topics might be controversial and unpopular, one thing you can't take away from him is his extraordinary musical talent!

In 2013, he released his twenty-first studio album, the rather aptly titled *Old Sock*. The title was born out of a conversation with David Bowie. McCartney plays bass and sings vocals on the song 'All Of Me'. It is a cover version of a 1931 jazz standard written by Gerald Marks and Seymour Simons. Other versions have been recorded by the likes of Louis Armstrong, Billie Holiday, Frank Sinatra and even Willie Nelson. It also inspired the Steve Martin film of the same name.

The album was also notable for containing the final recorded appearance from singer/songwriter JJ Cale before his passing in 2013.

Artist - Sir Bob Cornelius Rifo Presents The Bloody Beetroots Feat. Paul McCartney & Youth
Title - Out Of Sight

Year - 2013
Label - Ultra Records

Bob Rifo and Simone Cogo, AKA The Bloody Beetroots, are an Italian electronic dance music duo established in 2006 (though nowadays, it's just Rifo on his own). They have produced tunes in genres as diverse as electro house, dubstep and drum & bass, and have worked with the likes of Steve Aoki, playing at many major dance music festivals such as Tomorrowland and Ultra Music Festival. The duo are also known for wearing masks similar to the Marvel superhero Spider-Man.

In 2013, out of left-field, Paul collaborated with The Beetroots on the tune 'Out Of Sight '- a dubstep-inspired track that has more in common with Skrillex than The Beatles. While some more traditional Beatle fans may hate it, I personally think it's really good and pretty tasteful. Remember, this isn't the first time Macca has dipped into dance music - Paul is one half of the dance duo The Fireman (whose other member, Youth AKA Martin Glover, is also on this tune) and he has collaborated with Roy Kerr on the project Twin Freaks in 2004, which was a series of house and big beat remixes of songs from McCartney's solo career.

Artist - James McCartney
Album - Me
Year - 2013
Label - ECR Music Group

As you would guess from the artist's name, James McCartney is, of course, Paul and Linda's son, who was born in 1977. Like his father, he is also a musician and songwriter and also, like his dad, his first name is James.

In 2013, he released his debut album, *Me*. With the exception of 'Thinking About Rock & Roll', which features dad McCartney on backing vocals and guitar, it is not known which other songs Paul played on, but what is known is that it was recorded between Abbey Road, Hog Mill, Select, Avatar and Nevo studios and producing the album was David Kahne.

McCartney Jr is still performing and releasing records today. Like his father, he is a vegetarian and an animal rights activist.

Artist - Paul McCartney feat. Dave Grohl, Krist Novoselic and Pat Smear
Title - Cut Me Some Slack
Year - 2013

Label - Roswell Records

Nirvana were the main band in the American grunge music scene, and are probably best known for their massive, massive hit tune 'Smells Like Teen Spirit '(a true banger). They were led by their late vocalist, Kurt Cobain. Obviously, Cobain had sadly joined the "27 Club" in 1994, so a true reunion would not be on the cards, but it didn't stop a one-off semi-reunion of sorts happening in 2013.

Nirvana's drummer, Foo Fighter and all-round good guy Dave Grohl, had an idea for a documentary film about the history of the sound recording studios in Los Angeles where Nirvana recorded their legendary 1991 album *Nevermind*, and he invited several friends of his to help out on the film's soundtrack - one of these individuals was the Beatle legend himself!

After a three hour jam session, Grohl, McCartney and former Nirvana members Krist Novoselic and Pat Smear came up with the song 'Cut Me Some Slack'. The tune had its premiere in 2012 for a Hurricane Sandy Relief charity concert. In 2014 'Cut Me Some Slack 'won the Grammy Award for Best Rock Song.

A banging tune, which would have made Kurt Cobain proud, the song was released on the 12th March 2013 on the soundtrack album to the documentary film *Sound City* (see my previous book *Acting Naturally*) entitled *Sound City - Real to Reel*, which contains a segment on the recording of this piece.

Artist - Kanye West
Title - Only One
Year - 2014
Label - GOOD

A self-claimed "motherf***ing genius", Kanye West is a very popular and also very controversial figure in the hip-hop arena. Despite brimming with talent and creativity, he is also known for being "eccentric" at times, with his antics upstaging the music he has produced over the years.

Recorded during a two-day period in Mexico in September 2014, this was the first of the two rumoured collaborations between the two musical icons - Paul and Yeezy (nowadays known as Ye), with the other being the rather obscenely titled 'Piss On Your Grave '(unreleased). 'Only One 'was a tribute to West's daughter, North, with Kanye's wife at the time, Kim Kardashian, who says it's her ex-husband's favourite song. Providing backing vocals was singer and producer Ty$.

Despite being a good tune, Paul's vocals seemed to be buried in the background, making you wonder if McCartney's name was just put in to push more record sales?

The track was successful, reaching No.18 in the UK Singles Chart, and No.35 in the US *Billboard* Chart, but it was a bigger hit in Australia and New Zealand, reaching No.8 in those two countries respectively.

If you want to hear a song that actually does feature Paul McCartney rapping, there is an audio clip of Paul covering the old nursery rhyme 'Humpty Dumpty 'circa 1992 on YouTube. Additionally, if you want to hear a really good Beatles/hip-hop hybrid (with ironically more Macca), check out Danger Mouse's bootleg album *The Grey Album*, which mashes The Beatles '*White Album* with Jay-Z's *The Black Album* - it's dope!

Artist - Dr. Dre feat. Marsha Ambrosias and Kendrick Lamar
Title - Gone
Year - 2015
Label - Aftermath Entertainment

For fans of classic hip-hop, Andre Young AKA Dr. Dre is a total legend. He's probably best known for being one fifth of the legendary (and controversial) N.W.A., the guy who discovered Eminem and Snoop Dogg (among others), and outside of rap is probably best known as the guy who put his name to the bestselling line of headphones - Beats. As of 2023, he still hasn't released his long-awaited album *Detox*!

In 2015, he released his third studio album, *Compton* (obviously named to cash in on the N.W.A. biopic movie *Straight Outta Compton* that came out that year), and the track 'Gone 'features a sample of the Wings track 'Spirits of Ancient Egypt'. While not strictly a collabo between Macca and the D.R.E., Paul and Linda McCartney both receive a songwriter's credit.

Artist - Hollywood Vampires
Title - Come and Get It
Year - 2015
Label - UME

The Hollywood Vampires are a rock supergroup featuring Alice Cooper, Joe Perry, Tommy Henriksen and Hollywood actor Johnny Depp performing an array of cover songs. Their band name comes from an infamous drinking club which was frequented by the likes of John and Ringo Beatle,

Harry Nilsson, Keith Moon of The Who and Micky Dolenz of The Monkees.

Paul McCartney makes a guest appearance on their cover of Badfinger's 'Come and Get It', written by McCartney. "We're recording live... Alice looks at me with this befuddled little look and he's mouthing the words, 'Oh my god, that's Paul McCartney!' to me... Then I look over at Joe Perry - one of my guitar heroes from when I was a kid - and he looks at me and he says, mouthing it, 'Jesus - look, man, it's Paul McCartney!'" remembers Johnny Depp." It was great to see those two huge stars being starstruck." [23]

A great version of an already great tune, and it's amazing to think that things have gone full circle, as McCartney sang on the original Beatles demo version before giving it to Badfinger, and on this version, Macca is on lead vocals.

Artist - Paul McCartney, Jon Bon Jovi, Sheryl Crow, Fergie, Colbie Caillat, Natasha Bedingfield, Leona Lewis, Sean Paul, Johnny Rzeznik, Krewella, Angelique Kidjo, Kelsea Ballerini, Nicole Scherzinger, Christina Grimmie, Victoria Justice & Q'orianka Kilcher
Title - Love Song To The Earth
Year - 2015
Label - Friends Of The Earth

An all-star charity release with the sole purpose to save the world from the evil that is global warming. This was made to coincide with the COP21 conference that happened in November and December that year in Paris, France. Whether the politicians listened to them is up for debate.

"I'm glad to be a part of 'Love Song to the Earth, 'aiming to inspire people across the world to urge their leaders to act on climate change," McCartney told *Rolling Stone* magazine in 2015." We need to be fast and efficient, switching to renewable energy and eating less meat, for example. Big decisions will be made this week, so I am doing everything I can to make sure governments sign up to an agreement which can protect our planet. Now is the time to act. So please spread the woes and help keep our planet safe!" [26]

All proceeds of the song went towards the environmental group Friends of the Earth and the United Artists Foundations. Paul and his musical cohorts also donated their fees for this release.

Artist - Rihanna feat. Kanye West and Paul McCartney
Title - FourFiveSeconds
Year - 2015
Label - Roc Nation

Robyn Rihanna Fenty is a pop music icon, known for her very catchy tunes and her very sexy stage persona. Hailing from Barbados, she has had some really massive hits such as 'Umbrella', 'We Found Love', 'Diamonds 'and 'Don't Stop The Music'. As well as being a singer, she is also an actress, a fashion designer and she has her own range of cosmetics. Trying to get the hook of her song 'Disturbia 'out of your head is almost close to impossible, so be warned if you listen to it!

The collaboration between Macca, RiRi and Yeezy was recorded circa early 2014 at the Beverly Hills Hotel in Los Angeles, and producing the song was Kanye. Like his other collaborations with Kanye West, 'FourFiveSeconds 'is a possible attempt of Paul to be "down-with-the-kids", and it paid off, as the song was a massive commercial success, topping the charts around the world. Hopefully, more adolescents will become Beatles fans after hearing this song! It's also the most streamed non-Beatles Paul McCartney song on Spotify (as of 2023).

"I just threw ideas at [Kanye]. I had no idea about the end result or whether he would even use any of it until he sent me the three songs for listening. The first time I listened, I was pretty confused. I spoke to one of Kanye's people, Noah - an incredibly nice man - and asked him, 'Well, where am I? 'And he laughed and said, 'Well, the groove itself is your guitar, man!'" remembers McCartney." The icing on the cake was Rihanna. He had her added afterwards because he thought the song would be a good fit for her. Then I listened to it one more time. It worked. The next step was that we made a video. It was super, great fun. It was with this Dutch director couple that I forgot the names of. They have some impossible names to remember [Inez van Lamsweerde and Vinoodh Matadin], but they did a really fine job. The next step was that we played at the Grammys show in February… Rihanna is an excellent performer so it was a great pleasure. I have to say that I'm glad I jumped on the bandwagon." [24]

Artist - Kanye West
Title - All Day
Year - 2015
Label - GOOD

The third collabo between Macca and Ye. Like 'Only One', there isn't much involvement from McCartney other than a replayed sample of Macca whistling from the 1971 Wings song 'When The Wind Is Blowing', which was recorded in early 2014 at the Beverley Hills Hotel in Los Angeles. It was a commercial success, however, reaching the top 20 in many countries. Paul was happy with the song, but was dissatisfied that it contained 40 uses of the dreaded N-word.

Artist - Bernhard Welz
Title - Maybe I'm Amazed
Year - 2016
Label - Pure Rock Records

Bernhard Welz is a drummer, producer and drum teacher from Austria. He has been in bands such as No Bros, Schubert In Rock and The Mild Mannered Janitors.

In 2016, he released an album called *Stay Tuned 1.5.* for the charity Rock Against Cancer.

The album closes with a cover version of the old Macca classic 'Maybe I'm Amazed 'featuring Paul himself on vocals.

Artist - Foo Fighters
Title - Sunday Rain
Year - 2017
Label - Roswell Records

Ultra-popular alternative rock band founded by former Nirvana drummer and nice guy, Dave Grohl. They have received critical and commercial acclaim, and have sold out arenas and headlined festivals worldwide, and still do to this day. On September 15th 2017, they released their ninth studio album, *Concrete and Gold*, and for Beatle fans, it is notable for having Paul McCartney as a guest drummer on the song 'Sunday Rain'.

It was recorded around March-April 2017 at EastWest Studios in Los Angeles. Many Beatle fans think the opening of the song sounds somewhat similar to the Lennon solo composition 'How Do You Sleep? 'which, is ironically, a diss track aimed at Macca.

Artist - Charlotte Gainsbourg
Title - Songbird In A Cage

Year - 2017
Label - Because Music

Charlotte Gainsbourg is the daughter of the legendary French musical icon Serge Gainsbourg and English actress Jane Birkin. Paul wrote this song around 2011, and gave it to Charlotte, with the song being released in 2017 as part of her album *Rest*. It was recorded around 2016 at Electric Lady Studios in New York, and Paul provided additional drum work, guitar and piano parts.

"We had a very nice lunch about six-and-a-half years ago", recalled Charlotte. "I couldn't believe that I was actually sitting next to him. I told him that if he ever had a song for me it would be a dream come true. A few weeks later he sent this track. It was a demo. I didn't know what to do with it, because I wanted it to be part of the album. We had to reinvent it. Paul very sweetly came to Electric Lady. He did a bit of piano, some bass, a bit of guitar. It was incredible, just to see him work." [4]

Artist - Paul McCartney, Jimmy Fallon And The Roots
Title - Wonderful Christmastime
Year - 2017
Label - Capitol Records

A remake of an old Paul McCartney standard, featuring a comedic talk-show host and a really awesome alternative rap group. If you don't know who The Roots are, they are a jazzy hip-hop act (think A Tribe Called Quest or Gang Starr) who were formed in 1987 and are still going today; unlike most hip-hop acts, instead of sampling other records, they actually play their own instruments, and are probably best known as being Jimmy Fallon's house band, which explains this collaboration.

A very tasty (if a little on the short side) reinterpretation of a classic Macca tune with some nice barbershop-esque beatboxing and backing vocals. It was featured on Fallon's album *Holidays Rule Vol.2*.

Artist - Henry McCullough
Title - Live Long Rock & Roll
Year - 2019
Label - Jack Russell Music

The late Henry McCullough was a member of Paul McCartney's very successful second band, Wings. Despite his passing in 2016, his popularity saw the release of a posthumous album in 2019 on Jack Russell Music entitled *Ballywonderland*.

One of the songs on the album is a McCartney composition entitled 'Live Long Rock & Roll', and Paul also is on bass duties. This song was part of a one-shot supergroup, which consisted of Procol Harum singer Gary Brooker, Chris Stainton who drummed with Pink Floyd, Albert Lee, Paul Carrack, Paul Brady, The London Community Gospel Choir, Don Mascall and of course our Macca.

It was recorded around 2014 and executive producer Don Mascall remembers the day Paul came into the studio:" There are still some times when I'm on my own in the studio when I'll listen to Paul McCartney's bass on the track and think, 'If anyone brought magic to this track - it was Sir Paul McCartney. 'I have to hand it to him. This wasn't a rushed job. He put heart and soul into the bass line on the track. It's absolutely incredible." [15]

Artist - Thelma Plum
Title - Made For You
Year - 2019
Label - Warner

Thelma Plum is a soulful singer-songwriter from the home of wallabies, Kylie Minogue, philosophers (thanks Monty Python!) and The Sydney Opera House - Australia. In 2019, she released her debut album *Better In Blak* and the album closes with the song 'Made For You', which features none other than Macca playing a lovely guitar loop!

How the collaboration came about was when Plum was recording her LP, Paul overheard what she was doing, and was impressed and asked if he could "lay something down", so he provided a guitar part for the song.

"Paul McCartney came to the studio to pick something up after I'd gone one night and David [Plum's Producer] had' Made for You' on in the background on a loop and McCartney asked who it was," Plum told the *Sydney Morning Herald* in 2019. "He said, 'It's this Aboriginal woman from Australia named Thelma Plum and she wrote it with Paul Kelly, 'and McCartney knew who Paul Kelly was and he said, 'This is beautiful, do you mind if I lay some guitar down? 'And David's like, 'I don't think Thelma will mind, 'which I didn't!" [10]

Artist - Little Steven And The Disciples Of Soul
Title - I Saw Her Standing There

Year - 2021 (recorded in 2017)
Label - Wicked Cool Record Co.

Little Steven (birth name Steven Van Zandt) was a member of Bruce Springsteen's E Street Band, but in reality, he is not really that little (he stands at a respectable 5ft 7inches). He also has his own band called The Disciples Of Soul, which I think is one of the coolest names that anybody can think of for a group!

This was part of a 2021 live album called *Macca To Mecca*. As one would guess from the title, this is a cover version of that old Beatle standard we all know and love, performed live at The Cavern Club in Liverpool, and joining them is Paul himself. The rest of the performance is a collection of covers of Beatles songs. Despite the claim of being recorded at The Cavern Club, McCartney's guest spot was actually recorded at a gig at the famous Roundhouse venue in London in 2017.

Artist - Michael Bublé
Title - My Valentine
Year - 2022
Label - Reprise Records

Michael Bublé is a very famous Grammy and Juno award-winning Canadian latter-day crooner, who has sold over 75 million records worldwide. Despite his career starting in the 1990s, it was around 2005 when his career started to take off with the wild success of his album *It's Time*. Like a certain other good-looking Canadian singer, he attracts hordes of screaming girls, plus he once covered the Spider-Man theme!

In March 2022, Bublé released the album *Higher*, which was a commercial success, reaching No.1 in the UK album chart, and was then accompanied by a residency in Las Vegas and a UK tour in 2023. The LP also contains a rendition of Paul McCartney's 2012 ballad single 'My Valentine' (which Paul always dedicates to his wife, Nancy), produced by none other than McCartney himself. You may remember the original version for its music video, which featured Hollywood royalty, Johnny Depp and Natalie Portman, using sign language for the lyrics.

As you expect from Bublé, it's a beautiful and very cinematic rendition of a McCartney standard.

Artist - The Umoza Music Project
Title - Home

Year - 2022
Label - Right Track Records

The Umoza Music Project are a collective of international African musicians based in Malawi, who have been going since 2010. In 2022, they released the album *Home* on Right Track Records. Being a massive fan of African music, Paul was pleased to be involved on this LP, playing Hofner bass. As this was made in 2020, obviously Macca's bits were recorded at home. McCartney stated on his official website:" I've always loved African music so when I was asked to do this I jumped at the chance and ended up playing my Hofner bass on this cool song. It was great to collaborate with these excellent African musicians." [35]

A really delightful tune, and a brilliant gateway into the wonders of African pop music.

CHAPTER THREE – GEORGE

There was a misconception that George was the quiet Beatle, but he was far from it, certainly when it came to his workload helping out his music friends. One thing you will notice is that Harrison was very in-demand as a gifted slide guitarist, and contributed to many other acts' recordings. You will also notice he liked to play alongside his pal, Eric Clapton, despite them sharing the same wife at different times!

Artist - The Remo Four
Title - In The First Place
Year - 1968 (released 1999)
Label - Pilar

The Remo Four were a Merseybeat group who performed from 1959-1970. They were contemporaries of our Fab Four, and members Colin Manley and Dan Andrew actually went to the same school as Paul McCartney (the Liverpool Institute For Boys)! They had backed Tommy Quickly with the single 'Tip Of My Tongue', a Lennon/McCartney composition, which we will cover later in this book.

'In The First Place' was a song that was made to accompany the psychedelic movie *Wonderwall* (for which Harrison composed the soundtrack), and a lot of commentators have compared it to the *Magical Mystery Tour* cut 'Blue Jay Way'. Produced by Harrison, the sessions for this song began on 22nd December 1967 at EMI (Abbey Road) Studios, and the song was written by The Remo Four's keyboard player, Tony Ashton.

The song was unfortunately cut from the finished film, and the tune didn't receive a commercial release until 1999, when interest in a director's cut of the *Wonderwall* film emerged because of the popularity of the hit song of the same name by Britpop band Oasis. This time, 'In The First Place' was finally re-inserted into the film (plus the band got credited as well!), and the song was released as a charity single on Pilar Records. This was to help pay for the cancer treatment being undergone by member Colin Manley, who sadly passed away three months prior to the single's release.

Over time, 'In The First Place' has come to be seen as a lost gem of the psychedelic era. Tony Ashton and Roy Dyke would later form Ashton, Gardner & Dyke with Kim Gardner.

Artist - Blind Faith
Album - Blind Faith
Title - Exchange and Mart/Spending All My Days
Year - 1969 (released in 1986)
Label - Polydor

What happens when the groups Cream and Traffic merge together? You get the supergroup known as Blind Faith, consisting of Steve Winwood, Eric Clapton, Ginger Baker and Ric Grech! Despite the band only existing for a meagre few months, they had one very successful album, and a massive summer concert tour, which included their first gig in Hyde Park, where they played to a staggering 100,000 people.

Their one and only, self-titled album was released on Polydor in August 1969; while a massive success, selling over 8 million copies, it is also remembered for its rather tasteless cover featuring a topless 11-year-old model (which was thankfully changed in some regions).

When the album was reissued as a CD in 1986, it contained two previously unreleased songs, 'Exchange and Mart' and 'Spending All My Days'. George is said to have played guitar on those sessions.

Artist - Joe Cocker
Album - Joe Cocker!
Title - Something
Year - 1969
Label - Regal Zonophone
NOTE - It is not 100% known if George contributed to this album, but it is here for reference purposes.

Joe Cocker was a Sheffield-born blues-rock legend, known for his gritty, bluesy vocal delivery, with his signature song being his soulful, anthemic cover of The Beatles classic 'With A Little Help From My Friends', which might actually be more well known (and, sorry to say this, even better) than the Beatles original, thanks to its use as the theme song to the classic late 1980s coming-of-age dramedy series *The Wonder Years*.

In 1969, Cocker released his second studio album on Regal Zonophone records, *Joe Cocker!*, which received favourable reviews from critics. Riding high from the success of his cover of 'With A Little Help From My Friends', Cocker covers two Beatles cuts from their finale album *Abbey Road* - 'She Came In Though The Bathroom Window 'and 'Something'. Recorded at A&M Studios and Sunset Sound Studios in Hollywood, Harrison allegedly plays guitar on the latter, though in all likelihood, it's probably the work of Sneaky Pete Kleinow, who is credited on the album for playing pedal steel guitar. Kleinow would later work with Harrison (as well as John Lennon and Ringo Starr) on future solo projects.

Even if Harrison isn't involved, it's an amazing version of an already outstanding song. This version of the song would later be sampled in 2004 by British big beat DJ (and former Brighton neighbour of Paul McCartney) Fatboy Slim, for his hit single 'Don't Let The Man Get You Down'.

Artist - Cream
Title - Badge
Year - 1969
Label - Polydor

Cream were a very influential British rock trio performing from 1966-1969, best known for their psychedelic masterpiece 'Sunshine Of Your Love' among many others. They consisted of guitarist Eric Clapton (who played on 'While My Guitar Gently Weeps'), drummer Ginger Baker and Scottish singer and bassist, Jack Bruce. They were inducted into the Rock & Roll Hall of Fame in 1983.

1969 saw them release their single 'Badge', which was featured on their appropriately named final studio album, *Goodbye*. The song was co-written by Clapton and George Harrison.

On this track, a guy named Badge L'Angelo played a guitar part. That man was none other than George Harrison recording under an alias for contractual reasons. George (ahem) Badge L'Angelo's part was recorded on the 21st November 1968 at Wally Heider Studios in Los Angeles.

This is an amazing tune of psychedelic awesomeness with a fantastic bass line provided by Jack Bruce and of course the great guitar work provided by Badge L'Angelo and Eric Clapton. This will take you back to the summer of love!

Artist - Jack Bruce
Title - Never Tell Your Mother She's Out of Tune
Year - 1969
Label - Polydor

As stated previously, the late Jack Bruce was the singer and bassist for the 1960s megagroup Cream. In 1969, he released his solo album *Songs for a Tailor*, which contained the humorously named opening song 'Never Tell Your Mother She's Out of Tune'. George Harrison's guest guitar part was buried in the mix, and he was credited under his Badge L'Angelo pseudonym. It was recorded on the 11th May 1969 at Morgan Studios in London and it was produced by Felix Pappalardi from the band Mountain.

A great tune, and as always, Jack Bruce knows how to make a great bass line. Remember what he says, otherwise your mother will come after you!

Artist - Brute Force
Title - King Of Fuh
Year - 1969
Label - Apple Records

Brute Force was a pseudonym for Stephen Friedland, who was a member of The Tokens, best known for their rendition of 'The Lion Sleeps Tonight'. He also wrote songs for the likes of Del Shannon, Peggy March, The Chiffons, The Cyrkle and many more.

In 1967, he carved a solo career under the alias of Brute Force, and he released the album *I, Brute Force* on Columbia Records. His most infamous song would probably have to be the novelty tune 'The King Of Fuh '- a self-penned number that was also produced by The Tokens. It told the story of a monarch from the land of Fuh, who was constantly referred to in the song as the "Fuh King" (groan!).

Seeing as EMI or Capitol Records didn't want to release a song that contained repeated uses of a word that sounded similar to a certain four-letter word, it was released on Apple Records, where it got praise from Beatles John and George. George later acquired the original demo, and overdubbed eleven strings from the London Philharmonic Orchestra arranged by John Barham.

Seeing as 1969 ears were not ready yet for excessive pseudo-swearing, the single saw an extremely limited run of only 1000 copies and for obvious reasons didn't chart! The record is so rare that in 2019, a copy was sold at Sotherby's for the rather pricy £2,250 - Fuh King 'ell!

In 2018, Paul McCartney would later release the single 'Fuh You 'from his *Egypt Station* album. Lennon on the other hand actually said the real F-word on his song 'Working Class Hero'.

Artist - Radha Krishna Temple
Title - Hare Krishna Mantra
Year - 1969
Label - Apple Records

The Radha Krishna Temple is the British headquarters for the International Society of Krishna Consciousness (ISKCON), which has been active since the late 1960s. They gained recognition through George Harrison, who was embracing the Hindu religion and Krishna Consciousness around the time, and in 1969, he invited members of the collective to release a George Harrison-produced single entitled 'Hare Krishna Mantra'. It proved to be a surprise commercial hit, reaching No.12 in the UK Singles Chart, and even reached No.15 in West Germany. The collective even made an appearance on the infamous BBC TV series *Top Of The Pops* to promote the single, and they also filmed a video clip. Because of the song's unexpected success, The Radha Krishna Temple made many concert and festival appearances around the same time.

This is a classic record, and it was great to see a non-English-speaking tune that isn't a cheesy novelty record become a hit back in 1969!

Artist - Billy Preston
Title - That's The Way God Planned It
Year - 1969
Label - Apple Records

Other than George Martin, if there's one guy who should get the credit for fifth Beatle, it would be the late Billy Preston. He was a former child prodigy, and he was friends with our fabulous foursome since the Hamburg days. During the dark times of the *Get Back* sessions, he was key to getting the band back on track, plus he also helped out during the Abbey Road sessions. As a solo artist, he has penned some really great tunes such as 'Nothing From Nothing 'and that piece of repetitive funk awesomeness known as 'Outa Space '- seriously, listen to it... dayyymmnnn!!!

This Preston-penned number is probably his most famous song - 'That's The Way God Planned It'. It's a George Harrison-produced gospel track, and it was a smash hit worldwide, reaching No.11 in the UK Singles Chart. Preston also sang the song at the famous Concert For Bangladesh charity events organised by Harrison.

The tune was recorded at the legendary Olympic Sound Studios in south-west London in April 1969, and Harrison asked his friends, Rolling Stone Keith Richards and Cream members Eric Clapton and Ginger Baker, as well as gospel singers Doris Troy and Madeline Bell, to participate, much to Preston's delight.

As the song was quite long-ish (5 minutes and 34 seconds), it was cut down to 3 minutes and 22 seconds for the single release, with the tune being split into two parts for the A-side and B-side.

Artist - Billy Preston
Title - Everything's All Right
Year - 1969
Label - Apple Records

A great, upbeat Motown/Stax-esque tune from the guy who played on the *Get Back/Let It Be* sessions. It was produced by George Harrison, and it was also featured on Billy's album *That's The Way God Planned It*. It was co-written by singer Doris Troy, who herself would later become an artist signed to Apple Records.

Despite the song being brilliant, it sadly failed to chart, outside of a modest No.75 in Australia.

Artist - Derek & The Dominos
Title - Tell The Truth
Year - 1970
Label - Acto Records

Derek and the Dominos were a short-lived blues-rock supergroup featuring Eric Clapton, Bobby Whitlock, Carl Radle, Duane Allman and Jim Gordon. They were formed during the recording sessions of George Harrison's solo megahit album *All Things Must Pass* and are probably best known for a certain song of awesomeness called 'Layla', which all Clapton and George fans know is a song about Clapton's love for a certain Pattie Boyd, the then-wife of George Harrison. Unfortunately, the band's life was cut short after the tragic death of Duane Allman, who was killed in a motorcycle accident, and Clapton's downward spiral into depression.

On a lighter note, their debut release was a single entitled 'Tell The Truth'. It was written during the recording sessions of George's *All Things Must Pass* album, and it had guitar contributions from George, as well as Traffic's Dave Mason. Produced by Phil Spector, it was released in September 1970 on US label Acto Records, but for some reason the band had this version withdrawn from commercial release after only a short time. When it was reissued in November of that year, it was an alternate recording produced by Tom Dowd, and doesn't feature any of Harrison's guitar parts. The way to tell the difference between the two versions is that Spector's version is faster.

The original single version of 'Tell The Truth 'with Harrison's guitar part is now a collectors' item for both Clapton and Harrison fans alike.

Artist - Derek & The Dominos
Title - Roll It Over
Year - 1970
Label - Acto Records

George Harrison plays slide guitar on the B-side to 'Tell The Truth', which has nothing to do with the Oasis song released in 2000 of the same name.

As you would expect from Derek and his Dominos, it's pure unadulterated blues rock awesomeness. Also, like its A-side, it was produced by none other than the infamous Phil Spector.

Artist - Ashton, Gardner & Dyke
Title - I'm Your Spiritual Breadman
Year - 1971
Label - Capitol Records

Tony Ashton, Kim Gardener and Roy Dyke (Ashton and Dyke were formerly part of The Remo Four) were a rock trio from London, who were at their commercial height in the early 1970s, best known for their international one-hit-wonder 'Resurrection Shuffle'.

In 1971, they released the album *The Worst of Ashton, Gardner + Dyke* on Capitol Records, which had a sleeve that featured a group of misfits flicking an obscene two-fingered gesture.

It also contained the song 'I'm Your Spiritual Breadman 'with George Harrison on guitar. For a song featured on an album claiming to be "the worst of", it's actually very good, and believe me, there are MUCH WORSE records out there, some of which are featured in this book!

Artist - Badfinger
Album - Straight Up
Titles - I'd Die Babe/The Name Of The Game/Suitcase/Day After Day
Year - 1971
Label - Apple Records

On the 13th December 1971 in the US (February 11th 1972 in the UK - lucky Americans!) Badfinger released their fourth studio album, called *Straight Up*. This album was considered something of a departure from their normal sound, axing their latter day Beatle-esque style for something a bit more power pop-sounding. It led to the album getting mixed reviews at the time, though nowadays people consider it to be their best album.

The LP had a troubled production. Regular Beatles engineer Geoff Emerick initially handled the production duties, but he wasn't happy with the initial recordings. George Harrison then took over, only to be indisposed, thanks to his commitments regarding his famous Concerts for Bangladesh. The remainder of the album was handled by Todd Rundgren.

George was involved in four of the twelve songs featured on the album - these were 'I'd Die Babe', 'The Name Of The Game', 'Suitcase 'and 'Day After Day'. Harrison's productions were all recorded at Abbey Road studios in London, and member Joey Molland recalled that George had virtually "joined the band" by adding slide guitar during these sessions. Other guests on the album include Leon Russell, playing piano on 'Day After Day 'and guitar on 'Suitcase', Bobby Diebold playing bass guitar on 'Suitcase', Klaus Voormann playing electric piano on 'Suitcase 'and Al Kooper playing piano on 'Name Of The Game'. It is also rumoured that Gary Wright of 'Dream Weaver 'fame also played piano on 'The Name Of The Game', though this hasn't been confirmed.

Artist - The Edwin Hawkins Singers
Title - Children (Get Together)
Year - 1971
Label - Buddha Records

Edwin Hawkins was a US gospel artist who was one of the pioneers of the urban contemporary gospel sound. He was active from the 1960s-1990s and was best known for the hit song 'Oh, Happy Day'. Sadly, he passed away from cancer in 2018.

In 1971, his album *Children Get Together* (sometimes known as *Get Together Children*) was released on Buddha Records, and its lead single of the same name featured an uncredited lead guitar performance from George Harrison.

It's a beautiful tune, and definitely one you should have in your record box. The song would later be sampled in 2018 by Kanye West for his track 'No Mistakes'.

Artist - Billy Preston
Title - I Wrote A Simple Song
Year - 1971
Label - A&M Records

From Preston's 1971 album of the same name, and the double A-side to that piece of repetitive funky brilliance known as 'Outa Space',' I Wrote A Simple Song 'is an outstanding track similar to 'What's Going On'-era Marvin Gaye with a full orchestra, and playing slide guitar and dobro is George.

It reached No.77 in the US *Billboard* Top 100.

Artist - Ravi Shankar & Chorus
Album - The Concert For Bangladesh
Title - Joe Bangla/Oh Bhaugowan/Raga Mishra-Jhinjhoti
Year - 1971
Label - Apple Records

The Concert for Bangladesh was a pair of all-star benefit concerts masterminded by Beatle George and Indian music legend Ravi Shankar, which took place at New York City's Madison Square Gardens on the 1st August 1971, to help raise awareness and to fund relief for refugees from Bengali following the Bangladesh Liberation Civil War. A record of this historic event was released on Apple Records on the 20th December 1971, and was noted for featuring Bob Dylan's first major American concert appearance in five years. The album was a major critical and commercial success, and topped the charts in several countries around the world, and won a Grammy Award for Album Of The Year in 1973. A concert film directed by Saul Swimmer was released in 1972 (see my previous book, *Acting Naturally*).

On disc one, side one, we get a performance from Ravi Shankar teaming up with George. A little bit of backstory about Ravi: born on the 7th April 1920, he was probably the most famous musician to come out of India, and had been performing since childhood. By the 1950s, he was already a big figure in classical music circles, but he only became popular with western pop audiences in 1965, when Harrison befriended him, striking a lifelong friendship, and Ravi taught George to play sitar, thus interspersing the instrument into several Beatles compositions. Shankar then became a big draw on the festival circuit, despite his concerts at the time being nothing more than him and his sitar, and he became an icon in hippie circles. His popularity did fade somewhat in the 1970s but he didn't mind that, as his true hardcore fans remained. He continued releasing records until his passing in December 2012. His daughters, Anoushka Shankar and, most famously, Norah Jones, are successful musicians in their own right.

Artist - Ronnie Spector
Title - Try Some, Buy Some
Year - 1971
Label - Apple Records

The original bad girl of rock and roll, the late Ronnie Spector of The Ronettes was married to the controversial producer Phil Spector between 1968-1972. Despite their divorce in 1974, Ronnie was still performing under the Spector surname, and was still releasing records until her death from cancer in 2022.

In 1971, Spector released the single 'Try Some Buy Some 'on Apple Records - a George Harrison-penned number, dating back to the *All Things Must Pass* sessions. It was also a co-production between George and Phil. Mr. Spector bailed out during the recording sessions, thanks to his famous erratic and unpleasant behaviour, but one thing he did contribute was his famous "wall of sound" production technique, put to its absolute fullest effect. Phil's "wall of sound" technique consisted of bombastic, reverberating multi-tracked instruments, which constantly threatened to drown out the vocals.

Also playing on the record were Leon Russell, Gary Wright, Pete Ham, Klaus Voormann and Jim Gordon, and John Barman helped with the orchestral and choral arrangements.

The single was not a massive success (only reaching No.77 in the US *Billboard* charts, and it failed to reach the UK top 40), but it would later be revisited by Harrison in 1973 for his famous *Living In The Material World* album, and there was also a version released by David Bowie, which was featured on his 2003 album *Reality*.

Artist - Ronnie Spector
Title - Tandoori Chicken
Year - 1971
Label - Apple Records

The B-side to 'Try Some, Buy Some'. Like the A-Side, it was written by Harrison, and was a co-production between George Harrison and Phil Spector. While the A-side was a cinematic power ballad, 'Tandoori Chicken 'is a fun, back-to-basics rockabilly jam.

Artist - Gary Wright
Album - Footprint
Titles - Give Me The Good Earth/Two Faced Man/Love To Survive/Whether It's Right Or Wrong/Stand For Our Right/Fascinating Things/Forgotten/If You Treat Someone Right
Year - 1971
Label - A&M Records

Gary Wright is a famous singer/songwriter and keyboard player, best known for composing his hit records 'Dream Weaver '(you may have heard it on several films) and 'Love Is Alive'. He has worked with everyone from Joe Cocker, Phil Collins, Elton John, Steve Winwood to even working with hip-hop legends such as Eminem, Busta Rhymes and Salt 'N 'Pepa. His song 'Coming Apart 'would be sampled by American house music king, Armand Van Helden, for his hit dance floor banger 'My My My 'in 2004.

In 1971, Gary Wright released his second studio album, *Footprint*, on A&M Records. Despite it getting great reviews from the critics, the album sadly failed to sell, as it didn't chart in either Britain or the USA. This led to Wright rejoining his old band, Spooky Tooth, and it only resurfaced as a solo album with his comeback release *The Dream Weaver* in 1975, featuring the super-famous title track of the same name. Wright had previously played with George on his *All Things Must Pass* LP.

The album was co-produced by an uncredited George Harrison, and both George and Gary appeared on *The Dick Cavett Show* to help promote the album, performing the number 'Two Faced Man' backed by Cavett's short-lived house band, Wonderwheel. On the album Harrison also played electric and acoustic guitars, and many regulars on Beatles solo projects appeared on the LP, including Klaus Voormann, Alan White, Jim Keltner and Bobby Keys.

Artist - David Bromberg
Title - The Holdup
Year - 1972
Label - Columbia

David Bromberg is an American multi-instrumentalist who is known for his fingerpicking style, humorous and quirky lyrics, and the ability to play rhythm and lead guitar at the same time - a very talented guy indeed. He has worked with many famous musicians including Bob Dylan, Carly Simon, Jerry Jeff Walker, Willie Nelson, Ravi Shankar and our pal, Ringo Starr. He even played with my father, Tom Hoy, when he was in the band Magna Carta, on their 1977 album *Took A Long Time* (AKA *Putting It Back Together*) appearing on Dad's song 'Princess'.

On February 16th 1972, Bromberg released his self-titled debut album on Columbia Records, which he secured on the strength of his acclaimed work as a session musician, and his impromptu appearance at the 1970 Isle Of Wight Festival. While not commercially successful, the album was well received.

George Harrison guests on the LP playing slide guitar on the song 'The Holdup'- a very jolly and upbeat tune. The album also features Bob Dylan playing harmonica on the track 'Sammy's Song'.

Artist - Jesse Davis
Title - Sue Me Sue You Blues
Year - 1972
Label - Acto

Jesse Ed Davis was an overlooked Native American guitar legend, who was a very prolific session musician and solo performer, who worked with the likes of John Lennon, George Harrison, Ringo Starr, John Lee Hooker, B.B. King, Eric Clapton, Keith Moon, Harry Nilsson, Long John Baldry and Rod Stewart.

In 1973, George Harrison released the song 'Sue Me Sue You Blues', which came out on his well-received solo album *Living In The Material World*. As you would guess from the lyrics, it's about the turbulence that was going on relating to The Beatles 'disbandment.

Winding the clocks back to January 1972, the song was recorded by Jesse Davis, who Harrison met though fellow singer-songwriter Leon Russell and drummer Jim Keltner, both of whom appeared on Harrison's 1971 charity single 'Bangla Desh'. Davis was then suggested by George to replace Eric Clapton during the famous Concerts for Bangladesh after Clapton's severe bout of heroin addiction. Thankfully, Clapton recovered, and coincidentally, both Clapton and Davis appeared in the concert.

Jesse Davis 'rendition of 'Sue Me Sue You Blues 'is something of a departure from George's more well-known 1973 version, turning the song into a shuffle in the vein of Southern blues music. Davis 'rendition is also considerably shorter than George's version, clocking in at only 2 minutes and 25 seconds (George's rendition runs in at 4 minutes and 48 seconds) and it also doesn't contain the third verse that the Harrison recording includes. The personnel contributing to Jesse Davis' version included Jim Keltner, Dr. John and Buddy Rich.

Retrospectively, Davis wasn't happy with his music, and considers 'Sue Me Sue You Blues 'to be one of the few songs of his he actually liked!

Artist - Nilsson
Title - You're Breakin 'My Heart
Year - 1972
Label - RCA Records

A song that the book *The 7500 Most Important Songs for the Rock and Roll Era* describes as "terse and to the point", 'You're Breakin 'My Heart 'is a fun, potty-mouthed song by Beatle-buddy Harry Nillson from his 1972 album *Son Of Schmilsson*, which featured such pieces of lyrical brilliance as "I sang my balls off for you Baby" on the track 'Take 54'.

'You're Breakin 'My Heart 'is a song about Harry's break-up with his wife, Diane, and is probably best known for its profane refrain of "You're breaking my heart, you're tearin 'it apart/so f**k you", which was very risqué to say on a pop record back then! George contributed to this track by playing slide guitar, and the song also featured Klaus Voorman, Bobby Keys, Nicky Hopkins, Barry Morgan and Jim Price, as well as guitar legend Peter Frampton.

Peter Wolf from the J. Geils Band would later cover the song on the Harry Nilsson tribute album *For The Love Of Harry: Everybody Sings Nilsson*.

Artist - Rudy Romero
Album - To The World
Titles - If I Find The Time/Lovely Lady/Nothin 'Gonna Get You Down/Doin 'The Right Thing
Year - 1972
Label - Tumbleweed Records

Rudy Romero was an obscure American-based guitarist and percussionist, who was in the bands The Hard Times and The New Phoenix (whose one and only release, 'Give To Me Your Love', was produced by Mama Cass of The Mamas and the Papas fame). Very little is known about Romero, but one claim to fame was that he did once go out with a 1971 playboy centrefold. He tragically died in a car accident in LA in July 1982 - he was only 34.

Despite the fact that Romero was a pretty obscure figure of the 1960s/1970s music scene, he did somehow manage to collaborate with George Harrison on his one and only album in 1972, *To The World*, released on Tumbleweed Records. Despite not being credited, Harrison is said to have played guitar on the songs 'Lovely Lady', 'Nothin 'Gonna Get You Down 'and 'Doin 'The Right Thing'. George is also said to have made vocal contributions to the album's opener 'If I Find The Time'.

Artist - Bobby Whitlock
Album - Bobby Whitlock
Title - Where There's A Will, There's A Way/A Day Without Jesus/Back In My Life Again
Year - 1972
Label - Dunhill

Bobby Whitlock is a Memphis-based singer, songwriter and musician, who was a member of Eric Clapton's group, Derek & The Dominos.

After the splitting of the Dominos in 1971, he released his creatively titled solo album *Bobby Whitlock*. The LP opens with the song 'Where There's A Will There's A Way', which features guitar work from our George. Also playing on this track is Derek Domino (AKA Eric Clapton) on guitar, Klaus Voormann on bass, Bobby Keys on saxophone, Jim Price on trumpet and ex-Domino Jim Gordon on drums. It was recorded at Olympic Sound Studios in London. The songs 'A Day Without Jesus 'and 'Back In My Life 'share the same line-up.

>   Artist - Cheech & Chong featuring Tyrone Shoelaces
>   Title - Basketball Jones
>   Year - 1973
>   Label - Ode Records

As discussed in my previous Beatles book, *Acting Naturally*, this was a collaboration between George Harrison and comedians Cheech Marin and Tommy Chong.

George Harrison (assisted by Billy Preston, Klaus Voormann, Tom Scott and Carole King) performs on this novelty single by comedy act Cheech and Chong. The track is probably best known for being covered by Barry White and Chris Rock for the Looney Tunes film *Space Jam*. The Beatles make a cameo appearance in the animated music video singing along with the song, which was later featured in the 1979 Peter Sellers comedy classic *Being There*. This rather unusual collaboration came together because Lou Adler, the song's producer, played the track to George Harrison, who was recording in the studio next door, and George enjoyed the song and wanted to be a part of it.

>   Artist - Jesse Ed Davis
>   Album - Keep Me Comin'
>   Title - Unknown songs
>   Year - 1973
>   Label - Epic
>   NOTE - It is not known for sure if George was involved in this, but it's here for reference's sake!

According to the 1998 book *Beatles Undercover*, George Harrison allegedly made some contributions to Davis '1973 album, *Keep Me Comin'*, under the pseudonym of Bette Y El Mysterioso (which sounds like a Harry Potter spell!). Seeing as Davies has worked with Harrison on other projects, this claim does have some possible truth to it.

>   Artist - Nicky Hopkins
>   Album - The Tin Man Was A Dreamer

Title - Waiting For The Band/Edward/Speed On
Year - 1973
Label - Columbia

Nicky Hopkins was an English pianist and organist who was always in demand, and he worked with many of the greats including The Rolling Stones, The Who, The Kinks, Cat Stevens, Jeff Beck and Spinal Tap (luckily he didn't play drums for them!). Over the years, he has worked with all four Beatles on their solo projects, and even when they were together, he played on the single version of 'Revolution 'back in 1968.

In 1973, he released his studio album *The Tin Man Was A Dreamer*. George Harrison, under the alias of George O'Hara, played slide guitar on the album's second cut,' Waiting For The Band', a really funky number. Beatle associate Klaus Voormann is on bass. Harrison also played on the songs 'Edward 'and 'Speed On'.

Artist - Alvin Lee & Mylong Le Fevre
Title - So Sad (No Love Of His Own)
Year - 1973
Label - Columbia

A George Harrison-penned number, which would see a second life, appearing on his 1974 album *Dark Horse*. It's a song about losing Pattie Boyd to his buddy Eric Clapton, which he wrote in New York City during the cold winter of 1972. Alvin Lee & Mylong Le Fevre's version was released on Columbia Records in December 1973. High-speed guitar player Alvin Lee was the frontman of the band Ten Years After, who Harrison had befriended previously, and he offered the song to them. Playing on this version included George (under the rather lazy pseudonym of Hari Georgeson) on acoustic guitar, dobro, bass and harmony vocal, Ronnie Wood from The Rolling Stones playing 12-string acoustic guitar, and Mick Fleetwood (of Fleetwood Mac) on drums.

The song was well-received by critics, and George's own version was considered the highlight of an album that received mixed reviews. On George's version, Ringo Starr is on drums (see later in the book).

Artist - Dave Mason
Title - If You've Got Love
Year - 1973
Label - Columbia

Dave Mason was the co-founder of the 1960s psychedelic Beatles-esque band Traffic (who were originally going to appear in the infamous *Magical Mystery Tour* TV movie, before they got cut out). Other members of Traffic included Steve Winwood, Jim Capaldi and Chris Wood.

In 1973, Dave released his solo album, *It's Like You Never Left*, which contained the really lovely number 'If You've Got Love'. Playing acoustic guitar in a very 'Here Comes The Sun'-esque way was a man who called himself Son Of Harry, alias George Harrison under a pseudonym.

Artist - Don Nix
Album - Hobos, Heroes And Street Corner Clowns
Titles - The Train Don't Stop Here No More/I Need You
Year - 1973
Label – Stax

The Memphis-based producer, singer, songwriter, arranger, musician and author Don Nix is a lesser-known icon in the southern soul and southern rock genres, known for being a key figure in the Memphis soul sound (think Booker T. & The M.G.'s, Otis Redding, Al Green etc.). In his career, he helped George Harrison on the production of the famous Concert For Bangladesh shows, and he has worked with many big names throughout his lifetime including Eric Clapton, Jeff Beck, Brian May and Isaac Hayes (who younger people may recognise as the voice of Chef in *South Park*).

In 1973, Nix released the studio album *Hobos, Heroes And Street Corner Clowns* on the legendary record label Stax. George Harrison played slide guitar on two of the album's cuts, 'The Train Don't Stop Here No More 'and 'I Need You '(which is not a cover of the Beatles song of the same name). Also playing on this album on bass is solo-years regular Klaus Voormann.

Artist - Ron Wood
Title - Far East Man
Year - 1974
Label - Warner Bros. Records

Ron(nie) Wood is, of course, a member of that other ultra successful group of the 1960s, The Rolling Stones (he was previously in The Faces, and appeared in many other groups). In that turbulent year known as 1974, he released his first solo album *I've Got My Own Album to Do*. It is notable for containing the song 'Far East Man', which was made as a tribute to the Indian legend, Ravi Shankar.

The creation of this song, according to Beatles expert Robert Rodriguez, started at Ronnie Wood's home in The Wick, which was located in Richmond in Surrey - a location known for some very rock 'n 'roll get togethers between Harrison, Wood, Eric Clapton and members of The Small Faces. Harrison and Wood had previously collaborated on Alvin Lee's rendition of the Harrison number 'So Sad'.

The song was co-written by George and Ronnie, and George also played slide guitar and harmony vocal. Interestingly, George recorded his own version of 'Far East Man', which would be featured on his 1974 *Dark Horse* album. Despite getting an absolute critical bashing by Jim Miller from *Rolling Stone* magazine, 'Far East Man 'is nowadays viewed as a stellar track in the expanded Beatles and Rolling Stones canon.

Artist - Monty Python's Flying Circus
Title - The Lumberjack Song
Year - 1975
Label – Charisma

Me with the legendary Python himself - Michael Palin circa 2013. What a lovely bloke!

As stated in my previous Beatles book, *Acting Naturally*, Monty Python were basically the comedy world's answer to The Beatles. It is very well known that all four members of The Beatles were massive Python fans - John once said in an interview that he would have preferred to have been a

Python than a Beatle, Ringo made a cameo in a 1972 episode of the *Flying Circus* TV series and of course without George, we wouldn't have their cinematic magnum opus *The Life Of Brian*.

'The Lumberjack Song 'originally appeared in the ninth episode of the 1969 *Flying Circus* TV series 'An Ant - An Introduction', and lyrically, it's about a gentleman (played by the world's nicest man, Michael Palin), who expresses dissatisfaction with his current job (in the original 1969 version, it's a barber, but in the version we're covering today, it's a weatherman) and then launches into a hilarious, but controversial song about becoming a lumberjack, with a fetish for wearing women's clothing, much to the surprise of his "best girlie", played by Connie Booth, who in real life was married to Python member John Cleese.

When it was released as a single in November 1975, this song about a closet transvestite lumberjack was rerecorded with a proper band (the original just had a piano, and backing vocals by The Fred Tomlinson Singers), and producing this new version was none other than Python fanboy, George, under the credit of George "Ohnothimagen" Harrison. An earlier live recording at London's Camden Theatre had appeared on wax in 1970 on the BBC Records LP *The Worst of Monty Python's Flying Circus*. Because the chart buying public at the time didn't have a good sense of humour, the single failed to chart.

Harrison would especially become chummy with Michael Palin and Eric Idle and during one of Monty Python's live shows at the Civic Center in New York on 20th April 1976, Harrison would join them incognito as one of the backing singers during 'The Lumberjack Song' (in true Python style, nobody noticed!). Probably the greatest thing Harrison did for the Pythons was, of course, fund *Life Of Brian*, as every major film studio turned it down due to its controversial subject matter, and with the help of a £3 million budget set up by Harrison, which, according to Python Terry Jones was "world's most expensive cinema ticket", *Brian* was eventually made, and also gave birth to Harrison's own very successful film company, Handmade Films.

When the Concert For George gig happened in November 2002 at the Royal Albert Hall, London, on the first anniversary of Harrison's death, Monty Python reformed (with special guest star, Hollywood actor Tom Hanks) and played 'The Lumberjack Song'. Ringo even sang a verse of the song in an episode of the Thomas The Tank Engine spin-off TV series *Shining Time Station*, though this time, he sings "I'm a lumberjack, and I'm alright."

Artist - Billy Preston
Title - That's Life
Year - 1975
Label - A&M Records

It most certainly is!

Unlike what the title suggests, this isn't a cover version of the old standard, popularised by Frank Sinatra. This is, in fact, a really funky, almost-disco sounding number, which would get anybody up on the dance floor. A certain Hari Georgeson (I wonder who he is?) plays guitar, and it was featured on Preston's tenth studio album, *It's My Pleasure*, which also included guest appearances from the likes of Stevie Wonder and Shuggie Otis. It would later be covered by The Rolling Stones and U2.

This is a really great tune. Definitely one for your record box!

Artist - Tom Scott
Title - Appolonia (Foxtrata)
Year - 1975
Label - Ode Records

Tom Scott is a famous Californian saxophonist, who has played with Michael Jackson, The Blues Brothers, Steely Dan, Carole King, Robbie Williams, Lulu, Aretha Franklin, Frankie Valli, Neil Diamond, L.A. Express, Ringo Starr and of course, our George. He also performed on the soundtrack to one of my favourite films, *Toy Story 2*, with Randy Newman.

In 1975, he released the single 'Uptown & Country', which contained the B-side 'Appolonia (Foxtrata)', which featured slide guitar work from George Harrison. A very nice, smooth jazz-funk number which is similar to hip-hop crate digger favourite, Bob James, it was featured on Scott's 1975 album *New York Connection*, which coincidently includes the aforementioned Bob James.

Artist - Peter Skellern
Title - Make Love, Not War
Year - 1975
Label - Island Records

The late Peter Skellern was a British easy listening singer from Manchester, UK, with a very distinctive voice and delivery, who was popular in the 1970s, and who would later join a band in 1984 called Oasis (no, not that band!). He had a few hit singles including 1972's 'You're A Lady', 1975's 'Hold On To Love', and 1978's 'Love Is The Sweetest Thing'.

1975 saw him release the album *Hard Times*, which, despite gaining enthusiastic radio support, was sadly a commercial failure. The LP is notable for including the track 'Make Love, Not War', which has guest slide guitar from a certain Mr. George Harrison.

Coincidentally, Skellern's Oasis album featured guest vocals from Mary Hopkin, an early Apple Records artist.

Artist - Splinter
Title - Lonely Man
Year - 1975
Label - Dark Horse Records

Sharing the same name as the rat sensei of the Teenage Mutant Ninja Turtles, Splinter were a two-man vocal group consisting of William Elliot and Bobby Purvis, formed in the early 1970s. They were the first act to be signed to George Harrison's Dark Horse Records, and their sound has been compared to that of The Beatles themselves and the very Beatle-esque band Badfinger. Despite not having much of a big fanbase in the west, they did however see success in Japan and South Korea.

'Lonely Man 'is a track on Splinter's studio album *Harder To Live*, released on George's record label, Dark Horse Records. As well as being co-produced by Harrison, Billy Preston is on organ, and Jim Keltner plays drums. The band came to the attention of George Harrison through former Beatles roadie, Mal Evans. The song that George heard was an earlier version of 'Lonely Man', which he felt would be ideal for the film that he was producing, *Little Malcolm and his Struggle Against the Eunuchs* (featuring the late Sir John Hurt). Harrison then signed the band to Apple Records, and Splinter went to Apple Studios to record it, but this fell through when Apple Records was falling apart. This was when George set up Dark Horse Records, which resulted in the band recording their debut album *The Place I Love*.

The success of this led to the release of their second album, *Harder To Live*, which featured a new recording of 'Lonely Man '(the original 1973 prototype remains to this day unreleased, sans its appearance in the *Little Malcolm* film). It was eventually released as a single, and like the band's career as a whole, while not a big success in the western world, to quote an old rock cliché, it was "big in Japan", where the band recorded a new version in the Japanese language. As previously stated, Splinter would later see big success in that country.

They disbanded in 1984, and their catalogue has been out of print for some time, but a new album entitled *Never Went Back* came out in 2020 on Gonzo Multimedia. William Elliott sadly passed away in June 2021.

Artist - Larry Hosford
Album - Cross Words
Titles - Direct Me/Wishing I Could
Year - 1976
Label - Shelter Records

The late Larry Hosford was a forgotten country music artist, who was a member of the bands Snail and The E-Types. He was raised in the lettuce capital of the world, Salinas in California, and was signed to Shelter Records. Despite his connections, Hosford has sadly somewhat faded to obscurity in modern times, despite the high-quality output of his music.

'Direct Me 'and 'Wishing I Could 'are tracks from Hosford's album *Cross Words*. Playing slide guitar is George Harrison. Also playing is Leon Russell, who will be featured later in this book. It was unfortunately a commercial failure, with one website suggesting that his output was too country-sounding for a 1970s rock crowd, with his lyrical content being too idiosyncratic for country fans. It doesn't help that he was basically a country artist who was on a rock label!

Hosford sadly passed away in 2016, and his death received almost no news coverage, outside of the local Salinas and Santa Cruz regions of California.

Artist - Ravi Shankar
Album - Ravi Shankar's Music Festival From India
Titles Vandana/Dhamar/Tarana/Chaturang/Raga Jait/Kajri/Bhajan/Nanderdani/Dehati
Year - 1976
Label - Dark Horse Records

Ravi Shankar's Music Festival From India was an Indian classical music revue, led by the sitar legend that was Ravi Shankar. It was intended for western audiences to give them a flavour of the wonders of Indian classical music, and it was the first project undertaken by George Harrison's charity, the Material World Charitable Foundation. Harrison also took part in the LP's production.

Sixteen people played as part of the festival, including Haripasad Chauasia, Shivkumar Sharma, Alla Rakka, T.V. Gopalkrishnan, L. Shubramian, Sultan Khan and Laksmi Shankar (Ravi's sister-in-law), and many of them went on to big things as a result of the success of this event. This touring festival started in Europe in September 1974 (its opening night being at the Royal Albert Hall, with every hole being filled), and then toured North America in November, this time with George Harrison joining them (probably to boost ticket sales and interest).

If you didn't get to witness these door-opening concerts (I wasn't even born when they were happening!), the next best thing arrived in the form of a two-disc vinyl album released in March 1976 on George's Dark Horse Records. It was produced by Harrison, and in 2010, a recording of the 1974 Royal Albert Hall performance was released on DVD. A great introduction to the world of Indian classical music.

Artist - Splinter
Album - Two Man Band
Titles - Round & Round/Baby Love/I Apologize/Black Friday/New York City (Who Am I)/I Need Your Love/Motions Of Love/Silver/Love Is Not Enough/Little Girl
Year - 1977
Label - Dark Horse Records

In 1977, the dynamic duo of Splinter released the studio album *Two Man Band* on Dark Horse Records (George H's label). The cabaret-ish (and somewhat garish) cover features the pair dressed up in military uniforms, though not quite as colourful as the *Sgt. Pepper* ones.

This is a very eclectic affair, slowly ditching their folk rock roots and embracing everything from northern soul ('Black Friday') to down-and-dirty slow jams ('Baby Love', not to be confused with the Supremes hit of the same name) and classic rock ('I Apologize'). It received a mixed reception from Splinter fans.

George Harrison was the executive producer on this release (with Harrison providing a guitar solo on the song 'Round & Round') and despite all his best efforts, it didn't make much of a splash in the western world. Like most of their back catalogue, it was out of print for some time, though it was reissued in 2016 in Japan and South Korea (Splinter, as you are aware by now, were quite big there) and in 2017, it was reissued for the first time in the UK on Grey Market independent label, Grey Scale. After this release, Splinter would later resign from Dark Horse Records, with the label being exclusively for George Harrison solo releases.

Artist - Hall & Oates
Title - The Last Time
Year - 1978
Label - RCA

Daryl Hall and John Oates are a popular music duo who combined rock 'n' roll with funk, probably best known for the massive hits 'Maneater 'and the inspiration for Michael Jackson's 'Billie Jean', 'I Can't Go For That (No Can Do)'. Twenty-nine of their thirty-three singles released between 1974-1991 have charted in the US *Billboard* Singles Charts, and in 2003, the band were inducted into the Rock And Roll Hall Of Fame. They are still performing and releasing records today.

George Harrison plays guitar on the song 'The Last Time '(not a cover of the famous Rolling Stones single), which was featured on their album *Along The Red Ledge*. It was produced by David Foster, who is probably one of the most prolific producers in the music industry - it would be easier to list the big names he hasn't worked with!

I tried to contact the band for an interview for this book, but was unsuccessful. Word is their agent told the band to "say no go" to doing it!

Artist - Monty Python
Title - Always Look On The Bright Side Of Life
Year - 1979
Label - Charisma

"Cheer up Brian, y'know what they say…"

The closing song from Monty Python's cinematic masterpiece *The Life Of Brian*, sung by Mr. Cheeky (Eric Idle) to our (not) Messiah (but "very naughty boy"), Brian Cohen (Graham Chapman), just as they are about to be crucified by the Romans ("what have they ever done for us?"). It's a music hall sing-a-long, which is popular at football matches and funerals. The man providing the mix down was none other than George himself (who helped finance the film, but you knew that already) and the song's iconic whistling was provided by the late Neil Innes, who was a good friend to our four Fabs.

While not a chart hit initially, it reached No.3 in the UK Singles Chart in 1991, when the song had a reissue, thanks to it being championed by BBC Radio 1 DJ at the time, Simon Mayo.

Artist - Gary Brooker
Album - Lead Me To The Water
Titles - The Clyde/Mineral Man
Year - 1982
Label - Mercury

The late Gary Brooker OBE was the lead singer of the very successful British rock band Procol Harum (best known for their massive hit 'Whiter Shade Of Pale '- the most psychedelic track ever, according to John Lennon). He also toured for a couple of years with Ringo Starr's All-Starr Band between 1997-1999. He was also in the All-Star lineup for the Concert For George at the Royal Albert Hall in London in 2002, a memorial concert for our beloved Beatle.

March 1st 1982 saw Brooker release his album *Lead Me To The Water*. The LP included a huge array of famous guest stars helping out, including drum work from Phil Collins and guitar work from Eric Clapton. George Harrison also appears on the album, but it is unknown which tracks Harrison appears on, though some have speculated that he provided backing vocals on 'The Clyde 'and played guitar on 'Mineral Man'.

Brooker sadly passed away of cancer in February 2022 aged 76.

Artist - Jimmy Helms
Title - Celebration
Year - 1985
Label - London Records

Jimmy Helms is an American-born but British-based singer and musician, who is known for songs such as 1973's 'Gonna Make You An Offer You Can't Refuse'. He would work with the likes of Madness, Cat Stevens, Ben E. King, David Essex, Evelyn Thomas and Gloria Gaynor. He is also a member of the dance group Londonbeat, who had a huge hit with 'I've Been Thinking About You', which reached No.1 in many countries in 1991, making Helms one of the oldest people to have a No.1 hit record at the time, age 50!

1985 saw Helms release the song 'Celebration', which was written by George Harrison, and was the B-side to the song 'Freedom 'by Billy Connolly, Chris Tummings & The Singing Rebels Band (which we'll cover later in this book). Both these songs were released as a promotional single for the Handmade Films production *Water* directed by Dick Clement and starring Michael Caine. Both songs were featured in the film of the same name.

Artist - Alvin Lee
Title - Talk Don't Bother Me
Year - 1986
Label - 21 Records

Alvin Lee was a Nottingham-based guitar guru who was the lead vocalist and lead guitarist of the blues rock band Ten Years After. In 1986, he released the album *Detroit Diesel*, which contains the cut 'Talk Don't Bother Me', which featured our George playing slide guitar. Alvin was also in the line-up for 2002's The Concert For George.

Released as part of Lee's aforementioned LP, it's a solid piece of 1980s singer-songwriter music with powerful vocals, and a heavy blues/soul influence, not to mention a great solo from Beatle George.

Artist - Duane Eddy
Title - Theme For Something Really Important
Year - 1987
Label - Capitol Records

As previously stated in this book, in 1987, Eddy released the studio album *Duane Eddy*, which is notable for featuring two Beatles - Paul McCartney and George Harrison.

George plays slide guitar on the very Jeff Lynne/Travelling Wilburys-esque 'Theme For Something Really Important', which is rather apt, as it was produced by... you guessed it... Jeff Lynne! While doing research for this book, I couldn't find a movie or TV show called 'Something Really Important', unless it's so obscure that not many people know about it. In reality, it's probably just a show or film in the mind of a guitar genius but, think about it, I wonder what sort of show it would have been?

Artist - Duane Eddy
Title - The Trembler
Year - 1987
Label - Capitol Records

Another tune from the self-titled 1987 LP, and another collaboration between Eddy/Harrison/Lynne. Unlike the previous composition, this was actually featured in a real film - 1994's *Natural Born Killers*, directed by Oliver Stone and written by Quentin Tarantino. It's probably the most likely place you've heard this song, and it shared the soundtrack with the likes of

Leonard Cohen, Patti Smith, Bob Dylan and hip-hop artist Dr. Dre, making it a very diverse film soundtrack.

Artist - Eric Clapton
Title - Run So Far
Year - 1989
Label - Reprise Records

In 1989, George's mate, Eric Clapton, released his studio album *Journeyman* (which is said to be Clapton's favourite album). Released after a stint of alcoholism, the album was said to be a return to form, and it became a huge commercial success.

It contains the George Harrison-penned song 'Run So Far'. George also contributes to the song by playing guitar and singing harmony vocals. It reached No.40 in the US *Billboard* Mainstream Rock Charts. The song would later be covered by Czech artist Pavel Bobek in 1993.

Clapton also masterminded the Concert For George memorial gig in November 2002, bringing together all of George's musical buddies in a supergroup on stage at the Royal Albert Hall.

Artist - Sylvia Griffin
Title - Love's A State Of Mind
Year - 1988
Label - The Rocket Record Company

Sylvia Griffin is a singer who has worked with Marc Almond and Agnes Bernelle. Very little is known about Sylvia, other than she was previously in the rather suggestively titled new wave/syntb-pop band, Kissing The Pink (or KTP), who actually had a cult following and a No.1 hit on the US *Billboard* Dance Club Song Charts in 1987 with 'Certain Things Are Likely'.

In 1988, Griffin wanted to carve out a solo career, and she and George Harrison met at a party held by Elton and Renate John. Sylvia was already friends with Renate, meeting her a few years earlier during the time Renate worked as a tape op/sound engineer at Air Studios in London. The two of them started working on some songs together, and played some of them to George at that party. The tune he particularly liked was 'Love's A State Of Mind', and Harrison agreed to play slide guitar on the final recording. It was released in 1988 on Elton John's label, The Rocket Record Company. [7]

Sadly, Sylvia faded to obscurity after this release. Kissing The Pink however are still going today, though Griffin is no longer a member.

Artist - Gary Wright
Title - (I Don't Wanna) Hold Back
Year - 1988
Label - Cypress Records

1988 saw Gary Wright release the album *Who I Am*, which featured the song '(I Don't Wanna) Hold Back'. George makes a contribution by playing slide guitar. Other musicians involved in the session included Jimmy Johnson, Terry Bozzio, Steve Farris, Bruce Gaitsch and Mindy Lee.

It's a great Bryan Adams-esque tune, which brings out vibes similar to that of 'In The Air Tonight' by Phil Collins, even if the drum section isn't quite as epic.

Artist - Jim Capaldi
Title - Oh Lord, Why Lord
Year - 1989
Label - JAWS Records

The late Jim Capaldi was the drummer and founding member of the 1960s group Traffic. From 1971, he had a successful solo career, and he wrote for several artists and performed with many of the greats, including Eric Clapton, Jimi Hendrix, Steve Winwood and Mick Jagger.

In 1989, he released the single 'Oh Lord, Why Lord '(a cover of a song by The Pop Tops), featuring some guitar work from George Harrison. It was also on Capaldi's commercially unsuccessful album *Some Come Running*.

Artist - Belinda Carlisle
Title - Leave A Light On
Year - 1989
Label - Virgin

Belinda Carlisle is a member of the all-female punk/new wave band Go Go's, who are the most successful all-female rock band of all time, and were the first all-female band in history to write their own material, play their own instruments and have a No.1 album in the charts, making them real trailblazers for women in rock. Carlisle would also have a successful solo career with radio hits like 'Mad About You', 'I Get Weak', 'Circle In The Sand 'and 'Leave A Light On'. She also recorded the song 'I Won't Say (I'm In Love) 'for the 1997 Disney animated feature *Hercules*.

1989 saw her release the album *Runaway Heroes*, which contained the hit single 'Leave A Light On'. Playing slide guitar was none other than Mr. George Harrison himself.

"Rick [Nowels] said we should get someone cool and with a distinctive style to play the lead guitar part," remembers Carlisle." I thought for a moment and said 'What about George Harrison?' I had met George briefly a few years earlier in San Remo, Italy, and Morgan [Mason, Carlisle's husband] through his work on *Sex Lies and Videotape* [a film Mason had produced for Harrison's HandMade Films] knew someone who was close to [Harrison] and able to get word to him. George responded right away, saying he'd love to help out." [5]

The tune was commercially successful, reaching No.4 in the UK Singles Chart, and was a top five hit worldwide, selling over 200,000 copies in the UK alone. It would see many cover versions in the years to come.

Artist - Belinda Carlisle
Title - Deep Deep Ocean
Year - 1989
Label - Virgin

Another song from Belinda Carlisle's *Runaway Heroes* LP. George Harrison plays 12-string guitar in a song that has a very Jeff Lynne-esque feel to it, even though it was actually produced by Rick Nowels, who would later work with the likes of Adele, Madonna, Stevie Nicks, Cher, Mel C, Dua Lipa and Lana Del Ray.

Artist - Roy Orbison
Title - A Love So Beautiful
Year - 1989
Label - Virgin

Roy Orbison AKA The Big O AKA Lefty Wilbury was an immensely popular singer-songwriter of the 1960s, who had a really amazing and distinctive voice, and was a very prolific songwriter. In 1963, he toured with our beloved combo and in 1988, he co-founded the most awesome supergroup with Bob Dylan, Tom Petty, Jeff Lynne and George - The Travelling Wilburys. He unfortunately passed away in 1988 after suffering a heart attack, but he is still a popular icon in music today.

1989 saw the posthumous release of his critically and commercially successful album *Mystery Girl*, which is notable for having the hit single 'You Got It'. On the song 'A Love So Beautiful', Nelson Wilbury, better known to most people as George Harrison, contributed backing vocals, and it was also co-written by Jeff Lynne AKA Otis Wilbury.

'A Love So Beautiful' was also the name of a Roy Orbison remix album released in 2017, where Orbison's vocals were accompanied by The Royal Philharmonic Orchestra, which included the aforementioned title track.

Artist - Tom Petty
Title - I Won't Back Down
Year - 1989
Label - MCA Records

Charlie T. Wilbury Jr. AKA Muddy Wilbury, better known to most as Tom Petty, was a rock legend and a Heartbreaker. He was a member of the supergroup (with George, Bob Dylan, Roy Orbison and Jeff Lynne) known as The Travelling Wilburys, who, on their first and third albums (the second album doesn't exist!), made some amazing music together.

In 1989, Charlie T. Wilbury Jr, under his real life alias of Tom Petty, released his solo single 'I Won't Back Down' from his album *Full Moon Fever*. Co-written by Jeff Lynne, this single, which sounds ambiguously like the Wilbury hit 'Handle With Care', featured George on acoustic guitar and backing vocals. The tune was a commercial success, reaching No.12 in the US *Billboard* Top 100 and No.5 in Canada, and even reached No.1 in the US Mainstream Rock Charts.

For added flavours of Beatle, Ringo appears playing drums, though only in the song's music video. Petty was another member of the supergroup for the aforementioned Concert For George.

He sadly passed away on October 2nd 2017 of an accidental drug overdose. He was 66 years old.

Artist - Vicki Brown
Title - Lu Le La
Year - 1990
Label - Polydor

Vicki Brown was a backing singer who worked in pop, rock and even classical music. She was the mother of Sam Brown and wife of one of George's closest friends, Joe Brown, and she worked with the likes of Pink Floyd, Tina Turner, The Kinks, Dusty Springfield, Lulu, Olivia Newton-John, Slade, Elton John, Bryan Ferry, The Small Faces, Robert Palmer and many more. She sadly passed away in June 1991 of cancer. She was only 50 years old.

In 1990, she released her final album before her death, *About Love And Life*, and on the song 'Lu Le La 'George Harrison plays slide guitar. A beautiful song, which is sadly rather overlooked.

Her husband, Joe Brown, famously ended the Concert For George in 2002 singing, accompanied by his ukulele, 'I'll See You In My Dreams'.

Artist - Bob Dylan
Title - Under The Red Sky
Year - 1990
Label - CBS

If you are a fan of The Beatles, then you're probably also going to be a fan of Bob Dylan too. If you are one of the two people who don't know who Robert Zimmerman is, he's one of the most beloved and most influential people in pop and folk music, and is an American cultural legend, still massively successful today, plus he inspired a character in *The Magic Roundabout*! Seeing as I (and many people reading this book) are over 30 (see one of his famous quotes), he probably won't trust me, but if you're reading this, Bob, I hope you enjoy this book!

As Dylan was a friend of The Beatles since 1964 (he also allegedly was the catalyst for them getting into the more "illegal" recreational substances), it would make sense that he would team up with a Beatle sometime in his seven decade career, and guess what - he did! Out of all The Beatles, Dylan maintained probably the best relationship with George, and they even shared the bill sometimes; and of course, he was a member of that supergroup with George - The Travelling Wilburys, playing the role of Lucky Wilbury.

On his 1990 album *Under The Red Sky*, Beatle George played slide guitar on the title track. Dylan also played acoustic guitar, Don Was is on bass and Waddy Wachtel and Al Kooper emulate the Hammond organ sound of 'Like A Rolling Stone 'by playing keyboards.

Artist - The Jeff Healy Band
Title - While My Guitar Gently Weeps
Year - 1990
Label - Arista

The late Jeff Healy was a Canadian guitar legend who had a tragic life, having contracted cancer in the eye at one year old, which ultimately took his life. On a lighter note, he had a successful career in music, with his most popular record being the single 'Angel Eyes'. While not a hit in the UK, it was a massive hit in America, reaching No.5 in the *Billboard* charts, and it was covered by R&B singer Paulini in 2004, which ended up being a hit in Australia and New Zealand.

In 1990, he covered the Beatles classic 'While My Guitar Gently Weeps', which was a hit in Canada, reaching No.27, and it even reached No.7 in the US *Billboard* Rock Charts. This cover is notable, as it featured George Harrison himself on acoustic guitar and backing vocals. Also playing on this version was fellow Travelling Wilbury, Jeff Lynne, who also provided backing vocals and acoustic guitar work.

It appeared on Healy's studio album *Hell To Pay*.

Artist - Jim Horn
Title - Take Away The Sadness
Year - 1990
Label - Warner Bros. Records

Jim Horn is a very prolific LA-born saxophonist, woodwind player and session musician. He has worked with three of the four Beatles, and was particularly pally with George after appearing at his legendary Concert For Bangladesh in 1971. He has worked with Paul McCartney, Ringo Starr, The Rolling Stones, Michael Jackson, Stevie Wonder, The Beach Boys, Elvis Presley, Ike and Tina Turner, Herbie Hancock, Billy Joel, Diana Ross, Elton John, Frank Sinatra, Barbra Streisand, Little Richard, Lionel Richie, Garth Brooks, Harry Nilsson and many, many, many more - wow! Chances are, you have probably heard a record he has played on.

In 1988, Horn released the studio album *Work It Out* on Warner Bros. Records, and on the song 'Take Away The Sadness', George Harrison is on slide guitar. It's a very relaxing "smooth jazz" release that brings back nostalgic memories of browsing through the BBC Teletext service back in the day.

Artist - Jeff Lynne
Album - Armchair Theatre
Title - Every Little Thing/Lift Me Up/September Song
Year - 1990
Label - Reprise Records

On the 12th June 1990, Jeff Lynne released his first solo album, *Armchair Theatre*, on Reprise Records, recorded between 1989-1990 in Raindirk at Posh Studios in England. It is notable for reuniting Lynne with Richard Tandy from ELO, and Beatle George AKA Nelson Wilbury. Ringo Starr would also play drums on the song 'Blown Away '(which we'll cover later in the book). The album received decent reviews from critics.

George Harrison played acoustic guitar and backing vocals on the album's lead single 'Every Little Thing', as well as appearing in the song's music video, directed by Meiert Avis. While selling well in America, reaching No.9 in the US *Billboard* Mainstream Rock Charts, and reaching No.24 in Australia, the single failed to make an impact in the UK, only reaching No.59 in the UK Singles Chart.

On 'Lift Me Up', George is on slide guitar, and he also sings backing vocals. There is also a really lovely cover version of 'September Song', an American standard, originally written for the Broadway Musical *Knickerbocker Holiday* by Kurt Weill and Maxwell Anderson. George also plays slide guitar on that one too, as well as playing slide guitar on 'Stormy Weather', a cover version of a torch song from 1933, originally written by Harold Arlen and Ted Koehler.

Artist - Eric Clapton
Title - That Kind Of Woman
Year - 1990
Label - Warner Bros. Records

Not to be confused with the song by Dua Lipa, which obviously came much later, 'That Kind Of Woman 'was a George Harrison-penned number which was released as part of the charity album *Nobody's Child: Romanian Angel Appeal*, which was launched by Beatle wives - Barbra Bach, Yoko Ono, Linda McCartney and Olivia Harrison - to help Romanian children after the fall of communism. This charity album contained contributions from a large array of rock music greats including The Travelling Wilburys, a duet with George and Paul Simon, Stevie Wonder, Elton John, Van Morrison, the Bee Gees, Billy Idol and Guns N 'Roses, and the album ended with a live rendition of 'With A Little Help From My Friends' by Ringo Starr and His All-Starr Band.

Clapton's number, 'That Kind Of Woman', has a very Travelling Wilburys-esque vibe to it (which makes a lot of sense considering the time period), and if you like the Travelling Wilburys, I think you may like this one. As well as writing the song, George also played slide guitar.

Artist - Gary Moore
Title - That Kind Of Woman
Year - 1990
Label - Virgin

The late Gary Moore was an Irish blues and rock guitarist who was a member of Thin Lizzy, Skid Row and The Greg Lake Band. He had a very diverse career, and was considered a very influential guitarist in his field, earning the title of a virtuoso. His most famous track would have to be 'Parisian Walkways'.

1990 saw him release the album *Still Got The Blues* on Virgin Records, and it contained the George Harrison-penned number 'That Kind Of Woman '(which had also been recorded by Eric Clapton, see the previous entry in this book). As well as writing the piece, Harrison also played both slide and rhythm guitar, and also provided backing vocals. Like Clapton's version, despite not being a Travelling Wilburys song, it does sound very much like one, which is far from a bad thing!

Artist - Julian Lennon
Title - Saltwater
Year - 1991
Label - Virgin

Julian Lennon is the son of John and Cynthia Lennon. He was the inspiration for at least three of the songs in the Beatles discography - 'Lucy In The Sky With Diamonds', 'Hey Jude 'and 'Good Night'. In the 1980s and 1990s, he had a moderately successful solo career with two top ten hits, 1984's 'Too Late For Goodbyes 'and the tune we are covering in this book, 1991's 'Saltwater'.

It was part of Julian's 1991 album *Help Yourself*, and it reached No.6 in the UK Singles Chart. It is very similar to the sort of song his father would have made if he had survived, with lyrics about environmental conservation and poverty, and Julian's voice is eerily similar to John's. Julian initially wrote the song's guitar solo in the style of George Harrison, and under the suggestion of his producer, Bob Ezrin, he offered the solo to George. Unfortunately, Harrison turned it down, as he was consoling Eric Clapton, whose son had just recently passed away. Harrison eventually did then send a couple of riffs, though in the actual song's recording, they were played by Steve Hunter.

Harrison did get an acknowledgement in the liner notes for Julian's *Help Yourself* album.

Artist - Jimmy Nail
Title - Real Love
Year - 1991
Label - EastWest

Jimmy Nail is a singer-songwriter, actor, TV writer and film producer hailing from Newcastle-upon-Tyne. Outside of music, he is best known for playing Leonard "Oz" Osbourne in the classic British comedy/drama series *Auf Wiedersehen, Pet*, and working with fellow Geordies like Sting and Mark Knopfler.

In 1992, he released his second LP, *Growing Up In Public*, which contained the No.1 hit single 'Ain't No Doubt'. On this LP, he managed to get a group of big names to collaborate with him: Pink Floyd's David Gilmour, Gary Moore, Sam Brown and, on the tune 'Real Love '(not the 1996 Beatles "reunion" single of the same name), George Harrison plays slide guitar.

Artist - Del Shannon
Title - Hot Love
Year - 1991
Label - Silvertone Records

Del Shannon (real name Charles Westover) was a popular but sadly nowadays overlooked legend in rock 'n' roll, best known for the 1960 hit single 'Runaway'. At one time, he was considered to replace Roy Orbison in George's band, The Travelling Wilburys, though sadly this never came about, as he tragically committed suicide in 1990.

1991 saw the release of the posthumous single 'Callin 'Out My Name', and its B-side was a number entitled 'Hot Love', which was recorded on the 25th May 1988 at Weddington Studios in LA and produced by Del himself. You know I was saying that Shannon could have been a Wilbury - well, this tune includes Jeff Lynne, Tom Petty and yes, George Harrison providing backing vocals. Seriously, he should have joined up, as if you've heard his voice, he was quite something, and he had a very distinct Frankie Valli-esque falsetto.

>
> Artist - Alvin Lee
> Title - Real Life Blues
> Year - 1992
> Label - Castle Communications

The late, great Alvin Lee was a blues rock legend, who is best known for being the lead guitarist and singer with the hugely successful 1970s band Ten Years After.

In 1991, he released the solo single 'Real Life Blues', which featured George Harrison as guest guitarist, as well as the co-founder of Deep Purple, Jon Lord. It's a reflection of how messed up the world can be with war and the depressing nature of the news, but it seemed as if the chart going public at the time preferred mindless escapism to the blues of real life (it was released during the fallout of the Cold War and the first Gulf War).

>
> Artist - Alvin Lee
> Album - Nineteenninetyfour
> Title - The Bluest Blues/I Want You (She's So Heavy)
> Year - 1994
> Label - Viceroy Music

Back in the 1990s, Alvin Lee released the album *Nineteenninetyfour* (guess which year this came out?!) on Viceroy Music. George Harrison contributed to two songs on the album - 'The Bluest Blues 'and 'I Want You (She's So Heavy)'.

If 'Real Life Blues 'isn't your cup of tea, then how about 'The Bluest Blues'? George is on slide guitar, and it's very similar musically to his previous release,' Real Life Blues', though lyrically it's about a break-up with a woman. 'I Want You 'is a cover of that song of epic proportions from The Beatles 'grand finale studio album *Abbey Road*. Unlike the two blues songs, this is a lot more uplifting. George plays slide guitar and the track is also the album's closer.

>
> Artist - Mike Batt
> Title - The Hunting Of The Snark

Year - 1995 (recorded 1986)
Label - Epic

Mike Batt is a British musician, best known for discovering Katie Melua, writing the Art Garfunkel hit 'Bright Eyes 'from the "children's" film *Watership Down*... and for turning the animated TV characters of *The Wombles* into a novelty pop group.

In 1984, Batt made a musical version of Lewis Carroll's poem 'The Hunting Of The Snark 'with The London Symphony Orchestra. It was later revived in 1986 as an all-star concept album fearing George Harrison, Roger Daltrey (The Who), Art Garfunkel, John Hurt, Cliff Richard, Captain Sensible, and John Lennon's son, Julian. This version was performed as a live concert at the famous Barbican venue in London, but a recording was withheld from release because of a dispute with the record label (CBS), and it was not subsequently released until 1995 on Epic Records.

Other versions of the musical would be produced in 1990, 1991 and 1995.

Artist - Gary Wright
Title - Don't Try To Own Me
Year - 1995
Label - High Wave Music Inc.

It will cost 'ya!

1995 saw Wright release the single 'Don't Try To Own Me', which featured George Harrison singing backing vocals. A video clip of the recording session appears in the song's music video directed by Michael Schultz. It would later be featured on Wright's 1995 studio album *First Signs Of Life*.

While the song does sound more like something released in 1985 than 1995, if you like MOR power ballads, then this is a highly recommended tune.

Artist - Rubyhorse
Title - Punchdrunk
Year - 2000
Label - Horse Trade

Rubyhorse are an indie rock band that hail from Cork in Ireland. The members of the band - Joe Philpott, Decky Lucey, Owen Fegan, Gordon Ashe and David Farell - have been friends since nursery, and formed Rubyhorse when they were teenagers. They have toured with artists such as R.E.M., INXS, Culture Club and Def Leppard, and despite parting ways in 2003, reformed in 2016 and still perform shows today.

In 2000, they released the album *How Far Have You Come?*, which included the song 'Punchdrunk'. They subsequently signed to Island records, and recorded the album *Rise* in LA. Jay Joyce, the producer of the record, liked the song 'Punchdrunk', but suggested that it needed something special. George Harrison was staying in LA for a couple of days at the time, and a friend of the band played the track to Harrison when he was picking him up from the airport. George really liked what he heard, which led to him playing slide guitar on the new version, which was included on *Rise* when it was released in 2002.

It's a very beautiful and haunting piece, and in 2020 it was reissued as a single.

Artist - Bill Wyman's Rhythm Kings
Title - Love Letters
Year - 2001
Label - Roadrunner Arcade Music

Bill Wyman was the bass guitarist from 1962-1993 for that other really cool ultra-successful band of the 1960s, The Rolling Stones. He also has his own band called The Rhythm Kings, who are a collective of musicians who do cover version of blues, R&B and early rock and roll hits, as well as their own original compositions. I saw them live back in 2008, and they were awesome!

2001 saw them release the album *Double Bill* on Roadrunner Arcade Music and it contained a cover version of the 1945 song written by Edward Heyman and Victor Young, 'Love Letters', which was initially performed by Dick Haymes, and appeared in the movie of the same name.

It was later covered by the likes of Elvis Presley, Kitty Lester and Alison Moyet, and on Wyman's version, George Harrison contributed slide guitar; it also featured an amazing vocal track from Rhythm King member Janice Hoyte, who had previously sung on the Paul Hardcastle electro megahit '19'.

Artist - Electric Light Orchestra
Album - Zoom
Title - A Long Time Gone/All She Wanted
Year - 2001

Label - Epic

The Electric Light Orchestra (or simply ELO) are a Birmingham-based art rock collective, who have been having hits and selling out arenas for over 50 years. Their frontman is none other than the legendary Jeff Lynne, who is a major player in the Beatles story, as he produced their two "reunion" singles for the 1995 *Anthology* project,' Free As A Bird 'and 'Real Love', as well as being a member of The Travelling Wilburys supergroup with George Harrison.

2001 saw the band release their twelfth studio album, *Zoom*, which, despite a promise of the return of the classic ELO sound and receiving decent reviews, was a commercial failure, only reaching No.34 in the UK Albums Chart, and No.94 in the US *Billboard* Top 200 albums chart. The album is, however, notable for featuring contributions from two of The Beatles - Ringo Starr plays drums on the songs 'Moment in Paradise 'and 'Easy Money', which we'll cover later in the book, and playing slide guitar on the songs 'A Long Time Gone 'and 'All She Wanted 'was George Harrison. It was the final record appearance of Harrison to be released during his lifetime.

A great pair of tunes, and not a bad way to sign off the recording career of our beloved Beatle George.

CHAPTER FOUR – RINGO

Sir Richard "Ringo Starr" Starkey MBE is one hell of a drummer. As well as being both a Beatle and a successful solo artist, he has performed guest drums on many records past and present. Of course, he is the voice of many of our childhoods, as he was the narrator of *Thomas The Tank Engine* from 1984-1986. If you hear the phrase "Peace And Love" there's a 50/50 chance that our Ringo has said it!

Artist - Solomon King
Title - A Hundred Years Or More
Year - 1968
Label - Columbia

The late Solomon King was an American singer whose popularity was at its peak in the 1960s and 1970s. His biggest hit would have to be his cover of the Spanish standard 'She Wears My Ring', which was a top three hit in the UK, but failed to chart in his native America. He was also known for being very tall, and when he was interviewed on TV, he had to sit down, to make it easier for interviewers!

November 1968 saw him release the single 'Goodbye My Old Gal 'on Columbia Records, with its B-side being a tune entitled 'A Hundred Years

Or More', originally written by American songwriter Charles Tobias. It featured none other than Ringo. It was recorded on the 9th July at Abbey Road's Studio 2. Ringo's contribution was handclaps, which are at their most audible around 1 minute 18 seconds into the song.

> Artist - Solomon King
> Title - Have Nagila
> Year - 1968
> Label - Columbia

This was the B-side to his single 'Somewhere In The Crowd', and is a cover of a traditional Jewish folk song which had its first commercial recording in 1918 by A.Z. Idelsohn. It was recorded at EMI (Abbey Road) studios, and Ringo is said to have provided backing vocals and played tambourine.

> Artist - Stephen Stills
> Album - Stephen Stills
> Titles - To A Flame/We Are Not Helpless
> Year - 1970
> Label - Atlantic

Stephen Stills was a founder member of the cult American band Buffalo Springfield, and subsequently a member of the legendary singer-songwriter supergroup Crosby Stills, Nash & Young. He also had a solo career, and in 1970, released a self-titled LP on Atlantic Records. The tracks 'To A Flame 'and 'We Are Not Helpless 'feature the drum work of some guy credited on the album as Richie, but as we all know, this Richie fella is something of a "Starr" if you get my drift. Stills returned the favour by playing piano on Ringo's solo hit 'It Don't Come Easy'.

> Artist - Howlin 'Wolf
> Title - I Ain't Superstitious
> Year - 1971
> Label - Chess

Howlin 'Wolf (real name Chester Burnett) was a blues music legend. Many of his songs have become blues standards, and he was known for his booming voice and imposing physical presence.

In 1971, he re-recorded his 1962 single 'I Ain't Superstitious', which was originally featured on his album *Change My Way*. This new version appeared on his LP *The London Howlin' Wolf Sessions*, which was recorded in May 1970 at the Olympic Sound Studios in London. Ringo Starr is featured on drums and also joining Wolf on this tune are Steve Winwood, Klaus Voormann, Eric Clapton, Jordan Sandke, Dennis Lansing, Joe Miller and Rolling Stone Bill Wyman.

A remastered CD version of the album was released in 2003.

Artist - B.B. King
Album - B.B. King In London
Titles - Ghetto Woman/Wet Hayshark/Part-Time Love
Year - 1971
Label - ABC Records

As shouted out by our Fab Four in the song 'Dig It', "B.B," King (1925-2015, real name Riley B. King) was an American blues legend who was one of the most original and talented people in his field, and he was known for performing at least 200 shows per year. One could assume that the B.B. meant Bloody Brilliant, but it really meant 'Blues Boy'.

In 1971, B.B. cut the album *B.B. King In London*, which was recorded at the Olympic and Continental Studios between the 9th and the 16th June 1971. It was released on the 19th November of that year to coincide with the first date of King's tour of the UK. Opening for him on that tour was the tragic British blues musician Duster Bennett, who was best known for his association with Fleetwood Mac. Bennett was a cult figure in rock circles, who released six albums in his lifetime, and even played on John Peel's radio show *Top Gear* (nothing to do with the British TV show about cars). He was tragically killed in a car crash in 1976 aged only 29.

It's a really great album, and Ringo played on three of the tracks, 'Ghetto Woman', 'Wet Hayshark' and 'Part-Time Love'. Also playing on eight of the songs on bass duties was none other than Beatle buddy Klaus Voormann.

Interestingly, John Lennon was going to perform on some of the tracks, but sadly this fell through for unknown reasons. Starr would later be featured in the 2012 documentary about B.B. King's life story *The Life Of Riley*.

Artist - Peter Frampton
Album - Wind Of Change
Titles - The Lodger/Alright
Year - 1972
Label - Atlantic

Peter Frampton is a rock legend from groups such as The Herd and Humble Pie (with Steve Marriott of Small Faces fame), who has worked with a who's who of classic rock such as Ringo Starr, David Bowie, The Bee Gees, John Entwistle, Harry Nilsson, Jerry Lee Lewis, and Bill Wyman. His biggest hits would have to be from his bestselling live album *Frampton Comes Alive!* in 1976 -' Baby I Love Your Way', 'Show Me The Way', and an edited version of 'Do You Feel Like We Do'.

He is also the master of the talk-box, and when he appeared at the Hullabalooza Festival in Springfield, USA in 1996, Homer Simpson broke his inflatable pig for his finale (bought from Pink Floyd's Yard Sale), Cypress Hill stole his orchestra and Sonic Youth were stealing eats from his food cooler! He also played Billy Shears in the infamous *Sgt. Pepper* film from 1978!

In 1972, he released his debut album *Wind Of Change*, which was also produced by Frampton himself. On the album's opening number,' The Lodger', Frampton invited Ringo Starr to play drums. Starr appears again on the album's closing number,' Alright', which also features Beatle pals Billy Preston on piano and Hammond organ and Klaus Voormann on bass.

Frampton would later join Ringo, as a member of his All Starr Band.

Artist - Bobby Hatfield
Title - Oo Wee Baby, I Love You
Year - 1972
Label - A&M Records

Bobby Hatfield was a member of bands such as The Paramours and, most famously, The Righteous Brothers. He notably sang solo on the Righteous' 1965 recording of 'Unchained Melody', which was a hit worldwide, both in '65, and a re-recording in 1990, when it finally reached No.1 worldwide after appearing in the Jerry Zucker film *Ghost* featuring Demi Moore and Patrick Swayze.

In 1972, he released the single 'Oo Wee Baby, I Love You', which sounds a little bit too similar to 'Get Back', which makes you surprised that the Beatle lawyers didn't cotton on! Maybe it's because the guy playing drums is our good friend, Richard Starkey, as well as solo years regular

Klaus Voormann on bass. Producing the song was the famed Richard Perry, who has worked with everybody from Ringo, Harry Nilsson and Art Garfunkel to Diana Ross, Donna Summer and Barbra Streisand.

Despite sounding very similar to a very well-known Beatles hit, it's actually a really good song, and I highly recommend that you go out there and find a copy somewhere!

Artist - The London Symphony Orchestra and Chambre Choir
Album - Tommy
Title - Fiddle About/Tommy's Holiday Camp
Year - 1972
Label - Ode Records

Tommy was a rock opera by the famous rockers of awesomeness, The Who. It's the story of Tommy Walker and his experiences with life and his family, and despite being a deaf, dumb and blind kid, he sure does play a mean pinball!

The rock opera was adapted many times, including a film version in 1975, but the version we will be covering in this book was in the form of a concert, performed by the London Symphony Orchestra in 1972, at London's Rainbow Theatre. In this incarnation, Ringo Starr played the role of the perverted Uncle Ernie and sang on the songs 'Fiddle About 'and 'Tommy's Holiday Camp'. Also joining Ringo were Rod Stewart as the local lad and Steve Winwood as the father and when this incarnation was resurrected in 1973, the cast also included none other than the legendary Doctor Who himself, Jon Pertwee!

Artist - All Occasion Brass Band
Title - Oh Happy Day
Year - 1974
Label - MCA Records

The All Occasion Brass Band are a little-known group from the 1970s, with one of their members being Texas-based multi-instrumentalist, producer, engineer, arranger and songwriter, Jim Price. Recorded at the Olympic Studios in London in 1971, their one-and-only album, *In The Presence Of The Lord*, which contained a series of cover versions of religious-themed rock songs, was released in 1974 after three years of development hell. Many of the people playing on the album are famous musicians performing under alter egos, including Pietro Rampini alias Peter Frampton.

As well as featuring covers of the George Harrison hits 'My Sweet Lord 'and 'Isn't It A Pity', on their version of 'Oh Happy Day', originally by The Edwin Hawkins Singers, Ringo Starr makes an uncredited contribution playing drums. George was rumoured to have also contributed to this release, with the Sanskrit OM symbol being listed in the production credit, which he often used at the time, but this is proven not to be the case.

It wasn't the first time that Price crossed paths with a Beatle, as he was also a member of Delaney and Bonnie's backing band, who backed John Lennon at a 1969 UNICEF Concert at the Lyceum in London, and he shared the bill on a tour with George Harrison.

Artist - Colonel Doug Bogie
Title - Cokey Cokey
Year - 1975
Label - ABC Records/Ring-O

Colonel Doug Bogie is a man who was signed to Ringo's short-lived record label, Ring O' Records. He is probably best known for being a two-time bassist for Queen, and he only played a couple of gigs in 1971 before being sacked for trying to upstage Freddie Mercury. He subsequently became a sound engineer, with credits including Duane Eddy and Mungo Jerry.

Ringo once said that Bogie was one of his favourite performers, and he also had a famous fan in Harry Nilsson. Released on November 21st 1975, Colonel Doug Bogie's one-and-only single was a cover version of the traditional German standard 'Cokey Cokey '(better known to most as the 'Hokey Cokey') done reggae style. The 'Hokey Cokey', for the two people who don't know, is a traditional participation campfire song, whose origins date to at least the 1820s. Other people to have recorded hit versions of the song include The Showmen, Black Lace, and comedian Bill Bailey, doing it in the style of Kraftwerk!

It is said that Ringo is on drums, and on guitar is none other than Eric Clapton! A really left-field and bizarre release in the extended Beatles canon.

"Yes! I managed to get a one off deal with Ringo Starr's Ring O' Records," recalled Bogie for an *Italian Queen* fanzine in 2019." I had gone in to pitch a demo of a sci fi based concept album *House Up In The Stars* that never came to be. But I also had this novelty track I had arranged and recorded at CBS. Ringo was so nice and listened to it all, but I think he only took it on because when I went to in to pitch he was with Harry Nilsson who took a liking to it. Couldn't believe my good fortune – an advance of

£400 – bought a second hand colour TV for my mum and myself – we shared a flat in those days." [27]

Bogie is still around today, and nowadays appears at Queen fan conventions around the world.

Artist - Colonel Doug Bogie
Title - Away In A Manger
Year - 1975
Label - ABC Records/Ring-O

The B-side to 'Cokey '- another cover song, this time the classic Christmas carol reinterpreted in a rock style - weird!

Artist - David Hentschel
Title - Step Lightly
Year - 1975
Label - Ring O'Records

Back in 1975, as George had success with Dark Horse Records, Ringo had his own attempt at a record label with the rather "pun-tastic" name of Ring O' Records. It lasted until 1978 and suffered from distribution problems throughout its life. The label produced seventeen singles and seven LPs.

For the label's debut, British record engineer David Hentschel did something unique - an instrumental version of Ringo's most successful solo album *Ringo*. It was released under the name of *Startling Music* and is a very original and "out-there" entry in the expanded Beatles musical canon.

David Hentschel started his career around 1969/1970 working at the famous Trident Studios in London, and in 1983, he would compose the soundtrack to the Lewis Gilbert film adaptation of the 1980 Willy Russell stage play *Educating Rita*, starring Michael Caine, Julie Walters and Maureen Lipman, which won many awards. He may be best known for producing many tunes in Genesis 'discography. Coincidentally, the drummer on this release is a young Phil Collins and Flaming Youth's Ronnie Caryl plays guitar (Collins was also in this band before Genesis).

Recorded after (but released before) McCartney's instrumental album *Thrillington* (a lounge-inspired reinterpretation of the *RAM* album), this is another reimagining of a classic Beatles solo album, though musically it's more diverse, flipping genres like a John Peel radio show. Despite the Beatles connection, the album has been out of print since 1979 with no CD or digital release coming out any time soon.

As for Ringo's actual musical involvement in this release, he plays finger clips on the song 'Step Lightly'.

Artist - Keith Moon
Album - Two Sides Of The Moon
Titles - Solid Gold/Together
Year - 1975
Label - Track Record

Keith Moon was the absolute definition of a man who lived the rock 'n' roll lifestyle to the fullest. He was a wild and crazy guy, not to mention an amazing drummer, and he played in one of the greatest bands of the 1960s - The Who. He was also the inspiration behind the Muppets character Animal.

1975 saw the release of his single 'Solid Gold', and making a spoken word contribution is fellow drummer Ringo Starr. It was featured on Moon's solo album *Two Sides Of The Moon*. Ringo would also perform guest drums and a spoken word section on the album's closer,' Together ' (also co-written by Harry Nilsson). Coincidentally, the album contains a cover version of the classic Beatles song 'In My Life', and a cover of the lesser-known John Lennon number 'Move Over Ms. L' (the B-side to Lennon's cover of Ben E. King's 'Stand By Me'). The LP also featured Davie Bowie as a guest vocalist on the song 'Real Emotion 'and for Beatle fans, roadie Mal Evans arranged the horns on 'Move Over Ms. L'.

The album was a commercial failure, reaching only No.155 in the US *Billboard* Album Chart. The album has something of a "so-bad-it's-good" reputation - while Keith might be a great drummer, he isn't exactly Roger Daltrey when it comes to singing! The collaboration between Moon and Starr features the drummer legends exchanging some really corny turn-of-the-century vaudeville jokes in a spoken-word section on the tune 'Together', which makes Paul McCartney and Michael Jackson's exchange on 'The Girl Is Mine 'sound intellectual and thought provoking!

Zak Starkey (Ringo's son) is now the current drummer for The Who (as well as being in Oasis), having played with them since 1996, and he is still playing with them to this day. I've had the pleasure of seeing them in concert, and they were fantastic - Zak is an amazing drummer.

Artist - Nilsson
Album - Duit On Mon Dei
Titles - Kojak Columbo/Good For God

Year - 1975
Label - RCA Victor

Duit On Mon Dei ('Do It On Monday '- a pun on the British monarchy's motto 'Dieu et mon droit '-' God and My Right') is the eleventh studio album by that man who triumphed eclecticism when it came to music genres, Harry Nilsson! Despite the album getting a mixed reception from critics of the day, time has been kind to the LP, and more modern reviews have been more favourable.

Ringo appears on two of the cuts on this LP. He plays drums on 'Kojak Columbo', and even sings backing vocals on 'Good for God'. The album also features the song 'Easier For Me', which Ringo had sung previously on his album *Goodnight Vienna*, and the indispensable Klaus Voormann appears in all but two of the album's cuts playing bass.

Artist - Carly Simon
Title - More And More
Year - 1975
Label - Elektra

In 1975, Carly Simon released her fifth studio album, called *Playing Possum*, which is controversially best remembered for its rather risqué cover featuring Carly wearing only a black negligee, sheer-to-waist pantyhose and black boots.

Objectifying the female body aside, this album has some lovely singer/songwriter cuts, and track four on the album,' More And More', features our good friend Ringo Starr playing drums. As in a lot of 1970s Beatles solo projects, Klaus Voormann is on bass (and he also plays on the album's opener 'After The Storm'.). It's a really nice almost disco-sounding tune, which I would highly recommend, featuring some great vocals from Carly and lyrics that complement the album's famous sleeve.

Artist - Vera Lynn
Title - Don't You Remember When
Year - 1976
Label - EMI

The late Dame Vera Lynn was a very popular UK vocalist during the dark times of World War II, earning her the title of "The Forces 'Sweetheart". She is best known for hits like 'We'll Meet Again 'and 'The White Cliffs

Of Dover', and a compilation of hers is also notorious for knocking the remastered Beatles albums from the top of the UK Album Charts back in 2009!

In 1976, she released her comeback hit single 'Don't You Remember When', written by Lynsey de Paul and Barry Blue, especially for her. Ringo contributed to the tambourines on this track, and despite the song's popularity, it wasn't reissued on CD until 2007! It is now a staple of funerals and memorial services because of the song's nostalgic tone. Lynsey De Paul, who wrote this song, and was rumoured to be romantically involved with Ringo Starr, sadly passed away in 2014.

On a side note, Vera also covered The Beatles 'classic 'The Fool On The Hill 'in the 1970s.

Artist - The Manhattan Transfer
Album - Coming Out
Titles - Zindy Lou/S.O.S.
Year - 1976
Label - Atlantic

The Manhattan Transfer are an American funk and jazz group, founded in 1969 and still performing today, with their biggest hit being the No.1 single 'Chanson D'Amour', released in 1977. Ringo Starr appeared on two songs from their 1976 album *Coming Out*. One of these tracks was the almost hip-hop sounding 'Zindy Lou', whose song title sounds similar to 'Cindy Lou', which was the working title for the Buddy Holly hit 'Peggy Sue'. If you like proto-rap like Pigmeat Markham, you may enjoy this track. Ringo also played on the song 'S.O.S.', which is not the song by ABBA. As on 'Zindy Lou', Ringo plays drums.

Artist - Cat Stevens
Album - Cat Stevens
Titles - Blue Monday/I Just Want To Make Love To You
Year - 1976 (released 2001)
Label - A&M Records

'Blue Monday 'is a great cover version of the Fats Domino classic by the wonderful singer-songwriter Yusuf 'Cat Stevens' Islam. This is a studio outtake which was recorded in 1976 in Copenhagen, Denmark, during the time of his *Izitso* album, and it wasn't released until 2001 on a self-titled compilation. Ringo played the drums.

Cat also sang a version of the Willie Dixon blues classic 'I Just Want To Make Love To You', memorably covered by Etta James, whose version would famously be used in a soft drinks advert in 1996. Ringo also plays drums on this tune.

    Artist - Guthrie Thomas
    Album - Lies and Alibis
    Title - Good Days Are Rollin 'In/Band Of Steel/Ramblin' Cocaine Blues
    Year - 1976
    Label - Capitol Records

The very prolific Guthrie Thomas (1952-2016) was a man from Texas who wrote over 1000 songs and over 100 instrumental compositions, as well as releasing 60 albums, all within the span of 45 years! He was very good friends with Willie Nelson.

1976 saw Thomas release the country album *Lies and Alibis* on Capitol Records, which was recorded at Capitol Records Studio B in Los Angeles. Ringo Starr was a guest on three of the songs on this LP - 'Good Days Are Rollin 'In', where he played drums with Jim Keltner, 'Band Of Steel', which was also a Starr composition, and was a vocal duet with Thomas, as well as playing drums on 'Ramblin 'Cocaine Blues'.

The album was out of print for many years, until a remastered CD edition was issued in 2016... but only in Japan!

    Artist - The Alpha Band
    Album - Spark In The Dark
    Titles - Born In Captivity/Good News/You Angel You
    Year - 1977
    Label - Arista

The Alpha Band was a splinter group of Bob Dylan's band, the Rolling Thunder Revue, and they lasted for three short years between 1976-1979. They signed a huge recording contract with Arista Records, though ironically, the band were and remain relatively obscure, and are probably best remembered for being a launching pad for David Mansfield's career.

In 1977, they released their rhythmically titled second album, *Spark In The Dark*. Like Spinal Tap, the album contained an array of drummers (though thankfully none of them died in bizarre gardening accidents!) with one of them being the guest drummer Ringo Starr. He played on three cuts:

'Born In Captivity', 'Good News 'and 'You Angel You '(a cover of a 1974 song by Bob Dylan).

The album received mixed reviews from critics.

Artist - Attitudes
Title - Good News
Year - 1977
Label - Dark Horse Records

Attitudes were an LA-based band who were signees to George Harrison's Dark Horse Records label, and they released two albums and four singles, before disappearing into obscurity. Their genesis came about when they were session musicians for Harrison's *Extra Texture* album. They were Paul Stallworth, who played bass guitar and sang lead and background vocals, Danny Kortchmar, who played guitar and sang lead and background vocals, David Foster on keyboards and Jim Keltner (who had previously performed with The Beatles on their solo projects) on drums and percussion. They had mild success in the US *Billboard* Charts in 1976 with their single 'Sweet Summer Music', which reached No.94, but their biggest hit would have to be 'Honey Don't Leave LA', as it was covered by James Taylor, who had a minor hit with it in 1978, when it reached No.61 in the *Billboard* Hot 100.

In 1977, they released the album *Good News*, and on the title track, which closes the LP (and sounds rather ambiguously like Stevie Wonder's 'Isn't She Lovely'), our pal Ringo plays drums. For hip-hop crate diggers, Ringo's drums in the beginning are open, and are clear, ready for sampling - if you have the money to clear it, that is!

Artist - Delaney Bramlett
Album - Class Reunion
Titles - Locked Up In Alabama/I Wish It Would Rain/I Think I Got It/For Old Time's Sake/You Were The Light
Year - 1977
Label - Columbia

The late Delaney Bramlett was a guitarist and singer/songwriter who was influenced by the likes of Eric Clapton, J.J.Cale and Duane Allman. He was married to Bonnie Lynn, who was a backing singer for Tina Turner, and they even formed their own duo called Delaney & Bonnie, who went on to tour and record with Eric Clapton.

On Bramlett's 1977 album *Class Reunion*, produced by Jimmy Bowen and Ray Ruff, Ringo Starr did some uncredited drum work on five of the ten songs on the LP.

Despite the Beatles connection, the album appears to have been out of print for many years, with no indication of a reissue any time soon.

Artist - The Band
Title - I Shall Be Released
Year - 1978
Label - Warner Bros. Records

The Band were a Canadian rock band with probably the most uninspired name for any band in history, though ironically calling a band just simply The Band is actually fairly inspired in itself! They got their big break when they were backing Bob Dylan on his first tour of going electric (imagine how that would go down in the toxic social media climate of today!) and they ended up being a massively successful group in their own right.

In 1976 the band were in turmoil, and vocalist and guitarist Robbie Robertson was suffering from a severe neck injury, and opted to pull out of many tour dates. He urged The Band to call it quits, and conceived a grand finale concert to give The Band a big send-off entitled 'The Last Waltz' (spoilers - they reformed in 1983, and again in 1990 until disbanding for real in 1999).

On the LP version of their (not-quite) *Last Waltz* at Bill Graham's Wonderland Ballroom in San Francisco, they finished their set with an all-star version of one of their biggest hits - a cover version of the Bob Dylan classic 'I Shall Be Released'. Joining them on stage was Ringo, as well as Bob Dylan himself, Dr. John, Neil Diamond, Joni Mitchell, Neil Young, Van Morrison, Ronnie Hawkins, Richard Manuel, Eric Clapton and Ronnie Wood - wow, what a line-up that only The Travelling Wilburys could rival!

Artist - Lonnie Donegan
Album - Puttin 'On The Style
Titles - Have A Drink On Me/Ham 'n' Eggs
Year - 1978
Label - Chrysalis

Lonnie Donegan MBE was a Scottish music legend, and pioneer of the "skiffle" movement, which sowed the seeds for groups like The Quarrymen, who of course evolved into The Beatles - without him, our Fabs may not have even existed. He was inspirational to many groups that followed.

The king of skiffle was something of a hit-maker during the late 1950s and early 1960s, scoring some big tunes of the time, including 'Rock Island Line 'and 'Puttin 'On The Style '(a Quarryman favourite), and even some novelty singles, including 'Does Your Chewing Gum Lose Its Flavour 'and 'My Old Man's A Dustman'. Ironically, Donegan's fall from chart grace in the early 1960s coincided with the rise of The Beatles, and other acts in the British Invasion.

After surviving a heart attack in 1976, 1978 saw Lonnie release the comeback album *Puttin 'On The Style*, which was a series of reworks of his greatest hits featuring an array of big names accompanying him. These included Rory Gallagher, Leo Sayer, Brian May, Ronnie Wood, Klaus Voormann, Elton John, and on the remakes of 'Ham 'n' Eggs 'and 'Have A Drink On Me', Ringo Starr is on drums. The intention of this album was clearly to reintroduce Donegan to a contemporary audience, and he succeeded in that!

Artist - Ian McLagan
Title - Hold On
Year - 1979
Label - Mercury

The much-missed Ian McLagan (1945-2014) was a keyboard player who was a member of The Small Faces and an honorary member of The Rolling Stones. He released eleven albums with The Small Faces and ten solo LPs, and he was inducted into the Rock & Roll Hall Of Fame in 2014.

In 1979, McLagan released his debut solo album, *Troublemaker*, on Mercury Records, with Ringo providing guest drum work on the title 'Hold On'. It's a very fun rock 'n 'roll throwback, which is very similar sounding to The Plastic Ono Band's backing band, Elephant's Memory.

Artist - Bob Dylan
Title - Heart of Mine
Year - 1981
Label - Columbia

In 1981, Robert Zimmerman released his twenty-first studio album, *Shot Of Love*. Despite the record having received mixed reviews and modest sales, the LP has a big name fan in Bono from U2, who loves Dylan's singing on this one.

Ringo played drums (with Rolling Stone Ronnie Wood on guitar and Donald "Duck" Dunn of Booker T. and the M.G.'s on bass) on the song 'Heart Of Mine', which was released as a single. It would end up being covered by the likes of Norah Jones (who is the daughter of George's buddy, Ravi Shankar). Despite not charting in the UK or the US, it was a hit in Norway, where it reached the respectable No.8.

Artist - Guthrie Thomas
Album - Hobo Eagle Thief
Year - 1983
Label - Sawdust Records

As previously stated in this book, Guthrie Thomas was a very prolific but sadly overlooked country music legend.

In 1983, he released the album *Hobo Eagle Thief*, and apparently, Ringo is one of the drummers playing on tracks on this album. It is not known on which tunes he performs.

Artist - The Beach Boys
Title - California Calling
Year - 1985
Label - Caribou Records

In the year 1985, the well-loved Californian group released their twenty-fifth studio album. As they couldn't find a good title for it, they settled on calling it just *The Beach Boys* and it has the distinction of being the first album of theirs to be recorded digitally.

Ringo makes an appearance on the song 'California Calling', a song that's a nostalgia throwback, more like the early years of the group, rather than the more Brian-led tracks from the *Pet Sounds/Smile* era.

The album received mixed reviews from critics.

Artist - Artists United Against Apartheid
Title - Sun City
Year - 1985

Label - EMI

If you thought Paul teaming up with Kayne West was the first collaboration between a Beatle and a rapper, think again, as Ringo collaborated with the pioneers such as Run-DMC, plus two of the people who were there in the Bronx and practically invented hip-hop culture back in 1973, DJ Kool Herc and Afrika Bambaataa among others.

'Sun City' was an all-star charity release founded by activist and performer Steven Van Zandt and early electronic music pioneer Arthur Baker (of 'Planet Rock' fame) against the apartheid regime in South Africa at the time. One of the contributors to this charity single was none other than Ringo Starr, and joining him are a very eclectic bunch, including rock legends such as Bob Dylan, Keith Richards, Ronnie Wood, Bono, Bonnie Raitt and Lou Reed as well as the aforementioned early hip-hop pioneers such as Grandmaster Melle Mel and Kurtis Blow, and funk artists like George Clinton and Gil-Scott Heron - so something for everyone here!

The song was a commercial success, reaching the top 40 in many countries. It was, unsurprisingly, banned in South Africa. After the fall of apartheid, the song 'Sun City' is still considered to this day a major historical landmark in helping to overthrow these unjust laws.

Artist - John Cleese/Bill Oddie/Ringo Starr
Title - Naughty Atom Bomb
Year - 1986
Label - EMI

John Cleese is a very tall and very British man who was a member of the comedy troupe Monty Python, co-creator of *Fawlty Towers*, and has a very silly walk. Bill Oddie is one third of another highly successful comedic troupe, The Goodies, and a famous bird watcher/twitcher. Ringo Starr, on the other hand... well I think you all know who Ringo Starr is!

In 1986, the Python, the Goodie and the Beatle teamed up for a charity project for EMI Records called The Anti-Heroin Project. This project resulted in two singles and an album entitled *It's A Live-In World*. All proceeds were donated to the Phoenix House Charities for recovery centres throughout the UK to help eradicate use of heroin. The album also contained an anti-heroin message from Ringo himself entitled 'You Know It Makes Sense', and a contribution from Zak Starkey (Ringo's son) and Kate Robbins (Paul McCartney's cousin) on the album's title track; Paul McCartney also appears on the album, contributing a song entitled 'Simple As That'.

'Naughty Atom Bomb' was recorded in August 1986 at Ringo's Startling Studios, and it was written by Kenny Craddock and Colin Gibson. According to the book *The Ringo Starr Encyclopedia* by Bill Harry, fellow Python member, Michael Palin, also makes an uncredited contribution on vocals. In the words of an interview with Cleese in 1990, he has "no recollection" of Ringo's involvement in the song, with the consciousness being that Ringo's section was recorded in a different session, and was added into the final mix.

Artist - Buck Owens And Ringo Starr
Title - Act Naturally
Year - 1989
Label - Capitol Records

Buck Owens (1929-2006) was a Texas-based country artist who had a string of number one hits in his native America in the 1960s. Unlike his contemporaries, Owens would always have his own road band on his records, giving them a distinct "live" sound.

The song 'Act Naturally', written by Johnny Russell and Voni Morrison, was a hit for Buck and his band, The Buckaroos, back in 1963. It became a country standard and it was memorably covered in 1965 by our beloved foursome on their fifth studio album, *Help*, with Ringo on vocals. It was also the loose inspiration for the name of my previous Beatles book *Acting Naturally*.

In 1989, Buck and Ringo recorded a duet version, which reached No.27 in the US *Billboard* Country Charts. It's quite similar to The Beatles' version, and that, in my opinion, isn't a bad thing at all!

A music video was made, featuring Ringo wearing a really cool cowboy outfit.

Artist - Spirit Of The Forest
Title - Spirit Of The Forest
Year - 1989
Label - Virgin

Ringo's second foray into hip-hop, all in the good name of charity. This song was written by a group called Gentlemen Without Weapons, and it was released as both a 7 inch and 12 inch single on the 5th June 1989. The masterminds behind this release were Richard Branson (the very famous billionaire entrepreneur) and the Earth Love Fund (ELP) in conjunction with the U.N.E.P. (United Nations Environment Programme) and The United Nations. The single was double A-sided with each side containing a different set of vocalists. All the proceeds were donated to programmes dedicated to saving the world's rainforests.

Ringo, on this record, joined up with the likes of Fleetwood Mac, Brian Wilson, David Gilmour, Joni Mitchell, Kate Bush, Debbie Harry, Belinda Carlisle, Bonnie Raitt, Iggy Pop, The Ramones, Donna Summer, Lenny Kravitz, Afrika Bambaataa, The Jungle Brothers, The B-52's and more on the same record! Sounds amazing... well... at least it was for a good cause, as it was to help save the planet.

Unfortunately, this didn't pay off, as the single only reached the lowly position of No.86 in the UK Singles Chart!

Artist - Jeff Lynne
Title - Blown Away
Year - 1990
Label - Reprise Records

As stated previously in the George chapter, Jeff Lynne released his debut studio album, *Armchair Theatre*, in June 1990.

On the tenth track,' Blown Away', Ringo Starr guests on drums. Also on this track are Richard Tandy on acoustic guitar and Mette Methiesen and Phil Hatton on backing vocals. We are also treated to a posthumous guest appearance from the late, great Del Shannon on backing vocals. Sadly, Del took his own life four months before the release of this LP.

It's a lovely song, which has a vibe similar to The Travelling Wilburys, which makes sense, and Ringo's drum work is comparable to his work on the 1995 Beatles reunion hit 'Free As A Bird'.

Artist - Paul Simon
Title - Further To Fly
Year - 1990
Label - Warner Bros. Records
NOTE - Ringo didn't actually play on this tune, but it is here to clear things up.

What can I say about Paul Simon, other than what has already been said before? He is an extraordinary singer-songwriter, one half of Simon & Garfunkel - an ultra-popular pop music duo - not to mention, a massive solo star as well. He has earned 16 Grammy Awards, and is still performing and releasing records today.

In October 1990, Simon released his eighth solo album, *The Rhythm Of The Saints*, which received critical acclaim and won two Grammy nominations, one for Album Of The Year and another for Producer Of The Year (it was produced by Paul Simon himself). According to the album's liner notes, Ringo Star (note no extra R) plays guitar (wrong instrument for a start!) on the song 'Further To Fly'. This is a misprint, as the person actually playing is Rigobert Bamuldele - a souks guitarist from DR Congo who goes by the stage name of Rigo Star.

Artist - Little Richard
Title - Good Golly Miss Molly
Year - 1991
Label - Polydor

Little Richard (Richard Wayne Penniman), who actually stood a respectable 5'10", was one of the original pioneers of rock 'n' roll, and he was awesome. He was a very flamboyant figure, and was the man who coined the term "A whop bop-a-lu bop a whop bam boom!", which scientists today are still figuring out! Even in his later years, he was still performing and releasing records, and for us kids of the 1990s, he sang the theme tune for the cartoon series *The Magic School Bus*. He was the inspiration for the Beatles "Oohs" and Paul McCartney once won a Little Richard impersonation contest!

In 1991, Little Richard re-recorded his 1958 mega-hit 'Good Golly Miss Molly 'for the British David S.Ward comedy movie *King Ralph*, with John Goodman and Peter O'Toole (Goodman also sings the song in the film). This new version was produced by Jeff Lynne, who is a member of ELO and The Travelling Wilburys, as well as being the producer behind the two Beatles "reunion" singles, 'Free As A Bird 'and 'Real Love', and Ringo plays the drums. It was recorded at Rumbo Recorders at Canoga Park in California sometime in 1990.

It was released as a single with extremely limited distribution, and sadly failed to chart.

Artist - Nils Lofgren
Album - Silver Lining
Title - Walkin 'Nerve/Bein 'Angry
Year - 1991

Label - Rykodisc

Nils Hilmer Lofgren is a Chicago based singer/songwriter and multi-instrumentalist, who was a member of Bruce Springsteen's E Street Band from 1984, and also a former member of Ringo Starr's All-Starr Band. He also co-wrote many songs with Lou Reed, and was a member of Neil Young's Crazy Horse and the founder and frontman of the band Grin.

1991 saw Lofgren release the solo album *Silver Lining*. Ringo Starr plays drums on the song 'Walkin 'Nerve '(which also came out as a single) and sang vocals on 'Bein 'Angry '(which also featured honorary Beatle Billy Preston on organ).

Artist - Paul Shaffer & The Party Boys Of Rock 'N 'Roll
Title - Burning Down The House
Year - 1993
Label - SBK Records

'Burning Down The House 'was originally a hit song by one of the funkiest non-African American music acts - Talking Heads. In 1993, the song was covered by Canadian singer, multi-instrumentalist, actor, author and comedian, Paul Shaffer, who served as the musical director for American TV presenter David Letterman, and was also a musical director for The Blues Brothers.

Shaffer's instrumental version appeared on his album *The World's Most Dangerous Party*, and it featured a spoken-word introduction from the legendary hip-hop artist LL Cool J (in the context of the album, this is all meant to take place at a party, hence the LP's title). Closing the song is a spoken word skit from Ringo.

Artist - Leon Redbone
Title - My Little Grass Shack
Year - 1994
Label - Private Music

Leon Redbone (1949-2019) was a Cyprus-born Groucho Marx lookalike, who sang jazz, blues and vaudeville numbers, released eighteen albums and sang the theme tune to the 1985 TV series *Mr. Belvedere*. 1994 saw him release the album *Whistling In The Wind* and our Ringo duets with Redbone on track seven,' My Little Grass Shack'. Is it just me, or does it sound like something from a Disney film?

'My Little Grass Shack '(full title 'My Little Grass Shack in Kealakekua, Hawaii') was originally written in 1933, by Tommy Harrison and Billy Cogswell for Kona's Independence Day celebrations that year, and was first recorded in December '33 by Ted Flo Rito and his Orchestra. Many notable cover versions over the years have included Bing Crosby, Guy Lombardo, Ray Charles, Benny Goodman, Jesse Colin Young and Krusty The Clown.

Artist - Guthrie Thomas
Album - Ghost Towns
Year - 1999
Label - Mainstreet CD

In 1999, Guthrie Thomas (see previous entries in this book) released the studio album *Ghost Towns*. Ringo Starr is one of the credited guest performers on this LP, but it is unknown which songs he took part in.

Artist - Eric Burden & Billy Preston
Title - Power To The People
Year - 2000
Label - Lion Gate Films

A collaboration between Billy Preston and Eric Burdon, who was the vocalist for the UK rock band The Animals and the American multi-ethnic funk band of awesomeness, War. He is noted for his powerful, deep voice and his aggressive stage performances.

For the biopic film about the radical activist Abbie Hoffmann, *Steal This Movie* (released in 2000 and directed by Robert Greenwald), Burdon and Preston teamed up to do a very faithful cover version of the John Lennon solo hit 'Power To The People'. Also joining them on drums was Ringo Starr.

In 2020, Abbie Hoffman was played by comedic actor Sasha Baron Cohen in the acclaimed film *The Trial Of The Chicago 7*.

Artist - Electric Light Orchestra
Album - Zoom
Titles - Moment In Paradise/Easy Money
Year - 2001
Label - Epic

As previously stated in this book, ELO recorded the album *Zoom* in 2001, and it was sadly a commercial failure. As well as featuring the final recorded appearances of George Harrison released during his lifetime, Ringo appears as a guest drummer on two of the album's cuts,' Moment in Paradise 'and 'Easy Money'. They're both great songs, even if 'Easy Money 'does contain one use of a moderate swear word, so probably not for younger ELO fans!

>
> Artist - Jools Holland & His Rhythm & Blues Orchestra
> Title - Boys
> Year - 2003
> Label - Radar

Jools Holland OBE is a famous British musician, former member of the band Squeeze, and TV presenter, who presents to this day the acclaimed TV series *Later...With Jools Holland*. He tours round the country with his Rhythm & Blues Orchestra, and his band is pretty damn good!

In 2003, he released an all-star collaborations album *Jack O The Green: Small World Big Band Friends 3* featuring people as diverse as Smokey Robinson, Nick Cave, Prince Buster, Ruby Turner, Eric Clapton, Peter Gabriel, Solomon Burke and even girl group The Sugababes. Ringo makes a guest appearance, singing the song 'Boys', originally performed by The Shirelles and written by Luther Dixon and Wes Farrell. This wasn't the first time Ringo sang 'Boys', as it was originally part of The Beatles' live repertoire, and was famously performed to perfection on the Fab Four's iconic 1963 debut album *Please Please Me* with one of Richie's best vocal performances.

>
> Artist - Liam Lynch
> Album - Fake Songs
> Titles - Cuz You Do/Try Me
> Year - 2003
> Label - S-Curve Records

Liam Lynch is an all-American jack-of-all-trades - he's a musician, a director and a screenwriter, best known for the surrealist comedy series *The Sifl and Olly Show* for MTV. He has directed music videos for artists as diverse as The Foo Fighters and "Weird Al" Yankovic and, like myself, he is an avid *Doctor Who* fan!

In 2003, he released the album *Fake Songs* for S-Curve Records (which also shares the name of a different album he released in 2000 on 111 Productions), which included such songs as 'Fake Bjork Song', 'Fake David Bowie Song', 'Fake Depeche Mode Song 'and 'Fake Pixies Song', as well as a collaboration with *School Of Rock* star Jack Black. The album also featured a couple of songs with old Richie on drums, such as 'Cuz You Do' and 'Try Me'. These songs had originally featured in the album's 2000 prototype, but Ringo heard the originals, and was very impressed, so he appears as guest drummer.

The album received mixed reviews from critics.

Artist - Platinum Weird
Album - Make Believe
Titles - Make Believe/If You Believe In Love
Year - 2005
Label - Maniac Records

Platinum Weird are said to have been a long-lost 1970s rock supergroup, but were, in reality, a hoax created by Dave Stewart (of Eurythmics fame) and producer Kara DioGuardi. There was even a string of phoney websites, fake fan sites and even an elaborate mock-documentary covering the lives of this group, produced by VH1, which featured mock interviews with the likes of Mick Jagger, Christina Aguleira, Stevie Nicks and Ringo Starr.

October 2006 saw the fake band release the appropriately titled album *Make Believe*. Ringo is a guest drummer on 'Make Believe 'and 'If You Believe In Love'. Elton John and Steve Brown are the album's executive producers.

Artist - Mark Hudson
Title - So You Are A Star
Year - 2009
Label - No Label

Mark Hudson is a US musician, songwriter and producer who has worked with everybody from Cher, Aerosmith and Ozzy Osbourne to Celine Dion, Hanson, Harry Nilsson and many more. He was also a member of the musical trio The Hudson Brothers, with his brothers Bill and Brett, who were very popular back in the day.

From 1998, Hudson was a focal figure in Ringo Starr's continuing career as a solo artist, and he has co-produced nine of Ringo's solo albums, with

Hudson co-producing a total of eighty-two different compositions. This relationship however ended around 2007.

Despite their musical relationship being "over", Ringo made a guest appearance on drums on Mark's 2009 solo album *The Artist* on the track 'So You Are A Star '(which should have been called 'So You Are A Starr '- just saying!). This song was originally performed by Mark in 1974 with his group, The Hudson Brothers, for Casablanca Records, and it was a Top 40 hit in the US *Billboard* charts, and even went Top 5 in Canada.

Hudson's album also contains covers of the Beatles solo songs 'How ' (Lennon) and 'Let 'Em In '(McCartney).

Artist - Peter Kay's Animated All Star Band
Title - The Official BBC Children In Need Medley
Year - 2009
Label - Epic

Peter Kay is one of Britain's greatest comedy talents. Raised in Bolton, Lancashire, Kay got his big break at the end of the 1990s, with his absolutely hilarious stand-up shows (Garlic Bread?), and his beloved sitcoms such as 2001's *Phoenix Nights* and 2015's *Car Share*. Paul McCartney famously made a cameo in Kay's 2008 X-Factor parody programme *Britain's Got The Pop Factor… and Possibly a New Celebrity Jesus Christ Soapstar Superstar Strictly On Ice* mentoring the protagonist of the show, Geraldine McQueen (played by Kay).

In 2009, Kay assembled probably the greatest crossover with children's TV characters of all time, 'The Official BBC Children In Need Medley 'for the UK charity Children In Need. This mass-gathering of childhood greats had them all singing seven classic songs as part of a special medley, including the "na-na-na-nanana-naaaa" part of 'Hey Jude 'mashed with 'One Day Like This 'by Elbow for the finale.

Ringo Starr reprises his role as Thomas The Tank Engine (Ringo narrated the original Thomas series from 1984-1986) singing verses from the song 'Jai Ho! 'from the movie *Slumdog Millionaire*, originally performed by A.R. Rahman with an English interpretation by The Pussycat Dolls.

After around two years of hard work (including a music video of epic proportions), it all paid off big time, as the single was a huge commercial success, reaching No.1 in the UK Singles Chart and selling over 452,000 copies.

Interestingly, this was the second time Ringo had sung with Ken Barrie (who plays Postman Pat, another beloved UK children's character), as Barrie sang backing vocals on the 1968 *White Album* number 'Good Night'.

Artist - Jerry Lee Lewis
Title - Roll Over Beethoven
Year - 2010
Label - Sundazed Music

Jerry Lee "The Killer" Lewis (1935-2022) was a living rock 'n' roll pioneer (the last of his kind) who had great balls of fire, plus he once set his piano on fire on live television! He was a signee to Sun Records, and is no relation to the comedian Jerry Lewis.

In 2010, he released a collaborations album entitled *Mean Old Man*, which was a follow-up to the surprisingly successful 2006 collaborations album *Last Man Standing*. One of the songs featured on the LP is a cover of the classic rock 'n' roll standard 'Roll Over Beethoven '(which you may remember The Beatles themselves covering on their *With The Beatles* album in 1963), and providing backing vocals (and possibly also playing drums) is Ringo. Not much to say, other than it's a respectful and authentic reinterpretation of a classic.

Despite having a stroke in 2019, Lewis entered the recording studios once again with T-Bone Burnett to record new material. He sadly passed away on October 28th 2022, and his funeral was held on November 5th 2022 in his hometown of Ferriday, Louisiana.

Artist - Ben Harper
Album - Give Till It's Gone
Titles - Spilling Faith/Get There From Here
Year - 2011
Label - Virgin

Ben Harper is a singer, songwriter, multi-instrumentalist and a philanthropist. He is a three time Grammy Award winner and ten time nominee, and has released fifteen studio albums.

2011 saw him release his tenth studio album, *Give Till It's Gone*. It is notable for containing two collaborations with the guy best known to his mother as Richard Starkey - 'Spilling Faith 'and 'Get There From Here'. The album was a commercial success, reaching the top 10 in many countries. It also received mostly positive reviews from music critics.

Artist - Joe Walsh
Album - Analog Man
Titles - Lucky That Way/Band Played On

Year - 2012
Label - Fantasy

Joe Walsh is a Kansas-born guitarist and singer, who is probably best known for being a member of The Eagles, as well as working with the likes of The Who, The Beach Boys, James Gang and most notably for Beatle nuts, Ringo Starr and His All Starr Band. In 2012, he released the solo album *Analog Man*. It received mixed reviews from critics.

The LP was produced by Jeff Lynne. It came about as Walsh decided to record a new album thanks to the support of his wife, Marjorie Bach (who is coincidentally the sister of Ringo's wife, Barbara Bach), who gave him Jeff Lynne's phone number.

Ringo played drums on two tunes on the *Analog* album - 'Lucky That Way 'and 'Band Played On'. A pair of really great songs.

Artist - Mark Hudson
Title - For Love
Year - 2014
Label - Self Released

In 2014, Mark Hudson released his second solo album, *The Hooligan*, which was recorded at the legendary Abbey Road Studios. On the second song of the album,' For Love', Ringo is on drums, and is also the songwriter. Coincidentally, Starr had previously recorded the song 'For Love ' on his 2008 album *Liverpool 8*, and the producer for the original incarnation was none other then Hudson himself!

Interestingly, the first tune on the album is called 'Peace And Love', which is, of course, Ringo's catchphrase.

Artist - Mark Rivera
Title - Money, Money, Money
Year - 2014
Label - Dynotone Records

Mark Rivera is an acclaimed saxophonist who is best known for working with Billy Joel. He was also a member of Ringo Starr's All-Starr Band. In 2014, he released the album *Common Bond*, which contained the really funky number 'Money, Money Money '(not a cover of the ABBA song), which features great drumming from Ringo. A fantastic tune!

Artist - Benmont Tench
Title - Blonde Girl, Blue Dress
Year - 2014
Label - Blue Note

Benmont Tench was a founding member of Tom Petty's group, The Heartbreakers. He has worked with the likes of Bob Dylan, The Who and Stevie Nicks, and has written many hit records, such as Feargal Sharkey's hit record 'You Little Thief'.

The year 2014 saw Tench release a solo album on the famous jazz label, Blue Note, *You Should Be So Lucky*. Tench called recording the album "the most joyous 11-day period of my life."

Ringo plays tambourine on the song 'Blonde Girl Blue Dress', which also features acoustic guitar and harmony vocals from David Rawlings and Gillian Welch, Jeremy Stacey on drums and on bass, Tom Petty himself.

Artist - Middleman Burr
Title - When Ringo Joined The Band
Year - 2017
Label - Self Released

Middleman Burr are a wife and husband country duo consisting of Georgia Middleman and Gary Burr. Middleman had previously co-written the Radney Foster hit single 'I'm In' in 1998, and Burr had previously written many hit records featured in the US *Billboard* Hot 100. Both members are also part of the trio The Blue Sky Riders with Kenny Loggins.

In 2017, the couple self-released the album *MB* (which, of course, are the initials of their surnames), and the LP closes with the song 'When Ringo Joined The Band', which is lyrically about finding the final piece of the puzzle to give something that special magic i.e. Ringo joining The Beatles and Bob Dylan going electric. For added flavour, Ringo himself appears playing drums.

Artist - Sheila E.
Title - Come Together/Revolution
Year - 2017
Label - Stilettoflats Music

Sheila E. (The E stands for Escovedo) is an American singer, actress, percussionist and drummer, probably best known for playing drums with

Prince's band, The Revolution, from the years 1987-1989. On her 2017 album *Iconic: Message 4 America*, there are a couple of Beatles covers including 'Blackbird 'and most notably a medley of 'Come Together 'and 'Revolution'. This is notable as this cover features Ringo himself on drums. Probably the closest thing to a collaboration between The Fab Four and His Purple Badness.

PS: Have you ever seen the video of Prince's cover of 'While My Guitar Gently Weeps 'with Tom Petty, Steve Winwood, Jeff Lynne, and George's son Dahni - seriously, look it up on YouTube!

Artist - Jon Stevens
Title - One Way Street
Year - 2017
Label - BMG

New Zealand's Jon Stevens is a singer best known for his work with the band Noiseworks, and he played the role of Judas Iscariot in the Australian production of *Jesus Christ Superstar*. In 2017, he released the album *Starlight*, which debuted at No.16 in the Australian albums chart, making it his highest charting album there.

The song 'One Way Street 'has Ringo Starr on drums. A fantastic tune with some great vocals from Stevens himself, not forgetting the drum work from Ritchie!

Artist - Rodney Cowell
Title - You're Only Happy When You're Miserable
Year - 2019
Label - RC1 Records

Rodney Cowell is a country musician who has had five No.1 singles on the Hot Country Songs chart in America, all from his 1988 hit album *Diamonds and Dirt*. He has also won two Grammy Awards in his career, one in 1990 for Best Country Song for his hit 'After All This Time', and another in 2014 for Best Americana Album for *Old Yellow Moon*.

2019 saw Cowell release the album *Texas* on RC1 Records featuring an array of guest stars including Vince Gill, Lee Ann Womack and Steve Earle. Ringo is featured on the song with an oxymoronic title,' You're Only Happy When You're Miserable'. This collaboration came about as a result of a mutual friend trying to get Rodney and Ringo to write something for one of Cowell's albums. "Ringo's legacy and achievement is intimidating but as a human being he's a gentle, kind soul, funny and smart," recalled Cowell in *Uncut* magazine." He sets you at ease." [25]

Artist - Jenny Lewis
Title - Red Bull & Hennessy
Year - 2019
Label - Warner Bros. Records

Jenny Lewis is a Las Vegas-born American singer, songwriter and actress who was a member of the cult indie rock/emo band Rilo Kiley. Before being a successful musician, she was also a child actress, who appeared in films and TV shows such as *Troop Beverley Hills*, *The Twilight Zone*, *Baywatch*, and most infamously, the cult 100 minute Nintendo commercial 'The Wizard'.

In 2019, she released the single 'Red Bull & Hennessy 'on that antiquated format known as cassette (seriously, what's the appeal?). Appearing as guest drummer is none other than old Richie. It would later be featured on her 2019 album *On The Line*, which is going for really silly money in the vinyl aftermarket nowadays!

Artist - The Empty Hearts
Title - Remember Days Like These
Year - 2020
Label - Wicked Cool Record Co.

The Empty Hearts are an American garage rock revival supergroup consisting of Wally Palmar (The Romantics) on lead vocals and rhythm guitar, Andy Babiuk (The Chesterfield Kings) on bass and vocals, Elliot Easton (The Cars) on lead guitar and vocals, and Clam Burke (Blondie) on drums and vocals.

In 2020, they released their second album, rather appropriately titled *The Second Album*. It's lead single, the flower-power-esque 'Remember Days Like These', features guest drumming work from Ringo Starr. On the single's cover art, there is a photo of the band, with a picture of Ringo hanging on the wall, looking like he's photobombing the photo!

Artist - Graham Gouldman
Title - Standing Next To Me

Year - 2020
Label - Lojinx

Graham Gouldman (who once went under the pseudonym of Hilary) is a singer, songwriter and bassist who is the only constant member of the famous art rockers 10cc. In 2018, he became a touring member of Ringo's All Starr Band.

During the dark and gloomy days of March 2020, Gouldman released the album *Modesty Forbids*, featuring a peacock on the cover with its eyes censored. On the album's opening song,' Standing Next To Me', Ringo Starr guests on drums. It was also released as a single, which sadly failed commercially.

Artist - Ray Wylie Hubbard
Title - Bad Trick
Year - 2020
Label - Big Machine Label Group

Ray Wylie Hubbard is an Oklahoma country singer born in 1946, who has been active since 1965, and is still performing and releasing records today. In everybody's least favourite year, 2020, Hubbard released the collaborations album *Co-Starring*, in which the country legend teamed up with a variety of guest star(r)s - this included Ringo playing on drums on the album's opener 'Bad Trick', and also featured legendary producer Don Was, Eagles member Joe Walsh (formally of Ringo's All-Starr Band), and Black Crowes member Chris Robinson.

Artist - Steve Lukather
Title - Run On Me
Year - 2021
Label - The Players Club

Steve Lukather is a well-known American guitarist, singer, songwriter and record producer who was the founding member of Toto, and was once a member of Ringo's All-Starr Band. He is also known for his work as a session musician, most notably being involved in every tune on Michael Jackson's megahit album *Thriller*, as well as working with practically every big name in pop and rock including Elton John, Cher, Earth Wind And Fire, Leo Sayer, Aretha Franklin, Eric Clapton, Rod Stewart, Dolly Parton, Donna Summer, Diana Ross, and most notably Paul McCartney on his 1984 album *Give My Regards to Broad Street*... and he also worked with Spinal Tap!

In February 2021, Lukather released the solo album *I Found The Sun Again* on Dutch label The Players Club, and on the song 'Run On Me' Ringo plays drums and tambourine. A music video was made, which also featured an appearance from Ringo himself, and, as was the way in 2021, he was wearing a face mask, with his segment filmed in his LA home.

Artist - Ray Wylie Hubbard
Title - Ride Or Die (Montar Or Moeir)
Year - 2022
Label - Big Machine Label Group

After the success of 2020's *Co-Starring* album, Ray Wylie Hubbard released a follow-up album entitled *Co-Starring Too* in 2022. The album featured some very well known names in the world of country including Willie Nelson and Steve Earle, but on the track 'Ride Or Die (Montar Or Morier)' we get a massive ensemble of his mates teaming up with Hubbard, including Ann Wilson, Eliza Gilkyson, Steve Lukather (who you may remember from the previous entry in this book), Ray's son Lucas Hubbard, and most notably, our Beatle friend Ringo Starr on drums.

CHAPTER FIVE - OTHER MEMBERS

There were other people in The Beatles at one time or another who were not named John, Paul, George or Ringo. The Beatles have had at least 20 members since their conception - from The Blackjacks (later The Quarrymen) in the summer of 1956 to The Beatles 'official disbandment in 1970 (and that's not counting one-off members, who played for only one gig). In fact, The Beatles have had as many drummers as Spinal Tap! Like the four "canonical" Beatles, all these other members helped out with other people's releases - here are some of the ones I could find information on, but I'm sure there are a lot more.

Artist - Freddie & The Dreamers
Title - I Understand (Just How You Feel)
Year - 1964
Label - Columbia
NOTE - This tune has no involvement from any of The Beatles, but it is here to set the record straight!

Classic British Mancunian beat group led by Freddie Garrity, best known for their song 'You Were Made For Me 'and their amusing on-stage dance routines!

Some sources list this single as being written by original Beatles drummer, Pete Best, but in reality, it is a cover of a 1947 song written by Pat Best from the 1940s/50s pop group The Four Tunes.

Artist - Johnny Harris
Album - Beatlemania
Titles - I Want To Hold Your Hand/Roll Over Beethoven/From Me To You/Till There Was You/Please Mr. Postman/Twist And Shout/All My Loving/She Loves You/I Wanna Be Your Man/Love Me Do/ Please Please Me/Money
Year - 1964
Label - Top Six

This was a "bargain bin" release on Pye Records sub-label, Top Six, which specialised in budget cover versions, which later spun-off into the EMI budget label, Music For Pleasure. The first long-playing release on this label was an album called *Beatlemania*. It contained cover versions of various Beatles songs, and Johnny Harris, who arranged this release (as well as the other musicians) is uncredited. This release is notable as it actually contains a real Beatle playing drums - not Ringo, not even Pete Best, but the elusive Jimmy Nicol, who briefly replaced Ringo during their tour of Europe and Australia in 1964 during Ringo's bout of tonsillitis. As this release was made before Nicol got the gig, one would assume it was on the strength of this release that he was hired to replace Ringo.

After his brief fifteen minutes of fame being a Beatle, Nicol's career didn't really take off, and he left the music industry at the end of the 1960s. He is reluctant to talk about his time as a Beatle.

Artist - Lulu And The Luvvers
Title - Shout
Year - 1964
Label - Decca

Weeeeeeeellllllllllll . . . . .

An absolute stomper of a tune, originally performed by The Isley Brothers in 1959. Lulu's iconic version was released in 1964, and it reached No.7 in the UK Singles Chart.

Playing drums on this tune was a temporary member of The Beatles named Andy White. Andy was the one-off drummer for a brief period in 1962. White was brought in by George Martin to play drums, as Martin was unhappy with Pete Best's drumming. White would later end up playing on the commercially released versions of 'P.S. I Love You' and the album version of 'Love Me Do'.

The Beatles themselves recorded their own version for their TV special *Around The Beatles* (as covered in my previous Beatles book, *Acting Naturally*). The recording of their version was featured on the Beatles compilation *Anthology 1* in 1996.

Artist - Tom Jones
Title - It's Not Unusual
Year - 1964
Label - Decca

Sir Tom Jones is a music legend hailing from Wales with a great voice, who is still just as popular today as he has always been. One of his biggest hits (and his very first No.1) was 'It's Not Unusual', which you may remember Carlton Banks from *The Fresh Prince Of Bel-Air* lip-syncing and dancing to back in the day. He is one of the biggest selling artists in pop music history, selling over 400 million records worldwide.

According to sources, this No.1 hit single featured the drum work of temporary Beatle, Andy White.

Artist - Jamie Power
Title - She Don't Know/Love's Gonna Go
Year - 1965
Label - Jamie

Raymond Leslie Howard AKA Jamie Power AKA Duffy Power was a British blue-eyed R&B vocalist extraordinaire, who had a career that spanned from the late 1950s until his death in 2014. He was one of the first people to cover a Beatles song, with a reinterpretation of 'I Saw Her Standing There 'with The Graham Bond Quartet, and he even had a hand in the soundtrack to the acclaimed 1969 film *The Italian Job*.

1965 saw him release the double A-side single 'She Don't Know/Love's Gonna Go 'on the aptly titled Jamie Records. This is notable as the person playing the drums on this release was none other than one-time Beatle, Jimmy Nicol.

Artist - The Wurzels
Title - Combine Harvester
Year - 1975
Label - EMI

The Wurzels are a novelty act from Somerset, England, specialising in a genre called scrumpy and western - they are still performing today. Their most famous single would have to be their No.1 hit 'Combine Harvester ' (originally by Brendan Grace), which was a parody of the song 'Brand New Key 'by Melanie Safka. Why on earth would I include such a tune in a book about The Beatles? The (uncredited) drummer on this track was Andy White, who was a temporary Beatle in 1962! It was also recorded at Abbey Road studios, adding to the Beatles connection. White would later continue to play with The Wurzels on many other releases between 1975-1977.

Artist - Stuart Sutcliffe
Title - Love Me Tender
Year - 2011 ("recorded" in 1961)
Label - The Stuart Sutcliffe Estate
NOTE - The authenticity of this record was proven to be fraudulent, but it is here to set the record straight.

Anything to do with the elusive original bassist for The Beatles, the late Stuart Sutcliffe, would certainly attract interest and intrigue from people. In 2011, an alleged recording of Stuart Sutcliffe singing the Elvis Presley ballad 'Love Me Tender' was released as an MP3 by the Stuart Sutcliffe Estate.

Back in the Hamburg days, Stuart would sometimes get on the microphone and sing the aforementioned Elvis classic (usually dedicated to his girlfriend, Astrid Kirchherr), and he also sang Carl Perkins' 'Matchbox' (later given to Ringo, as heard on the 'Long Tall Sally' EP) and another Elvis song,' Wooden Heart'. Sadly, no known recordings of The Beatles with Stuart on vocals have been released to the public, but back in 2009, Stuart's estate was alerted to a copy of Stuart supposedly singing 'Love Me Tender' in Hamburg circa 1961 surfacing. According to Stuart's sister, Pauline, this was the real deal, and she believed that it was really her brother singing. The story goes that this was recorded after Stu had left The Beatles, and the band backing him was a German band called The Bats, who also played at The Star Club around the time of The Beatles.

When the MP3 was released in public in 2011, fans were sceptical about whether this was an authentic recording of Stu singing. Sadly, after some deep detective work, the recording was confirmed by fans to be a forgery. It was, in reality, a 1966 recording by British covers group The Boston Show Band, albeit in low quality. The original high-quality version of The Boston Show Band's interpretation was featured on their 1966 album *Piccadilly Band*, which was released on Cornet Records.

Artist - The Quarrymen
Album - The Quarryman Live! In Penny Lane
Year - 2020
Label - Scorpion Productions

I think most moderate-hardcore Beatle fans will know that The Beatles evolved from John Lennon's skiffle group, known as The Quarrymen. Believe it or not, The Quarrymen reformed in 1990 and despite their advancing years are still going strong and playing live shows today (catch them every year at Beatle Week in Liverpool in August).

In 2020, they made a "live" album called *The Quarrymen Live! In Penny Lane*, which was recorded at the John Lennon Recording Studios in Penny Lane, Liverpool (which makes sense, as performing to crowds wasn't really a thing that year). This CD of rock 'n' roll covers is notable as it features a guy on bass and vocals called Chas Newby. Newby was, for a very brief period, the bassist for The Beatles, and played when Stuart Sutcliffe resigned to focus on his art career. Because of university commitments, Newby left the band, and the bassist became a certain Paul McCartney. In 2016, Newby became a full-time Quarryman, and is now a permanent member.

Artist - The Smithereens
Title - Love Me Do/P.S. I Love You
Year - 2020 (recorded in 2008)
Label - Tollie Records

The Smithereens are an American rock band who were formed in 1980 and have had many hits from the late 1980s to mid 1990s such as 'Only A Memory', 'A Girl Like You 'and 'Too Much Passion'. In 2008, they recorded versions of The Beatles 'debut release 'Love Me Do/P.S. I Love You 'with guest drum work from session musician and one-time Beatle Andy White.

Despite being released in 2020, five years after White's passing, this release came out in his memory, as well as the memory of Smithereens member Pat DiNizo. To give this release even more authenticity, it was released on Tollie Records, the independent US label that released 'Love Me Do 'in that country.

CHAPTER SIX - JOHN AND PAUL

John and Paul, Lennon and McCartney, McLennon (well, maybe not that one!) - they are basically the Batman and Robin of songwriting teams, responsible for some of the greatest songs ever conceived in the history of recorded music... and 'Revolution 9'! With two amazing talents combining together, magic happens, and here are examples of their magic in motion. Saying that, many of the songs listed here were only written by one of them, but for contractual reasons, the songs listed were always credited to being written by both.

Artist - The Fourmost
Title - Hello Little Girl
Year - 1963
Label - Parlophone

A classic Lennon/McCartney composition written all the way back in 1957, around the time they had first been introduced; it's possibly the first song they wrote together. The Beatles performed the song on January 1st 1962 at their unsuccessful audition with Decca Records, but the song needed a home, and that home was with another Merseybeat group...

The Fourmost were formed in 1961, and despite many line-up changes over the years are still performing today. If you come across those package tours featuring various 1960s groups performing in your local theatre, you may come across The Fourmost. During their "classic" phase, their line-up was Brian O'Hara, Joey Bower, Mike Millward and Dave Lovelady.

Their version was recorded on the 3rd July 1963 at EMI Studios (now Abbey Road Studios) and producing it was none other than the fifth Beatle himself, Sir George Martin. The Beatles were also present in the recording studio, and it was The Fourmost's debut release. It reached No.9 in the UK Singles Chart. Interestingly, Gerry and The Pacemakers also recorded a version around the same time, but it didn't see a commercial release until 1991.

Artist - The Fourmost
Title - I'm In Love
Year - 1963
Label - Parlophone

Another Lennon/McCartney piece for The Fourmost, though this time it was tailor made exclusively for them. Like their previous release, it was produced by George Martin, and reached the moderate heights of No.17 in the UK hit parade. It was popular enough to inspire a few cover versions, including one from Billy J. Kramer (which was never released) and another by short-lived American band The New Breed, which was a regional hit in the Californian Bay Area.

The Fourmost would later cover the song 'Here, There And Everywhere' from the *Revolver* album in 1966, though sadly, their version didn't chart.

Artist - Billy J. Kramer & The Dakotas
Title - I'll Be On My Way
Year - 1963
Label - Parlophone

Billy J. Kramer (real name William Ashton - the J doesn't stand for anything) is an English pop singer from Liverpool who was managed by Brian Epstein, and who sang many original compositions by the dynamic duo of pop songwriting - Lennon & McCartney. His biggest song would have to be the No.1 hit 'Little Children', written by J. Leslie McFarland and Mort Shuman, and he had previously covered 'Do You Want To Know A Secret' from The Beatles '*Please Please Me* album, and others.

'I'll Be On My Way' is a Lennon/McCartney composition written during the Quarrymen days circa 1959, though this was just listed as that for contractual reasons, as in reality, it's a Paul solo composition, written on his first guitar - a Framus Zenth acoustic guitar, which he also used while composing songs such as 'I Saw Her Standing There' and 'Michelle'.

It sounds rather ambiguously like a Buddy Holly song, and in fact the famous musicologist, Ian MacDonald, believes that if the song is played a little faster, 'I'll Be On My Way' owes a debt to Holly's rudimentary three-chords scheme. When our Fabs performed it live, John sang the lead vocal as a harmony duet with Paul.

Lennon hated the song, so McCartney sent it to Billy J. Kramer and his Dakotas, where it was made into the B-side to the cover of a Beatles song, 'Do You Want To Know A Secret'. The Dakotas recording was made on the 14th and 21st March 1963, with the release coming out on the 26th April. It was their debut release, and reached No.2 in the UK Singles Chart, ironically being held off the top spot by 'From Me To You' by The Beatles!

Artist - Billy J. Kramer & The Dakotas
Title - I'll Keep You Satisfied
Year - 1963
Label - Parlophone

'I'll Keep You Satisfied' is a Lennon/McCartney composition. Despite being credited to both of them, Macca did most of the work. It would later be featured on Billy J's album *Little Children*, and it was recorded on the 14th October 1963, with the producer for the session being Beatles regular George Martin.

It was released on Parlophone Records on the 1st November 1963 and reached No. 4 in the UK Singles Chart; it stayed in the charts for 13 weeks. It's a really fun number, which has a similar feel to *Please Please Me* or *With The Beatles* era Fabs.

Artist - Billy J. Kramer & The Dakotas
Title - Bad To Me
Year - 1963
Label - Parlophone

A lovely Lennon and McCartney composition, which has the carefree innocence of the *Please Please Me/With The Beatles* era of our Fabs. Accounts of how this tune was conceived tend to vary, with John initially saying he wrote it in the back of a van with Paul, saying he did the lion's share of the work. In later years, though, Lennon would claim he wrote it on holiday in Spain. Regardless of the song's origins, it was initially made around May 1963, as Lennon's original demo was recorded on the 31st of that month (and was later featured on the album *The Beatles Bootleg Recordings 1963*, a 2013 compilation album that was made to extend the copyright on Beatles recordings, and to prevent them from becoming public domain).

Billy J's version was a massive hit, and went to No.1 in the UK hit parade. It reached No.9 in the US *Billboard* Charts. It was produced by George Martin, and Paul was said to have been present during the recording sessions at EMI Studios (nowadays Abbey Road Studios). It would later see cover versions from the likes of Terry Black, Graham Parker and Australian Beatles tribute band The Beatnix.

Artist - Tommy Quickly
Title - Tip Of My Tongue
Year - 1963

Label - Piccadilly

Tommy Quickly (real name Thomas Quigley) is a fellow Liverpudlian beat musician who was also managed by Brian Epstein. His debut single was the Lennon/McCartney composition 'Tip Of My Tongue', which was initially recorded by The Beatles in November 1962, but George Martin was unhappy with how the recording went. The tune was then given to the up-and-coming Tommy Quickly, and was released on Piccadilly Records (a sub-label of Pye). Despite being released when Beatlemania was finally taking off, it was sadly a commercial failure. He did however have one legitimate hit in 1964 with a cover of the Hank Thompson song 'Wild Side Of Life', which reached the modest heights of No.33 in the UK Singles Chart.

Despite the song's lack of success, it was later covered by Swedish band Mascots in 1965, and was also recorded by The Badbeats in 1979, Bas Muys in 1989 and The Beatnix in 1998.

Quickly's life would later be portrayed in the 2020 biopic short *Humpty F*cking Dumpty*, in which he was portrayed by British actor Andrew Gower. It was about his mental breakdown after the failure of his music career.

Artist - Cilla Black
Title - Love Of The Loved
Year - 1963
Label - Parlophone

Pricilla White AKA Cilla Black (1943-2015) was a very popular British singer and light-entertainment icon, not to mention a fellow Liverpudlian, also managed by Brian Epstein; and she was famously the cloakroom girl at The Cavern Club in Liverpool. She was good friends with The Beatles, and has had nineteen Top 40 hits in the UK (with several No.1's), and in 1968, became a popular presenter, fronting her own variety series, *Cilla* (more on that later in the book), and most famously the dating game show *Blind Date* from 1986-2003.

For her debut single, she was given a previous Lennon/McCartney composition called 'Love of the Loved', which was also a tune that The Beatles performed on their unsuccessful audition with Decca Records in early 1962. Like the songs with The Fourmost, it was produced by George Martin. It was only a modest hit in the charts, reaching No.35 in the UK hit parade.

Despite this, the song would later be covered by artists such as The Popettes and RollerCoaster and Australian Beatles tribute band The Beatnix, who emulated it in a way The Beatles would have performed it.

Artist - Cilla Black
Title - It's For You
Year - 1964
Label - Parlophone Records

When Cilla was recording her breakthrough single,' Anyone Who Had A Heart '(a cover of the Dionne Warwick song composed by Burt Bacharach), Paul McCartney was present in the recording studio, and with John Lennon thought about doing a song that was similar to 'Heart 'but not quite. On the 3rd June 1964, Paul recorded his initial demo, which he presented to Cilla and George Martin, and they were impressed. Cilla's version was recorded on the 2nd July 1964 at EMI (Abbey Road) Studios with the release of the song happening on the 31st of that month on Parlophone Records. Black's vocals on this track are far more soulful and powerful, and I feel superior to her first single. It reached the very healthy No.7 in the UK Singles Chart.

Paul's initial demo version resurfaced in 2016, following Black's passing a year earlier, because of her collection being sold off.

Artist - The Applejacks
Title - Like Dreamers Do
Year - 1964
Label - Decca

'Like Dreamers Do 'is an early composition from the world's most awesome writing team of Dr. Winston O 'Boogie and Apollo C. Vermouth AKA John Lennon and Paul McCartney, which was written in 1959. It was initially performed by The Beatles for their unsuccessful audition for Decca Records on the 1st January 1962. McCartney has said in retrospect that it isn't a song he particularly likes, and considers it almost "throwaway".

In 1964, Lennon and McCartney gave the song to a fellow beat group called The Applejacks, who hailed from the historic market town of Solihull. Their line-up consisted of Al Jackson on vocals, Phil Cash on rhythm guitar, Don Gould on organ, Gary Freeman on drums, and - something rare at the time - a female member, Megan Davies, on bass. Their biggest hit was their debut single 'Tell Me When', which reached No.7 in the UK Singles Chart.

The Applejacks 'version of 'Like Dreamers Do 'was a moderate success in the hit parade, reaching No.20. It was produced by Mike Leander, who has worked with a who's who of 1960s legends including The Rolling Stones, Billy Fury, Joe Cocker, Marc Bolan, The Small Faces, Lulu, Van Morrison, Shirley Bassey, Jimmy Page, Ben E. King, The Drifters and even our beloved Beatles, as Paul requested him to arrange the orchestra on the track 'She's Leaving Home 'on the *Sgt. Pepper* album, upsetting their old friend, George Martin, who was unavailable at the time.

The Beatles 'own version of 'Like Dreamers Do 'would later be officially released on their 1995 compilation album *Anthology 1*.

>Artist - Billy J. Kramer & The Dakotas
>Title - From A Window
>Year - 1964
>Label - Parlophone

The last of six Lennon/McCartney compositions that were recorded by Billy J. Kramer & The Dakotas. Paul makes a sneaky little cameo, harmonising the final word. It was recorded on the 29th May 1964 at EMI (Abbey Road) Studios, and was produced by George (the legend) Martin. A really chipper, happy song that takes you back to the "innocent" and "carefree" days of 1964, even if you (like myself) never got to experience those halcyon times.

The song was a commercial success, reaching No.10 in the UK Singles Chart, though it was their last Top 10 hit, and their subsequent releases were not quite as successful. As with the previous Billy J. Kramer tunes written by Lennon and McCartney, Australian tribute band The Beatnix did their own version, in the style of how our Fabs would have performed it.

Kramer is still performing today.

>Artist - Peter And Gordon
>Title - A World Without Love
>Year - 1964
>Label - Columbia

Peter and Gordon's debut single was a John & Paul piece entitled 'A World Without Love'. It was initially written by Paul when he was 16 years old; later on, when he was dating Peter's sister, actress Jane Asher, back in 1963, she asked if her brother and his friend Gordon Waller could perform the song, as they had just signed a recording deal with Columbia. McCartney agreed. It's a classic tune (even if the organ solo is a little bit "end-of-the-pier").

The song was a huge commercial success, and it reached No.1 in many countries including the UK, US, Canada, Ireland and New Zealand. It would later be covered by The Supremes, Bobby Rydell, Terry Black, The Mavericks and Del Shannon.

Interestingly, the guy who played lead guitar (Vic Flick) would also play the guitar lick for the iconic James Bond theme.

Artist - Peter and Gordon
Title - Nobody I Know
Year - 1964
Label - Columbia

Another Lennon/McCartney composition (though Paul did all the work) which was written with the intention of providing a follow-up to 'A World Without Love'. While the song was well-received and sold well, it didn't have quite the same impact as its predecessor, but still reached a decent No.10 in the UK and No.12 in the US Singles Charts. It's a lovely early-1960s record, which really takes you back, not to mention something of an earworm.

Interestingly, Petula Clark did a cover version in French called 'Partir, il nous faut '('We Must Leave'), which was featured in a 1965 French language EP, 'Dans Le Temps (Downtown) 'for Disques Vouge.

Artist - Peter & Gordon
Title - I Don't Want To See You Again
Year - 1964
Label - Columbia

A Paul McCartney composition (credited to Lennon/McCartney) that was given to Peter and Gordon. It was a success in the US *Billboard* Charts, reaching 16, but sadly didn't make a dent in the UK Singles Chart. It's a very nice tune, which would have fitted in during the latter Beatlemania phase of the Fabs 'career.

Peter Asher later became a prolific music producer, working with people like James Taylor, Linda Ronstadt, Bonnie Raitt, Cher, Diana Ross, Olivia Newton-John, Morrissey, Billy Joel, Randy Newman, Neil Diamond, and most notably for us Beatle fans, Ringo Starr.

After an unsuccessful solo career, Gordon Waller of Peter & Gordon had a brief stint as a theatre actor. He returned to recording in 2002 and released a solo album in 2007, but sadly passed away in July 2009. He was 64 years old.

Peter and Gordon last performed together on the 2nd February 2009 at the Surf Ballroom in Iowa, United States, as a part of a Buddy Holly tribute concert.

Artist - The Strangers With Mike Shannon
Title - One And One Is Two
Year - 1964
Label - Phillips

Learn nursery level mathematics with the help of obscure 1960s beat group, The Strangers, and vocalist Mike Shannon. This catchy little number was written by John and Paul, but unlike The Beatles, this tune failed to chart.

Not much is known about The Strangers and Mike Shannon, though according to some sources, the band might have been based in South Africa. The song itself was originally written for Billy J. Kramer, only to have it turned down, then offered to The Fourmost, only for it to be rejected again.

According to Lennon in a 1980 interview for *Playboy*, it was, in his own diplomatically immune words "another of Paul's bad attempts at writing a song." Though in all honesty, it's not that bad at all. It's a jolly little number, which, while nothing to write home about, has a very catchy and infectious tune; it's what would probably be described best as a "guilty pleasure".

Artist - P.J. Proby
Title - That Means A Lot
Year - 1965
Label - Liberty

James Marcus Smith, better known to most of the world as P.J. Proby (the P.J. doesn't stand for anything) is a US singer, songwriter and actor who was big in the 1960s and still performs in the UK in package tours with other 60s acts. He also has his own independent record label entitled Select Records.

During the time of the *Help* movie, Paul McCartney wrote the song 'That Means A Lot', and while it was credited as a Lennon-McCartney tune, John claims that Paul wrote it all. Neither of them were keen on it, so Brian Epstein gave the song to Proby, who released his version in September 1965. It was arranged and conducted by George Martin (though it was produced by Ron Richards) and ended up being moderately successful, reaching No.30 in the UK Singles Chart.

The Beatles 'own version would eventually see an official release in 1996 on part 2 of the acclaimed *Anthology* compilation series. Alternate takes have appeared on various bootleg releases.

Artist - Cilla Black
Title - Step Inside Love
Year - 1967
Label - Parlophone Records

In 1967, Macca was approached by TV producer Michael Hurll to write the theme tune to Cilla Black's BBC TV series, *Cilla*. It was a light-entertainment series which ran from 1968-1976. It was a showcase of entertainment talent of the time, and as with many TV shows from that period, unfortunately some of the episodes were wiped during the 1970s BBC archival culls.

Paul's original demo of the show's theme was recorded with just his vocal, an acoustic guitar, and only one verse complete. The initial Black recording was used for the first few weeks of the show, until they decided it needed an additional verse," You look tired, love", which came from Paul observing Cilla looking tired during the long rehearsal period. Paul then added a third verse, with the completed single release having its premiere on the 5th March 1968 edition of her show. The single release came out three days later. The tune was a commercial success, reaching a respectable No.8 in the UK Singles Chart. It was however banned in South Africa due to fears of the lyrics containing sexual elements. It would also be featured in Black's rather humorously titled album *Sher-oo!* released in April 1968, and the tune would later see an official remix in 2009 by DJ Ronstar.

The Beatles themselves recorded their own version of 'Step Inside Love 'during a *White Album* era jam session on the 16th September 1968. This version would later be released on the Beatles compilation *Anthology 3* in 1996 and the 2018 50th Anniversary edition of *The White Album* as a bonus track.

Artist - The Rolling Stones
Title - We Love You
Year - 1967
Label - Decca

1967 saw the other big band of the swinging sixties release the single 'We Love You '(aww, thanks Mick!). It was written during the aftermath of

Mick and Keith being arrested for owning illegal recreational substances, and the song is lyrically considered something of a pastiche of The Beatles hit 'All You Need Is Love '(coincidentally, Mick and Keith provided backing vocals on 'All You Need Is Love').

It was recorded during the sessions of their *Sgt. Pepper*-esque album *Their Satanic Majesties Request* in July 1967 at the Olympic Studios in London. It's a very trippy psychedelic tune, comparable to *Sgt. Pepper* era Beatles, and it featured the late Brian Jones playing the Mellotron. On backing vocals are our Beatle heroes, John and Paul, and they provide handclaps too.

The song was a commercial success, reaching No.8 in the UK Singles Chart.

Artist - The Rolling Stones
Title - Dandelion
Year - 1967
Label - Decca

The more conventional and commercial B-side to 'We Love You': a very fun tune, with backing vocals provided by John and Paul, which harkens back to classic British nursery rhymes. The original demo was recorded in November 1966 and was called 'Sometimes Happy, Sometimes Blue ' when it was being developed. The song has never been performed (as of 2023) in any Rolling Stones concerts.

Artist - The Black Dyke Mills Band
Title - Thingumybob
Year - 1968
Label - Apple Records

Hailing from Queensbury in West Yorkshire, The Black Dyke Mills Band are one of the oldest and best-known brass bands in the whole world, who have been entertaining people since 1855. They were signed to Apple Records in 1968, with the theme song to the sadly-lost TV sitcom *Thingumybob*, which I covered previously in my other Beatles book, *Acting Naturally*. The tune was produced by Paul McCartney, and was credited as a Lennon/McCartney composition, possibly for contractual reasons. The B-side was a rather cinematic cover of the old Beatles favourite 'Yellow Submarine'. 'Thingumybob' is a delightful little number, which reminds me of the music in the classic 1996 dramedy film *Brassed Off*.

Artist - Mary Hopkin
Title - Goodbye
Year - 1969
Label - Apple Records

The follow-up to Hopkin's mega-hit 'Those Were The Days', and it shows, as this song is very similar in tone. Despite being credited to Lennon/McCartney, only Paul had serious involvement, and in retrospect, he has very little recollection of making the song, other than it being written to capitalise on the success of 'Days'.

Despite being very similar to 'Those Were The Days', the song still proved to be very successful, reaching No.2 in the UK Singles Chart, No.6 in the US *Billboard* Chart and even No.1 in Ireland and the Netherlands. While recording international versions of the song, as per 'Days', Hopkin would meet her future husband, Tony Visconti - they had two children, but sadly divorced in 1981, and in 1989, Visconti married John Lennon's "lost weekend" companion, May Pang, with whom he had two children; they got divorced in 2000.

Artist - Plastic Ono Band
Title - Give Peace A Chance
Year - 1969
Label - Apple Records

The ultimate anti-war anthem, and in many ways a forerunner to rap music. Written during John and Yoko's famous 'Bed-In 'honeymoon at the Queen Elizabeth Hotel in Montreal, Canada, the song was recorded there on the 1st June 1969, accompanied by many of John and Yoko's friends, including Timothy Leary, Rabbi Abraham Feinberg, Joseph Schwartz, Rosemary Woodruff Leary, Petula Clark, Dick Gregory, Allen Ginsberg, Roger Scott, Murray The K and The Beatles 'press agent, Derek Taylor. This was credited as a Lennon/McCartney composition, though the reason for Paul's name being on the release was as a "thank you" for him helping John record 'The Ballad Of John and Yoko 'at short notice.

Released on the 4th July 1969 on Apple Records, the tune was a huge commercial success, reaching No.2 in the UK and even No.1 in the Netherlands. Like all Plastic Ono Band singles, it was accompanied by a B-side sung by Yoko Ono, with her song being entitled 'Remember Love'. It's surprisingly very accessible for a Yoko song, and it was even included as a bonus track for reissues of that 1968 "experiment" known as *Two Virgins*.

It remains to this day one of the ultimate peace anthems. There was some controversy surrounding the lyrics, as the third verse contained a reference to a very private recreational activity, which was altered to say "mastication" in the lyrics sheet. Ono would later revisit the song in 1991, featuring an all-star line-up, as a response to the first Gulf War, and again in 2008. Both Paul and Ringo have performed the song themselves in live concerts, with Ringo often finishing his sets with it.

Artist - John Lennon, Paul McCartney and friends
Album - A Toot and a Snore in '74
Titles - Lucille/Stand By Me/Cupid/Chain Gang/Take This Hammer
Year - 1974 (released 1992)
Label - Mistral Music

Around the time John Lennon was producing Harry Nilsson's LP *Pussy Cats*, during Lennon's infamous 'lost weekend 'period, former bestie Paul McCartney dropped in after the first night of the sessions at Burbank Studios in LA on the 28th March 1974. Joining them were Harry Nilsson, Jesse Ed Davis, Bobby Keys, Linda McCartney, Lennon's partner at the time, May Pang, producer Ed Freeman and even Stevie Wonder for a wild impromptu jam session.

One would naturally assume that with this amount of talent in the room, musical awesomeness would result, but sadly this wasn't the case. What came out of these sessions was pretty terrible, with Lennon sounding like he was high on something illegal, and not even Stevie could help save this session from being, in my opinion, woeful.

The songs played included so-called covers of 'Lucille 'and 'Stand By Me 'as well as a medley which included 'Cupid', 'Chain Gang 'and 'Take This Hammer'.

Unless you are a very die-hard Beatle mega fan who wants to listen, out of curiosity, I wouldn't recommend it… gosh I need a stiff drink!

CHAPTER SEVEN - JOHN AND GEORGE

After the disbandment of our beloved Fabs, John was still very pally with George Harrison, and occasionally, they would collaborate with each other (sadly, the same can't be said for Lennon and McCartney at the time).

Artist - John Lennon
Title - Instant Karma!
Year - 1970
Label - Apple Records

One of the stand-out tracks made during Lennon's tumultuous solo career, produced by the controversial Phil Spector. Written in one hour and recorded on the 27th January 1970, and released one week later on the 6th February, one would assume that a song made during this very short period of time would feel rushed and weak, but this proved to be the opposite, and it was a critical and commercial success, going top five in many countries around the world and selling a million copies in the United States alone! Lennon performed the song on the BBC TV show *Top Of The Pops* on the 11th February 1970, which is memorable for featuring Yoko crocheting while blindfolded with a sanitary towel on her head, and holding up random cards, at points during the song, containing one-word statements like "Smile", 'Peace", "Love", 'Hope" and "Breathe". Our favourite eccentric couple of pop also wore denim jackets during this performance with armbands that said" people for peace".

Helping John out on this track included George Harrison on electric guitar, piano and backing vocals, and Beatle buddies Klaus Voormann on bass guitar, electric piano and backing vocals, Alan White on drums, piano and backing vocals, Billy Preston on Hammond organ and backing vocals, former road manager Mal Evans on tambourine, former manager Allen Klein on backing vocals and of course Yoko providing backing vocals.

Artist - John Lennon
Album - Imagine
Titles - Crippled Inside/I Don't Want To Be A Soldier, Mama/Gimme Some Truth/Oh My Love/How Do You Sleep?
Year - 1971
Label - Apple Records

John Lennon's second (or fifth if you count those weird experimental ones with Yoko) solo LP, *Imagine*, was a massive critical and commercial success. Its title track (and also John's signature song) is timeless and iconic, with a beautiful message, and is easily one of the best solo Beatles tracks, and had one of the most memorable accompanying videos. The LP is also known for some other fan favourites including 'Jealous Guy '(as famously covered by Roxy Music, becoming a massive hit for them), and it has also inspired many documentary movies about the album's conception. It might possibly be the most famous of all the Beatles solo albums. As covering the whole album in this book would make a book in itself, we will only be covering the songs where John and George collaborated.

On the song 'Crippled Inside', George plays an instrument called a Dobro, which is a special type of resonator guitar invented by a company appropriately called Dobro, which is now owned by Gibson. It was recorded on the 26th May 1971 at Ascot Sound Studios, and the melody of the song's bridge has been observed by some to be very similar to Koerner, Ray & Glover's interpretation of the folk song 'Black Dog'.

'I Don't Want To Be A Soldier, Mama', which was recorded around February 1971, has the unique distinction of having a vocabulary of only 25 words (think 'I Want You (She's So Heavy) 'from the *Abbey Road* album or 'Love Me Do'). It was recorded in various sessions from February-July 1971 and was produced by the infamous Phil Spector. It was the only song to use Spector's trademark 'wall of sound 'production technique to its fullest extent. George Harrison, being the slide guitar guru that he was, played the aforementioned instrument in this composition.

'Gimme Some Truth', meanwhile, is a rather punky blues rant - if you doubled the time signature on the drums, it would easily be a punk rock song! As well as featuring George on slide guitar and electric guitar, John expresses his frustration with Tricky Dicky (Richard Nixon), and chauvinists (ironically, John was one in a previous life), and there's a reference to the classic nursery rhyme 'Old Mother Hubbard'. Recording for this tune took place at Ascot Sound Studios on May 25th 1971.

On 'Oh My Love 'George plays electric guitar. This song was originally conceived around the time of the *White Album*, but then was reinterpreted as a Lennon solo composition. Recorded on the 25th May 1971, Harrison's guitar work on this song echoes the work that he did on 'Julia 'and 'Happiness Is A Warm Gun', and it has even been used in a few films, notably the 1980 film *Little Darlings*, and 2001's *Heartbreakers*.

The last Lennon/Harrison collaboration, 'How Do You Sleep? 'is a "diss" track, aimed at Paul McCartney. This came about as the songs 'Too Many People 'and '3 Legs 'from Paul's *Ram* album were allegedly digs aimed at John, though Macca has denied this. As a response, John recorded 'How Do You Sleep? '- a tune which referenced various Paul songs, and even the infamous "Paul Is Dead" urban legend. Also contributing to the song included George Harrison playing slide guitar, Nicky Hopkins on Wurlitzer electric piano, John Tout on piano, Ted Turner, Rod Linton and Andy Davis on acoustic guitars, Klaus Voorman on bass, Alan White on drums and an act called The Flux Fiddlers on strings.

The album was produced by Phil Spector.

CHAPTER EIGHT - JOHN AND RINGO

The first person and the last person to join The Beatles.

    Artist - Plastic Ono Band
    Title - Cold Turkey
    Year - 1969
    Label - Apple Records

A really funky John song with his new group, The Plastic Ono Band, which was formed in 1968. They were a loose collective of musicians with the ringleaders being our favourite eccentric pop music couple of 1969, John Lennon and Yoko Ono. People who took part in the POB project over the years included Eric Clapton, Klaus Voormann, Alan White, Billy Preston, Jim Keltner, Keith Moon, Delaney & Bonnie and friends, and former Beatles, George and Ringo. The project ended in 1974, but was revitalised (obviously without John) with Sean Lennon from 2009-2015 under the title of Yoko Ono Plastic Ono Band (Ono Ono!) with new "members" such as Mark Ronson, The Scissor Sisters, Paul Simon and rather appropriately, Lady Gaga.

This song is about John's withdrawal from that awful drug known as heroin (it's bad m'kay - to quote Mr. Mackey from *South Park*) and John initially presented the song for Paul as a potential *Abbey Road*-era single, only to be rejected, and so it was released as a Plastic Ono Band single.

While the song was far from a flop, it was only a moderate success compared to other Beatle-related tracks at the time, reaching No.14 in the UK Singles Chart. When Lennon returned his MBE, he quipped by saying "I am returning this MBE in protest against Britain's involvement in the Nigeria-Biafra thing, against our support of America in Vietnam, and against 'Cold Turkey 'slipping down the charts. With love, John Lennon of Bag." [2]

Despite not being a Beatles song, Ringo contributed by playing the drums. Also playing guitar is Eric Clapton, and on bass is Klaus Voormann.

On the live version featured on Lennon's *Some Time In New York City* album, George Harrison joins him on guitar (as well as playing on the live version of 'Don't Worry Kyoko'). This was a recording from December 15th 1969 at the Lyceum Ballroom in London as part of a charity concert for UNICEF.

Artist - Plastic Ono Band
Title - Don't Worry Kyoko (Mummy's Only Looking For A Hand In The Snow)
Year - 1969
Label - Apple Records

As per tradition with Plastic Ono Band singles, John sang the A-side (PLAY LOUD), while Yoko sang the B-side (PLAY QUIET). One of her most famous compositions is this blues-ey hard rock number entitled 'Don't Worry Kyoko '(Kyoko was Yoko's daughter from a previous marriage to Anthony Cox). Beginning with her trademark screaming, the song has Ms. Ocean Child yell 'Don't Worry 'over and over and over and over! Ringo provides the drum work on this song, and it is probably one of her better-known tracks. To be truthfully honest, I'd pick the A-side any day (sorry Yoko!).

Artist - Yoko Ono
Album - Yoko Ono/Plastic Ono Band
Titles – Why/Why Not/Touch Me/Paper Shoes
Year - 1970
Label - Apple Records

Yoko's debut solo album *Yoko Ono/Plastic Ono Band* came out at the same time as John's solo album *John Lennon/Plastic Ono Band* in an act of total confusion, as the albums have almost identical covers, probably to help Yoko's album gain more sales.

The opening track is a song entitled 'Why', which actually sounds very ahead of its time, as it was pretty much punk rock before punk rock (though it could be said that Hamburg-era Beatles were the punk of their day.) It's a very chaotic tune, with Ringo on drums. Yoko sings the song in a unique Japanese vocal technique taken from Kabuki Theatre called Hetai. It is also symbolic of the primal scream therapy that John and Yoko were taking at the time.

The second track from Yoko's debut featuring Ringo on drums was appropriately titled 'Why Not '(coincidentally, Ringo would release an album entitled *Y Not* in 2010). Like the previous song, probably not suited for mainstream tastes, but a stand-out song in its field. Like 'Why', Yoko sings this song in her unique Hetai way. This is then succeeded by 'Touch Me '- a rather risqué tune, with Ringo on drums and John on guitar. John also produces it. The last Lennon/Starr collaboration on the album was a number entitled 'Paper Shoes'. Have your ever worn paper shoes? I wouldn't advise it!

While not to everybody's taste, one thing you to admire about this album is its originality and creativity.

Artist - Michael Viner's Incredible Bongo Band
Title - Unknown Tracks
Year - 1972-1974
Label - MGM Records

The Incredible Bongo Band was a collective of session musicians curated by American film and record producer, Michael Viner, consisting of "kitsch-y" instrumental funk cover songs with heavy bongo-led percussion, hence the band's name. They are probably best remembered for their cover version of the 1960 instrumental 'Apache', which was also covered by fellow beat group The Shadows. The Bongos' version has a very long percussion breakdown. It got a second life in the latter half of the 1970s, as it was later picked up by early hip-hop pioneers such as DJ Kool Herc and Grandmaster Flash, as this breakdown (AKA the "get down" part or "breakbeat") was ideal for rappers to put their rhymes over and for breakdancers to breakdance, hence "breakbeat".

According to Michael Viner himself:" ...we also had people from Harry Nilsson to John Lennon and Ringo Starr - all sorts of people coming by and helping on a few tracks. John actually helped on the album, Ringo helped on percussion on one of the tracks. I can't even remember which one. John actually helped us with the mixing. When we were mixing he was there. And it was a wonderful time." [1]

It is unknown which tracks Lennon and Starr contributed to (though Ringo is said to have contributed to the track 'Kiburi'), but it is fascinating to think that The Beatles had a secret hand in sowing the seeds for hip-hop culture!

Artist - Harry Nilsson
Album - Pussy Cats
Title - All My Life/Loop De Loop/Subterranean Homesick Blues/Mucho Mungo/Mt. Elga
Year - 1974
Label - RCA

If you've read earlier chapters in this book, you will have learnt that John Lennon produced the Harry Nilsson album *Pussycats*. On some of the songs, Lennon has his Beatle buddy, Ringo Starr, help him out.

'All My Life' is a great tune arranged by John Lennon, with Ringo on drums and Beatle companion Klaus Voormann on bass. On Chinese wood block is Keith Moon from The Who. Also on the album is 'Loop De Loop', a cover version of a Johnny Thunder song written by Teddy Vann and Joe Dong. Ringo is on drums for this track and also for' Subterranean Homesick Blues', a cover version of a Bob Dylan classic, produced by John Lennon. It was the second single from *Pussy Cats* and as well as featuring Lennon as producer, other Beatle collaborators on the track included Klaus Voormann, Keith Moon, and others. The final Lennon/Starr team up on the album is a number entitled 'Mucho Mungo/Mt. Elga' with Lennon producing and Ringo on drums.

Artist - Ringo Starr
Album - Goodnight Vienna
Titles - (It's All Down to) Goodnight Vienna/All By Myself/Only You (And You Alone)
Year - 1974
Label - Apple Records

In 1974, Ringo Starr released his fourth studio album, *Goodnight Vienna*, named after the slang phrase meaning "it's all over". The album's cover portrayed Ringo dressed up as a spaceman standing next to what looks like a member of Daft Punk. This was actually a remnant of an unmade Ringo Starr TV movie, which was going to be a collaboration between Monty Python's Graham Chapman and the acclaimed comedic sci-fi writer Douglas Adams of *Hitchhiker's Guide to The Galaxy* fame (more on that in my other Beatles book, *Acting Naturally*). Despite the album being released in a year that many would consider to be one of the worst in music history (still, it could be worse, it could be 2020!), the album received mostly positive reviews from critics, and sold decently commercially.

The album's upbeat opener, which is also the title track, was written by John Lennon, who also played piano. Billy Preston played clavinet alongside Klaus Voormann on bass, Jim Keltner on drums, Carl Fortina on accordion and Lon Van Eaton and Jesse Ed Davis on guitar. The song had its origins during the infamous "lost weekend" period of Lennon's life, and the lyrics are a depiction of Lennon, Starr and his friends enjoying crazy wild nights of hedonism in Los Angeles. While not successful in the UK when released as a single, it did however do well in the US, reaching a healthy No.31 in the US *Billboard* Charts.

Another song on the album which had involvement with Lennon was the Ringo-penned number 'All By Myself', featuring Lennon on piano, as well as 'Only You '- a cover of the song by The Platters, which was a top five hit in 1954. Ringo's version was recorded under the suggestion of John Lennon, and was released as a single; it reached No.6 in the US *Billboard* Charts, making it the most successful song on the album. John played acoustic guitar, and on backing vocals is Beatle friend Harry Nilsson. An alternate version with Lennon's demo vocals was featured on the *John Lennon Anthology* box set in 1998.

    Artist - Ringo Starr
    Title - Cookin '(In The Kitchen Of Love)
    Year - 1976
    Label - Polydor

In 1976, Ringo Starr released his rather oddly titled fifth studio album, *Ringo's Rotogravure* (FYI a Rotogravure is a printing process in which paper is rolled through intaglio cylinders). It was the final Beatle project to have involvement from all four Beatles, as John was tragically assassinated in 1980. The album didn't get fantastic reviews, and was a moderate success, reaching the modest heights of No.28 in the US *Billboard* Album Chart.

    For John's contribution to the album, he wrote a song entitled 'Cookin ' (In The Kitchen Of Love)', and he played piano. Also performing in the session was Jim Keltner on drums, Mac Rebannack on organ and guitar, Danny Kortchmar on guitar, King Errison on percussion and Will Lee on bass. It's a surprisingly upbeat song for a tune written by Lennon post-Beatles, free of politics and Yoko laments - a happy, uplifting, if slightly tongue-in-cheek track.

CHAPTER NINE - JOHN, PAUL AND GEORGE

Chapter Nine,
Chapter Nine,
Chapter Nine,
Chapter Nine,
Chapter Nine…
The Beatles sans the drummer.

Artist - The Silkie
Title - You've Got To Hide Your Love Away
Year - 1965
Label - Fontana

The Silkie were a 1960s folk-rock group whose name was derived from an Orcadian song 'The Great Silkie of Sule Skerry'. Their classic line-up was Sylvia Tatler (vocals), Mike Ramsden (guitar and vocals), Ivor Aylesbury (guitar and vocals) and Kevin Cunningham (double bass). Like The Beatles, they were discovered after an appearance at The Cavern Club in Liverpool, and were signed by Brian Epstein, and Alistair Taylor became their manager.

While their first single,' Blood Red River', failed to make an impact on the British hit parade, their follow-up was a cover of The Beatles' classic 'You've Got To Hide Your Love Away', which was originally made for the 1965 film *Help!*. This tasteful cover version was assisted by three of the four Beatles. John Lennon produced, Paul was on guitar, and George was on guitar and played the tambourine. Lennon was impressed, and he played it over the phone to Brian Epstein, and told him they had recorded a No.1 hit; though in reality, it reached the more moderate heights of No.28.

The Silkie never really made it massively, and their first US tour in 1965 had to be shelved as the band were not able to obtain the necessary visas and work permits (this had included an appearance on both *American Bandstand* and *Ed Sullivan*). One year later, the band became a two-piece, now consisting of the husband and wife team of Mike Ramsden and Sylvia Talter. The band would eventually finish in 2004 following the passing of Ramsden. Talter later passed away in 2018.

CHAPTER TEN - JOHN, GEORGE AND RINGO

The Beatles without the cute one.

>Artist - Yoko Ono
>Title - Greenfield Morning I Pushed An Empty Baby Carriage All Over The City
>Year - 1970
>Label - Apple Records

A track from her solo album *Yoko Ono/Plastic Ono Band*, the song's title is a reference to the awful miscarriage Yoko had in 1969 (the heartbeat of the unborn baby was sampled in her 1969 album with John, *Life With The Lions*). This tune has the unique distinction of having every Beatle not named Paul McCartney playing on it. Ringo is on drums, George is on sitar, and of course John plays guitars. Filling in for Paul is Klaus Voormann, and seriously, if it was Paul instead of Klaus, it could have been a Yoko Ono feat. The Beatles track, though seeing as it was recorded in 1970, this wouldn't have been possible. It's a very haunting track, and for some reason, the tune reminds me vocally of dub reggae, but that is only because of the echo chamber effects used in the vocals. The song ends with some beautiful sounds of birds singing.

>Artist - Ringo Starr
>Title - I'm The Greatest
>Year - 1973
>Label - Apple Records

An immodestly titled song that was the opening track to Ringo Starr's 1973 solo album *Ringo*. As we all know, The Beatles parted ways in 1970, and even in the immediate aftermath of their disbandment, there were rumours rife of a reunion, and the closest thing to a reunion was in this Ringo solo song. An autobiographical song written by John at the start of the 1970s, the song's title is a shout-out to the catchphrase of legendary boxer and Beatle acquaintance Muhammad Ali (who they met in 1964), and this song was a project of Lennon's between 1970-1973. As Ringo was working hard on his third LP, Lennon (with the help of Yoko Ono) gave the song to

Ringo, and Ono amended the lyrics to talk about Ringo's wife (Maureen) and children.

Despite having John, George and Ringo contributing to this track, there was one piece in the puzzle that was missing - the absence of Paul; but luckily, Beatle associate Klaus Voormann would come in to fill in the blanks on bass duty. Also playing organ and electric piano was none other than Billy Preston, who you may remember from the final two Beatles albums, *Let It Be* and *Abbey Road*. This quasi-Beatles line-up would later be dubbed by the press at the time as The Ladders, and there was much speculation as to whether this would lead to a real reunion. The tune was well-received by critics, and is considered to be a spiritual successor to *Sgt. Pepper* era Beatles, as it evokes the concept of a stage-show, and would later be featured on various Ringo Starr compilation albums.

CHAPTER ELEVEN - PAUL AND GEORGE

Cute and Quiet.

> Artist - James Taylor
> Title - Carolina On My Mind
> Year - 1968
> Label - Apple Records

As mentioned previously, one of the very first signees to Apple Records was the now-legendary singer/songwriter, James Taylor. On December 6th 1968, Taylor released his self-titled debut album, produced by Peter Asher (brother of Jane), and on the front cover, he sports a spiffy moustache. The album also contains a song entitled 'Something In The Way She Moves '- this sounds awfully familiar doesn't it, and Taylor himself always makes reference to this fact in his stage shows when he sings it.

'Carolina On My Mind 'featured Paul McCartney (credited) playing bass guitar and George Harrison (uncredited) on backing vocals, and was recorded at Trident Studios mid-1968. Lyrically, the song is about James Taylor feeling homesick, and despite the song getting rave reviews, it wasn't a success commercially; but it did fare a little better when it was rereleased in 1970. It's now a staple in his concerts, and one of his best known tracks. He considers it to be his favourite song - an absolutely classic and timeless record. This song really shows how awesome James Taylor is and if you do get chance to see his stage show - do, it's amazing!

CHAPTER TWELVE - PAUL AND RINGO

The two survivors. McCartney and Starr are still good friends today, and they still make awesome music together.

Artist - Alma Cogan
Title - It's You
Year - 1964
Label - Columbia

Alma Cogan was a pop starlet who died of cancer way too young. In her short 34 year life, she became known as the "girl with the giggle in her voice", and had a string of hits including 'Bell Bottom Blues', 'I Can't Tell A Waltz From A Tango 'and the No.1, 'Dreamboat'. She apparently had a fling with John Lennon (who was a fan of hers when he was growing up) and was also friends with the other Beatles too, especially Paul McCartney, who first played the melody of 'Yesterday 'on her piano.

1964 saw the release of her single 'It's You', which was produced by George Martin. Ringo provided the drum work, but was uncredited. It's said that Paul McCartney also played tambourine. It's a lovely little number, and it's a shame that her life was cut short, as she could have still been making hits today.

Cogan would later cover four Beatle classics, 'Help!', 'I Feel Fine', 'Eight Days A Week 'and 'Ticket To Ride'.

Artist - Alma Cogan
Title - I Knew Right Away
Year - 1964
Label - Columbia

The B-side to the previously mentioned 'I Knew'. Ringo is on drums, and Paul McCartney provides some tambourine work, but is uncredited. It's a really fun rock 'n' roll number, which has something of a Lulu-esque vibe to it.

Artist - Mary Hopkin
Title - Que Sera, Sera (Whatever Will Be Will Be)

Year - 1970
Label - Apple Records

A cover version of the classic Jay Livingston and Ray Evans number (later becoming a worldwide football/soccer anthem) sung by Doris Day in the 1956 film *The Man Who Knew Too Much*. The tune was produced by Paul McCartney, and was hand picked by him for Hopkin to sing. As well as Paul playing acoustic, bass and lead guitar, Ringo also lent a hand by playing drums. It was recorded on the 17th August 1969 at EMI (Abbey Road) Studios.

According to Hopkin herself:" At the time, it was just one of Paul's fun ideas. It was one sunny afternoon, we were sitting in Paul's garden, and he said, 'Do you like this song?' I said, 'Well, I used to sing it when I was three!' And he said, 'My dad likes it, let's go and do it.' And so Ringo came along; it was all done in an afternoon. I was sort of swept along with Paul's enthusiasm, really. By the time I was halfway through the backing vocals, I said, 'This is awful.' I really thought it was dreadful and I didn't want it released." [18]

Contrary to Hopkin's belief, it's not half bad, though unlike her string of mega-hits previously, 'Que Sera, Sera 'failed to chart in the UK, and only charted moderately in other countries. It did sell well in New Zealand, where it reached No. 10.

Artist - The Rolling Stones
Title - Shine A Light (early version)
Year - 1970
Label - Unreleased

'Shine A Light 'was a song from the Rolling Stones 'album *Exile On Main St.* which was written in tribute to founding member Brian Jones, who tragically passed away aged only 27 in 1969. The melody of the song was later "borrowed" by Britpop band Oasis for their 1994 smash hit 'Live Forever'.

In January 1970, an early version of the song was recorded at Olympic Studios in London featuring Ringo Starr on drums, Paul McCartney on bass and Leon Russell on organ. The only Stones present at the recording were Mick Jagger on lead vocal and Keith Richards on electric guitar.

It's a classic Rolling Stones tune, and the song's title would later inspire the 2008 Martin Scorsese Stones documentary of the same name.

Artist - Ringo Starr
Album - Ringo
Titles - You're Sixteen/Six O'Clock
Year - 1973
Label - Apple Records

As stated previously in this book, Ringo released an album entitled... well... *Ringo*, which was notable for having contributions from all four Beatles.

'You're Sixteen 'is a cover version of the single by Johnny Burnette, written by Robert B. and Richard M. Sherman, which reached No.3 in the UK Singles Chart in 1961. Ringo covered this song for his 1973 album *Ringo*, and Paul chipped in playing the rather divisive instrument, the kazoo, for a solo. Also joining him for this recording session was Harry Nilsson on backing vocals and Nicky Hopkins played piano. It was a commercial success, and while it reached top five in many countries, it reached No.1 in America, earning this record the unique distinction of being one of the few hit records to have a kazoo solo!

Ringo would revisit the tune again for his infamous 1978 *Ringo* variety TV special, this time a duet with *Star Wars* actress and sci-fi sex symbol, the late, great Carrie Fisher. As stated in my previous book, *Acting Naturally*, it's probably the closest thing to a duet between Thomas The Tank Engine and Princess Leia. Ringo would return to this song in 2009, when he played drums on Klaus Voormann's version for his LP *A Sideman's Journey*.

On the song 'Six O'Clock', Paul and Linda McCartney both helped out on the songwriting duties. It was the first time Paul and Ringo had worked together since The Beatles '1970 breakup. It has a very Wings-esque vibe (which makes an awful lot of sense) and lyrically, it's about a friend or lover to whom Ringo confesses not showing enough attention. The synthesisers are a little bit 70s, but overall, it's a melodically cheerful little number.

According to Beatle historian Bruce Spizer, Paul also played piano, synths, backing vocals, flute and string arrangements; Linda McCartney was on backing vocals, Vini Ponica on acoustic guitar and percussion and Klaus Voormann on bass.

Artist - Ringo Starr
Title - Pure Gold
Year - 1976
Label - Polydor

As you will know by now, Ringo released an album entitled *Ringo's Rotogravure*, which is notable for having contributions from all four Beatles (like his 1973 long player, *Ringo*).

For Paul's contribution, he wrote the ballad 'Pure Gold'. It was recorded on June 19th 1976 at Cherokee Studios in Hollywood, California, during a day off in McCartney's Wings Over America Tour. I quite like this one, especially the almost Motown-esque string section!

Artist - Ringo Starr
Album - Stop And Smell The Roses
Titles - Private Property/Attention/Sure To Fall
Year - 1981
Label - RCA

Stop And Smell The Roses was Ringo Starr's eighth studio album, released on October 27th 1981 on RCA Records in the UK and Broadwalk Records in the US. Despite featuring collaborations with Paul and George, Rolling Stone member Ronnie Wood and Harry Nilsson, it was a commercial flop, and received mixed reviews from critics. One really sad thing about this album was that John offered a song to Ringo called 'Life Begins At 40 ' - talk about harsher in hindsight.

Paul wrote a song for the album called 'Private Property', which was the opening track. He also produced it and played on it, and it was recorded between July 11th-21st 1980 at Super Bear Studios in Berre-Les-Aplies in France. On backing vocals is Linda McCartney, Howie Casey is on saxophone, Laurence Luber on guitar and Lloyd Green on pedal steel guitar.

In July 1982, an elaborate music video was made entitled 'The Cooler', which was directed by Lol Creme and Kevin Godley, who were members of 10cc. This was conceived by Paul, and Ringo plays a prisoner who is caught and thrown into the cooler, where he fantasises about the commandant, played by his wife, the lovely Barbra Bach. It was the official British entry in the short film category at the Cannes Film Festival on the 24th May 1982.

Paul also wrote the songs 'Attention 'and 'Sure To Fall', which was produced by him, and he played bass and piano. This was recorded at the same time as 'Private Property 'and all three songs share the same line-up of musicians.

The album would not appear on streaming services until March 2021.

Artist - Paul McCartney
Title - Take It Away
Year - 1982
Label - Parlophone Records

Celebrated at the time of its release as being a partial Beatles reunion, Paul McCartney's single from his 1982 LP *Tug Of War* featured Ringo on drums. The track was a relative commercial success, reaching No.10 in the US *Billboard* Hot 100 and No.15 in the UK Singles Chart. It was recorded at AIR Studios in Montserrat, and as well as featuring Paul and Ringo, Linda McCartney provides backing vocals, Eric Stewart (10cc) provides guitar and backing vocals, Steve Gadd (top session musician) also plays drums, and it was produced by none other than the fifth Beatle himself, George Martin (who also plays electric piano). Beatles era veteran Geoff Emerick (with help from Mike Stavrou) were the engineers for the recording sessions.

The main recording session took place between February 16th-18th 1981, with overdubs being mixed on the 23rd March. The final mix down took place circa December 1981.

The song's music video featured an appearance from the acclaimed actor, the late Sir John Hurt, who had previously worked with George Harrison on the film *Little Malcolm and His Struggle Against The Eunuchs* in 1974.

Artist - Paul McCartney
Album - Give My Regards To Broad Street
Titles - Wanderlust/Not Such A Bad Boy/No Values
Year - 1984
Label - MPL Records

1984 saw Paul release his cinematic solo debut in *Give My Regards To Broad Street*. It wasn't a success critically or commercially, but one thing that the film did have going for it was the soundtrack album, which was a mixture of remakes of Beatles classics (produced by George Martin) and some original songs. Ringo played drums on a remake of the song 'Wanderlust', which had originally appeared on 1982's *Tug Of War* album, as well as two original songs 'Not Such A Bad Boy 'and 'No Values'. They were recorded at AIR Studios in London around February-March 1983.

These songs are debatably much better than the movie for which they there made.

Artist - Recording Artists Against Drunk Driving (R.A.D.D.)
Title - Drive My Car
Year - 1994
Label - RADD

Drunk driving was (and still is) a big issue. There is an American charity called R.A.D.D. (Recording Artists Against Drunk Driving, formally Rockers Against Drunk Driving), which is the entertainment industry's voice for road safety. It was founded in 1986 by a number of DJs and radio personalities, and is dedicated to saving lives and reducing injuries, through the often misunderstood medium known as edutainment. As of 2023, the organisation is still running.

In 1994, the organisation released the all-star ensemble charity single 'Drive My Car', which, as you would have guessed from the title, is a cover version of the 1965 Beatles song from their fantastic *Rubber Soul* album. This version of the song featured Paul and Ringo, as well as John Lennon's son, Julian, Phil Collins, Little Richard, Los Lobos, Melissa Enterbridge, Trisha Yearwood and in his final record appearance before his death, Beatle friend Harry Nilsson.

The song had its premiere at the American Music Awards in February 1994, and the single release was dedicated to the memory of Nilsson, Stevie Ray Vaughn, Deirdre Gentry, Ross Marino, Randy Bachman, Bill Graham and John Lennon's mum, Julia.

Artist - Paul McCartney
Album - Flaming Pie
Titles - Really Love You/Beautiful Night
Year - 1997
Label - Capitol Records

Macca's tenth studio album, *Flaming Pie*, was released just after the huge commercial comeback of The Beatles, thanks to the *Anthology* project, and the success of that album paid off, as this LP sold well, going top 20 in many countries, and received positive reviews from critics. The album's title is a reference to John Lennon's mythical explanation of how the name The Beatles came into being. According to Lennon "I had a vision when I was twelve. And I saw a man on a flaming pie, and he said, 'You are the Beatles with an A.' And so we are."

On the rather funky track 'Really Love You', Ringo played drums. It was the first song to feature the songwriting credit reading Paul McCartney/Ringo Starr, and the song also featured Jeff Lynne providing backing vocals and electric guitar. It was recorded on the 14th May 1996 at Hog Hill Studios in Rye, and the engineer for the session was the legendary Geoff Emerick, with Keith Smith acting as assistant engineer. The song would later be remixed in 2004 as part of Macca's Twin Freaks remix project.

The other McCartney/Starr collaboration was a song called 'Beautiful Night', which, as well as including Ringo on drums, had Sir George Martin adding a beautiful orchestral arrangement, as well as guitar and backing work from Jeff Lynne, and the engineer for the session was none other than Geoff Emerick - talk about an all-Starr line-up (groan!). A music video was made by the famous Julian Temple, which received some minor controversy, as it featured a brief glimpse of a girl skinny-dipping.

Artist - Ringo Starr
Album - Vertical Man
Titles - La De Da/What In The...World/I Was Walkin'
Year - 1998
Label - Mercury

Hot on the heels of the mega-success of The Beatles' *Anthology*, Ringo recorded his commercial comeback with *Vertical Man*. The album contained an "all-Starr" cast of guests including Brian Wilson, Scott Weiland, Alanis Morissette, Tom Petty, Ozzy Osbourne, Joe Walsh and Timothy B. Schmit from The Eagles, Steven Tyler from Aerosmith and former Beatles Paul and George. Unlike Paul McCartney's *Flaming Pie* album a year earlier, Ringo's album got a mixed reception from critics, and was sadly a commercial failure, and according to *The Ringo Starr Encyclopedia* by Bill Harry only sold a reported 2000 copies.

Its lead single was a catchy little ditty entitled 'La De Da', on which Paul played bass guitar. It was recorded in September 1997 at Paul's Hog Hill recording studios, and clips of this session were featured in the promotional music video. On the song 'What In The...World 'Paul plays bass and also provides backing vocals. The overdubs were recorded on September 29th 1997 in Rye.

The album also contained a remake of that old Beatle favourite 'Love Me Do'.

Artist - Klaus Voormann
Album - A Sideman's Journey
Titles - I'm In Love Again/You're Sixteen
Year - 2009

Label - Voormann Office

If you know your Beatles, then you will have probably heard of a cool German guy named Klaus Voormann (he's mentioned once or twice in this book and many others!). He has been friends with The Beatles since the early Hamburg days, plus he has performed on their solo records and he also designed the covers for the albums *Revolver* and *Anthology*.

In 2009, he released his own album entitled *A Sideman's Journey*, which was released around the time of the documentary movie made about him, *All You Need Is Klaus*.

The opening song, 'I'm In Love Again', is a treat for Beatles fans, as it features both Paul and Ringo playing on it. It's a lovely blues number, which has a great rock 'n' roll vibe to it. The album also has Yusuf Islam (formerly Cat Stevens) covering the George hit 'All Things Must Pass 'and a soulful cover of 'My Sweet Lord 'with Bonnie Bramlett on vocals. Ringo appears on the song 'You're Sixteen', which he previously played in his solo years.

Artist - Ringo Starr
Album - Y Not
Titles - Peace Dream/Walk With You
Year - 2010
Label - Hip-O Records

At the turn of the 2010s, Ringo released his sixteenth studio album, *Y Not*. Recorded in 2009, but released in January 2010, the LP is noted for closing with a duet with the sultry soul siren Joss Stone. I love Ringo, but to be truthfully honest, Joss's vocals are in a totally different league to Ringo's, making this collaboration seem rather strange.

On the song 'Peace Dream', Paul McCartney is on bass duties, as well as providing backing vocals. "Paul was doing the Grammys, so he came over to the house and was playing bass on 'Peace Dream'," recalled Ringo for *The Guardian* newspaper in 2009." So I played him this other track ['Walk With You'] and Paul said, 'Give me the headphones. Give me a pair of cans. 'And he went to the mic and he just invented that part where he follows on my vocal. That was all Paul McCartney, and there could be nothing better. He makes it bigger and he makes it fuller. It makes the song like a conversation between us, and that was Paul's idea to do his part, one beat behind me. That's why he's a genius and incredible bass player." [29] The song also contained a shout-out to fallen Beatle and fellow peace campaigner, John Lennon, with one of his quotes, and a reference to Lennon's famous song 'Give Peace A Chance 'with the line "So try to imagine/If we give peace a chance…"

Ringo also teamed up with his old Beatle bestie on the tune 'Walk With You '- a lovely number about the power of friendship. As well as singing, Paul also plays bass. The song would later be featured on the Beatles solo years compilation EP 'John, Paul, George, Ringo'.

Artist - Ringo Starr
Title - Grow Old With Me
Year - 2019
Label - UM

In the summer of 1980 on a holiday in Bermuda, John Lennon wrote one of his final songs,' Grow Old With Me '- a really lovely piece, which was originally intended for inclusion on his last album, *Double Fantasy*. It would eventually see a commercial release in Lennon's posthumous album *Milk And Honey* in 1984.

In 1994, Yoko Ono attempted to revive the song for The Beatles' *Anthology* project, and have the other Beatles overdub in the style of their "reunion" hits, 1995's 'Free As A Bird 'and 1996's 'Real Love'. This project fell through, as they thought that Lennon's original demo required extra work to bring it up to standard for a proper release.

The song would later be covered by Ringo in 2019 for his album *What's My Name*. In this new version, Paul McCartney sang backing vocals and played bass, while Jack Douglas, who produced Lennon's *Double Fantasy* LP, arranged the string section, which quotes the George composition 'Here Comes The Sun'. Ringo said "So in a way, it's the four of us." [6]

Artist - Ringo Starr
Title - Here's To The Nights
Year - 2020
Label - UM

A Ringo Starr solo composition that was released on December 16th 2020, two days before McCartney's solo album *McCartney III*. It's a song about unity and being together (something that was hard to do in 2020), and it features two Beatles, Sheryl Crow, Jenny Lewis, Joe Walsh, Chris Stapleton, Benmont Tench, Dave Grohl, Ben Harper, Lenny Kravitz, Finneas, Yola, Black Pumas and Corinne Bailey Rae.

"Diane Warren wrote it," Ringo told *Rolling Stone* magazine." Here's to the nights we won't remember, with the friends we won't forget. So it has a beautiful sentiment. It's about us all coming together, so it seems appropriate for today. Everybody I know, we've all had quite a few nights we don't remember. And we've all had them with friends we won't forget. All these people joined in and helped me out. We got Paul McCartney, he's on board. Joe Walsh, Sheryl Crow, Jenny Lewis, Chris Stapleton, Benmont Tench. Dave Grohl, and Ben Harper were the first ones up. Lenny Kravitz came on at the last minute. We got Finneas, Yola, Black Pumas. Corinne Bailey Rae sings her heart out. Everybody has a little shout-out." [30]

The tune would later be featured on Ringo's 2021 EP 'Zoom In'.

CHAPTER THIRTEEN - GEORGE AND RINGO

While George once described this pair as being "economy class Beatles" in an interview, I would totally have to disagree, as both George and Ringo have made some amazing contributions to the world of popular music. Here is a taster of what this incredible duo have to offer.

Artist - George Harrison
Title - Ski-Ing
Year - 1968
Label - Apple Records

George's solo debut album was a rather unconventional one, as it wasn't a traditional rock record as such, but the soundtrack to the bizarre Joe Massot film *Wonderwall*, which is probably remembered best today for begetting the name of one of Britpop band Oasis 'biggest hits. George's whole album has an Eastern vibe to it, which makes sense considering Harrison's embracing of Indian culture around this time.

The piece 'Ski-Ing 'features some uncredited drum work from Ringo. On electric guitar, Eric Clapton also appears in the song, credited under the not-so-subtle pseudonym of Eddie Clayton, and on banjo is Peter Tork, best known for being a member of The Monkees, making this the closest thing to a collaboration between The Beatles and The Monkees, which in my opinion would have been awesome.

The song would also be used in an Apple Records promotional video in 1968.

Artist - Radha Krishna Temple
Title - Govinda
Year - 1970
Label - Apple Records

'Govinda 'was the second single released by the Radha Krishna Temple, who had a surprise hit in 1969 with the single 'Hare Krishna Mantra'. It is a musical adaptation of what is considered by many to be the world's first known poem. Like 'Hare Krishna Mantra', it was produced by George Harrison (and he also played lead guitar), and the recording for this single took place in January 1970 at Trident Studios in London. Joining Radha Krishna

Temple in the session included (according to member Shyamasundar Das) Ringo Starr playing some percussion, Klaus Voormann on bass guitar, and according to member Joshua Greene, Billy Preston, Donovan and Mary Hopkin were also present in the recording session.

Released on the 6th March 1970, it reached the healthy No. 23 in the UK Singles Chart, and it was very well received. In fact The Beatles 'press officer, Derek Taylor, said it was the best record ever made. It would later be featured in the album *The Radha Krishna Temple*, which came out in May 1971.

Artist - George Harrison
Title - My Sweet Lord
Year - 1970
Label - Apple Records

George's beautiful ode to the man upstairs, and the first Beatles solo single to reach No.1 in both the UK and the US. It's easily one of the most iconic Beatles solo singles, and my personal favourite. The song was originally written by George for Edwin Hawkins (who never recorded it), but the first version of the song was by fellow Apple Records artist and good friend of The Beatles, Billy Preston (who coincidentally played piano in the more famous Harrison rendition). Released in September 1970 as a single, where it was a minor success in Europe, it was featured in Preston's fantastic Apple album *Encouraging Words*.

Harrison's more well-known version was released two months later on the 23rd November 1970, and was featured on Harrison's acclaimed solo album *All Things Must Pass*. Produced by the notorious Phil Spector using his wall of sound technique, Ringo plays drums on this fantastic song, which also includes musical contributions from Eric Clapton, Pete Ham, Tom Evans, Joey Molland, Peter Frampton, Gary Wright, John Barham, Klaus Voormann, Jim Gordon and Mike Gibbins. The tune was a humungous commercial success, reaching No.1 in pretty much every country around the world, and it's very understandable why - the song is amazing!

It would later be covered by people as diverse as Elton John, Andy Williams, Edwin Starr, Nina Simone and Boy George. Despite being an amazing tune, it did however receive some controversy, as the song sounded ambiguously like Ronnie Mack's 1963 song for girl group The Chiffons, 'He's So Fine'.

After George's tragic passing in 2001, the song was re-released again in January 2002, reaching No.1 in the UK and Canada.

Artist - Billy Preston
Title - All That I've Got (I'm Gonna Give It To You)
Year - 1970
Label - Apple Records

A REALLY funky number from Billy Preston, released on the 30th January 1970 on Apple Records. According to George, this was Billy's response to critics who said he had dropped his black soul roots by "going with the whiteys" and embracing rock music, but in all fairness, it doesn't matter what sort of music you do or what skin colour you have, as long as it's done right!

The co-writer of the song was fellow Apple Records artiste, Doris Troy, and as well as having Preston on vocals, piano and Hammond organ, we have George Harrison on bass guitar and Ringo Starr on drums. Unfortunately, the tune failed to chart in the UK, and only reached No.108 in the US *Billboard* Charts, which is a real tragedy, as this is such a great number, which would certainly have had the approval of James Brown!

Artist - Billy Preston
Album - Encouraging Words
Titles - Right Now/Little Girl/Use What You Got/My Sweet Lord/Let The Music Play/The Same Thing Again/I've Got A Feeling/Sing One For The Lord/When You Are Mine/I Don't Want To Pretend/Encouraging Words/All Things (Must) Pass/You've Been Acting Strange
Year - 1970
Label - Apple Records

Encouraging Words was Billy Preston's fifth studio album, which was released on the 11th September 1970. It was the final album that Preston released on Apple Records, and the LP was entirely co-produced by George Harrison. One interesting fact about this release - it was the public debut of two of Harrison's most famous solo compositions,' My Sweet Lord 'and 'All Things Must Pass', released a couple of months before Harrison's own versions! While sadly not a massive commercial hit (I'm ashamed of you for not buying it!), it is easily the greatest album ever put out by Apple Records that wasn't by any of The Beatles.

As well as featuring early-bird appearances from the aforementioned Harrison solo numbers, there is also a really soulful Al Green-esque version of 'I Got A Feeling'. The personnel on the album included Eric Clapton, Delaney Bramlett, Klaus Voormann, Carl Radle, Jim Gordon, Bobby Keys,

Jim Rice, The Edwin Hawkins Singers, members of The Temptations and Sam & Dave's tour band and, on drums, the legend that is Richard Starkey!

There are three words I will leave you with before we go onto the next release - BUY THIS ALBUM!

Artist - Leon Russell
Album - Leon Russell
Titles - Dixie Lullaby/Shoot Out on the Plantation/Hurtsome Body
Year - 1970
Label - A&M

The late Grammy award-winning legend Leon Russell was an American singer/songwriter extraordinaire, who has played with every big name in classic rock and pop including Eric Clapton, Elton John (who considered him to be his "mentor"), Bob Dylan, Frank Sinatra, The Rolling Stones and George and Ringo Beatle. He also liked top hats.

In 1970, he released his acclaimed solo debut album on Shelter Records, which is notable for containing the famous song 'A Song For You', which Elton John calls an American Classic. As well as Elton, it would be covered by the likes of Andy Williams, The Carpenters, Willie Nelson, Ray Charles, Whitney Houston and Amy Winehouse.

What is less known about this LP is that George and Ringo played on three of the songs on the album. These songs were 'Dixie Lullaby', 'Shoot Out On The Plantation 'and 'Hurtsome Body', with George on guitar and Ringo on drums. The album also contains contributions from Beatle buddy Klaus Voormann, who played bass on 'New Sweet Home Chicago', Rolling Stones Mick Jagger and Charlie Watts, and Eric Clapton.

Artist - Doris Troy
Album - Doris Troy
Titles - Ain't That Cute/Special Care/Give Me Back My Dynamite/You Tore Me Up Inside/Games People Play/Gonna Get My Baby Back/I've Got To Be Strong/Hurry/Is Far/Exactly Like You/You Give Me Joy Joy/Don't Call Me No More/Jacob's Ladder
Year - 1970
Label - Apple Records

Doris Troy was a Bronx-based soul queen whose biggest hit was the 1963 single 'Just One Look '(as later covered by The Hollies in 1964, reaching No.2 in the UK Singles Chart). She also sang backing vocals on Pink

Floyd's 1973 bestselling magnum opus *The Dark Side Of The Moon*. In 1970, she released her second album, which was also her debut long player for Apple Records, entitled simply *Doris Troy*, and despite the album's mixed reviews, it's actually really, really good. To help put this album together, it was co-produced by none other than George Harrison, and on drums is Ringo Starr. George also co-wrote four of the songs on the album, 'Ain't That Cute', 'Give Me Back My Dynamite', 'Gonna Get My Baby Back '(also co-written by Ringo) and 'You Give Me Joy Joy'.

Many famous people helped put the album together including Billy Preston, Peter Frampton, Eric Clapton, Stephen Stills and Leon Russell. Some versions of the album contain a tasteful cover version of the Beatles classic 'Get Back'. Also, the album's front cover photograph of the great lady was taken by Beatle roadie, Mal Evans.

The album was reissued twice: firstly in 1992, and again in 2010 with some bonus tracks. It's a stellar release in the extended Apple Records discography, and like Billy Preston's *Encouraging Words*, it's more than just highly recommended.

Artist - Nicol Williamson
Album - Nicol Williamson
Titles - Unknown
Year - 1971
Label - CBS
NOTE - The likelihood of Harrison and Starr's involvement has been debunked, but it is here to set the record straight!

Nicol Williamson (1936-2011) was an acclaimed Scottish actor who John Osbourne described as "the greatest actor since Marlon Brando." He was probably best known for his work in Shakespeare adaptations, as well as his prolific work on film and TV, and he was nominated for several BAFTA awards in his lifetime.

By the accounts of Roy Young (who previously sang that awesome cover version of 'Got To Get You Into My Life', see the Paul chapter), George Harrison and Ringo Starr (as well as Eric Clapton and Klaus Voormann) played on Williams 'self-titled 1971 album, which consisted of orchestrated spoken-word easy-listening music (think William Shatner), which sounds as un-Beatle-esque as you can get! According to Young, "I worked with George Harrison and Eric Clapton on a strange project with the Shakespearean actor Nicol Williamson, who couldn't sing. I guess it was a tax write-off. It was Eric, Ringo, George, Klaus Voormann, and myself. It was quite funny. Nicol Williamson just could not sing. We were doing all these old rock and roll songs like 'Be-Bop-A-Lula' and 'Shakin' All Over', and we'd play half the song and he'd go, That's enough! That's enough! Let's have a drink! and bring out these cases of champagne. It was just an excuse for a huge pisser." [31]

The book *Beatles Undercover* is doubtful that Young's recollections are correct, and he may be referring to a session that was never commercially released, as the music he describes sounds nothing like what was released, though saying that, it would have been interesting to hear two Beatles making elevator music while a Shakespearian actor "sings" 1950s rock 'n 'roll standards!

Artist - Ringo Starr
Title - It Don't Come Easy
Year - 1971
Label - Apple Records

One of the best solo singles from an ex-Beatle. It was actually written by Ringo himself in late 1968 under the working title of 'You Gotta Pay Your Dues', just after finishing his first composition,' Don't Pass Me By', though George also had a hand in writing 'Easy'. Following John's departure from The Beatles in 1969, Ringo wanted the lyrics to reflect where he was in that moment, rather than the stereotype of him being the downtrodden drummer. George also suggested that the last verse should be about God, and have a shout-out to Hare Krishna. Ringo protested, and the lyrics were changed to be about peace.

Produced by Harrison, it was recorded over an extensive period. It was initially laid down in February 1970, with retakes being done in March of that year, and overdubs being recorded in October. It was eventually released on the 9th April 1971 to positive reviews, and reached No.4 in both the UK and US singles charts.

Interestingly, George's version of the song has surfaced on bootleg albums. As expected, Hare Krishna gets a shout out!

Artist - Bobby Keys
Title - Bootleg
Year - 1972
Label - Warner Bros. Records

The late Bobby Keys was a tenor saxophonist who played on many Beatles solo projects. He played the iconic sax riff on John Lennon's solo single

'Whatever Gets You Thru The Night', as well as playing on George's legendary *All Things Must Pass* album and Ringo's *Ringo* and *Goodnight Vienna* LPs. He also played sax with the likes of The Rolling Stones, Marvin Gaye, Keith Moon, Harry Nilsson, Barbra Streisand, Chuck Berry, B.B. King and Sheryl Crow.

In 1972, he released a self-titled solo album on Warner Bros. Records, and the song 'Bootleg' featured guitar work from George and Ringo playing drums. On bass is Beatle associate Klaus Voormann. The track 'Bootleg 'is a cover, and was originally played in 1965 by Booker T and the M.G.'s, which was sampled by hip-hop band Cypress Hill on their song 'Born To Get Busy'.

Artist - Ringo Starr
Title - Back Off Boogaloo
Year - 1971
Label - Apple Records

A T-Rex-inspired single from Sir Richard Starkey - this was rather apt, as Starr had just directed the T-Rex documentary film *Born To Boogie* (see my other Beatles book, *Acting Naturally*). There are even rumours that Marc Bolan himself from T-Rex had ghostwritten the song, but nothing concrete has been confirmed regarding this. There are also rumours that some of the song's lyrics could be interpreted as a "diss" at Paul McCartney, as the middle eight goes "Get yourself together now/And give me something tasty/Everything you try to do/You know it sure sounds wasted". Ringo wasn't so keen on McCartney's *RAM* album (something I disagree with, as I think it's the best Beatles solo album) and the "sounds wasted" line was a reference to Paul's alleged overindulgence on chronic. What is true however is that the line "give me something tasty" is a shout-out to UK football (soccer) commentator, Jimmy Hill (who had an enormous chin), who referred to a footballer's playing as "tasty".

Recorded in September 1971 at Apple Studios in central London and released on the 17th March 1972, the track was a critical and commercial success, reaching No.2 in the UK Singles Chart, making it Ringo's most successful solo single. The personnel on the song included George Harrison on slide guitar and acoustic guitar, Gary Wright on piano, Klaus Voormann on bass and saxophone, and Madeline Bell, Lesley Duncan and Jean Gilbert on backing vocals.

Ringo still performs this track in his concerts today.

Artist - Lon & Derrik Van Eaton
Album - Brother
Titles - Sweet Music/Another Thought
Year - 1972
Label - Apple Records

Lon & Derrick Van Eaton were a duo of musical brothers from Trenton in New Jersey, USA, who were signees to The Beatles 'record label, Apple Records. After getting a series of rejection letters from various record companies, they eventually approached Apple Records with a demo tape, and within two weeks, got a letter from Apple's A&R, Tony King, saying they'd passed it to George Harrison, who took the tape to LA. Two more weeks followed; Harrison then called the band to say that he loved their music, and would be interested in signing them to Apple Records.

In 1973, they released their critically acclaimed George Harrison-produced debut album *Brother*, which was co-produced by Beatle associate Klaus Voormann. The album was notorious for being out of print for many years, and was finally reissued on RPM Records in 2012. The long player is considered a cult classic in the field of overlooked classic rock.

Ringo Starr played drums on two of the songs, 'Sweet Music 'and the closing track 'Another Thought'. They are both great numbers, and certainly live up to the critical praise that this album deserves.

Artist - Ringo Starr
Album - Ringo
Titles - Photograph/Sunshine Life for Me (Sail Away Raymond)/You and Me (Babe)
Year - 1972
Label - Apple Records

As stated previously, *Ringo* was the third studio album for the world's greatest rock drummer, Ringo Starr. It was a commercial success, and is noted for having collaborations with all four Beatles, sparking (false) rumours of a Beatle reunion around the corner.

The collaborations with Beatle George on the LP were 'Photograph', 'Sunshine Life for Me (Sail Away Raymond) 'and 'You and Me (Babe)'.

'Photograph 'was written by Ringo and George on a luxury yacht in the South of France in May 1971, and lyrically centres around Ringo lamenting about lost love. The studio version of the track was recorded in March 1973 at Sunset Sound Recording Studio in Los Angeles, and was sung in the key of E, which Beatles author Ian Inglis describes as having an "easy melody" that allows for Ringo's limitations as a singer (cheeky!). George also provided backing vocals, as well as playing a 12-string acoustic guitar. It ended up being one of Ringo's biggest solo hits, when released as a single, reaching No.1 in America, Canada and Australia, and didn't do too shabbily in his home country, reaching No.8 in the UK Singles Chart. It is easily one of my favourite Ringo solo pieces and contrary to what Inglis says, Ringo's voice is pretty good on this one. 'Photograph 'was sung by Ringo in 2002 for the Concert for George at the Royal Albert Hall, giving it some extra poignancy.

While 'Photograph 'was really well-received,' Sunshine Life for Me (Sail Away Raymond) 'had more of a mixed reception. This slightly tongue-in-cheek number shows that Ringo is quite good at doing country music, and it was originally written in 1971 by George when he was on holiday in Ireland with his ex-wife Pattie Boyd, when they stayed over with Donovan, during his tax exile. As well as featuring Harrison on electric guitar and backing vocals, Robbie Robertson and Rick Danko from The Band also play on this tune, as well as Levon Helm, David Bromberg, Garth Hudson, Vini Poncia and Klaus Voormann. Despite the song's reception at the time, people have been kinder to this tune over the years, complimenting the song's lively and upbeat nature.

Harrison also helps out on the LP's closer,' You and Me (Babe)'. Like *Sgt. Pepper*, the song's lyrics are about the album coming to the end, and also Ringo drinking wine and getting high (!), and like Harry Nilsson's albums, it closes with a spoken message from Ringo, giving shout-outs to everyone who played on the album, including the other three Beatles. George also played electric guitar, providing a great solo. It's a lovely way to finish the album, and it's a shame LPs today don't do this, as it makes it feel more like a film or a musical, and it's a great way of involving the listener.

Artist - Nilsson
Title - Daybeak
Year - 1974
Label - RCA Victor

1974 saw the release of the critically and commercially unsuccessful Apple feature film *Son Of Dracula*, which is so obscure it hasn't seen an official DVD or Blu-Ray release as of 2023 (see my previous book, *Acting Naturally*). One positive thing the film did bring was the soundtrack album, which features a Nilsson number made especially for the film, entitled 'Daybreak'.

It's a great, uptempo song, which features Ringo on drums and George on lead guitar, and on bass is none other than Beatles friend Klaus Voormann. It's arguably a lot better than the film that it accompanies!

Artist - Shankar Family & Friends
Title - I Am Missing You
Year - 1974
Label - Dark Horse Records

A lovely song, written by Ravi Shankar, and sung by his sister-in-law, Lakshmi. Unlike most of Shankar's compositions, the song was designed with the western market in mind, with lyrics in the English language, and it was the lead single to the 1974 album *Shankar Family & Friends*. It was the first single to be released on George Harrison's own record label, Dark Horse Records.

The production of this title mimics that of Phil Spector, and lyrically it is a love song dedicated to the famed Hindu God, Krishna. As well as the song being produced by George Harrison, he also provided acoustic guitars and autoharp. Also providing instrumentation, Ringo Starr and Jim Keltner play drums, Billy Preston is playing organ, Nicky Hopkins is on piano, Tom Scott plays flute and soprano saxophone, Emil Richards plays kartal and shakers, while Kamala Chakravarty and Shivkumar Sharma provide backing vocals.

Despite the song having commercial potential and lots of baggage behind it, it sadly failed to chart.

Artist - Ringo Starr
Title - I Still Love You
Year - 1976
Label - Polydor

A beautiful ballad from Ringo's commercially unsuccessful studio album *Ringo's Rotogravure* (an album title that helps expand your vocabulary, something I forgot to mention the last time!).

This George Harrison-penned number had its origins back in 1970, as a song for the famous Welsh singer legend, Dame Shirley Bassey, who had previously covered The Beatles 'classic song 'Something'. George's original version (entitled 'When Every Song Is Sung') was recorded around the time of Harrison's megahit album *All Things Must Pass*, but ultimately has never been released officially. The song went from singer to singer including Ronnie Spector, Cilla Black, Mary Hopkin and Leon and Mary Russell - all (but one) unfinished and unreleased.

The song would eventually find a home in 1976 under the new (and in my opinion more generic) name of 'I Still Love You' with Ringo on vocals. It was always a song that he admired, and his version was recorded circa April-July 1975 at Cherokee Studios in Los Angeles. The line-up for the recording session included Lon Van Eaton on electric guitar, Jane Getz on piano, Arif Martin on ARP string synthesiser, Klaus Voormann on bass, Jim Keltner on drums, David Lasley on backing vocals, and a string section arranged by Gene Orloff.

Ultimately, after six years of "development hell", 'I Still Love You' received a mixed response from contemporary music critics, considering the song to be a parody of a George Harrison record with bad lyrics. However, over time, the reception of the song has been more kind, with many critics considering it to be a highlight of an otherwise mediocre LP. Cilla Black's version of the song under its original title 'When Every Song Is Sung' would be released in 2003, as a bonus track to the Black compilation *Cilla - The Best Of 1963-78*, while Harrison's original 1970 version is doing the rounds on the bootleg circuit.

Artist - Ringo Starr
Title - Wrack My Brain
Year - 1981
Label - RCA

A George Harrison-penned number from Ringo Starr's 1981 album for RCA Records, *Smell The Roses*. George wrote this tune to express his frustration at the music industry, and pressure from Warner Bros. to write the sort of cookie-cutter pop that Warner Bros. Records wanted. George played the song to Ringo, who loved it, and Harrison helped out by playing guitar, and also sang backup vocals.

On keyboards is Al Cooper of the band Blood Sweat & Tears. His parts (alongside another tune from the album,' You Belong To Me') were recorded at George Harrison's home in England. It was Herbie Flowers (a famous session bass guitarist) who hooked them up, and initially, he thought that being asked to work with two Beatles was nothing more than just a mere prank, but Flowers was actually being serious. George even asked Cooper what sort of keyboard he would prefer, from his choice of a Hammond B3 organ, a Fender Rhodes, a Wurlitzer piano and an ARP Omni. Also playing on the session was the uncredited Ray Cooper (who was a good friend of Harrison), and it was produced by Phil McDonald, who was also the engineer for the session.

When it was released as a single, it failed to chart in the UK, but did well in Switzerland, where it reached No.10, and also did healthily in Canada, reaching No.32. It also reached No.38 in the US *Billboard* Chart.

Artist - Billy Connolly & Chris Tummings & The Singing Rebels Band
Title - Freedom
Year - 1985
Label - London Records

One of the most beloved stand-up comics in Great Britain is a man they call "the Big Yin" AKA Scottish comedy legend Billy Connolly. He has been delighting audiences since the late 1960s, and remains incredibly popular today, even if his live career was cut short by Parkinson's disease. The single 'Freedom' was made for the 1985 film *Water* (produced by George Harrison's Handmade Films) and backing him were the fictional band The Singing Rebels, which consisted of none other than two of the Beatles - George and Ringo. Also playing guitar was Eric Clapton. This reggae-inspired record appeared at the end of the film during the 'Concert For Cascara' scene (Cascara is the fictional island that appears in the film), but unfortunately, the tune failed to chart.

Connolly would later cover the Beatles song 'Being For The Benefit of Mr. Kite!' for the 1998 George Martin-produced Beatles covers album *In My Life*, featuring celebrities covering Beatles tracks.

Artist - George Harrison
Title - When We Was Fab
Year - 1988
Label - Dark Horse Records

A hark-back to the glory days of the psychedelic era of The Beatles. It's a stand-out tune on George's comeback album *Cloud Nine* and produced by ELO maestro and fellow Travelling Wilbury, Jeff Lynne. To give it an extra bit of *Sgt. Pepper* era authenticity, Ringo provides the drums, and when they shot the music video for this tune (directed by Godley & Creme), Paul even made a small appearance in a walrus costume playing the bass (also watch out for Jeff Lynne's big afro, as well as cameos from Elton John, Paul Simon, and for all hardcore Beatle buffs, roadie and professional ghost-signer Neil Aspinall).

When the song was being made, the working title of the tune was 'Aussie Fab', as the song was written during a trip to Australia for the Adelaide Grand Prix, and the song sounded very Beatle-esque. Because of this, Harrison made the tune a nostalgia throwback to the psychedelic era of 1966-67, in contrast to the more sanguine Beatles throwback, 1981's tribute to John Lennon,' All Those Years Ago'. As well as Ringo Starr on drums, Gary Wright played piano. As expected, there are loads of Beatle references. There is also a reference to either Bob Dylan or Badfinger with the line "It's all over now, Baby Blue", which may be a shout-out to the song 'Baby Blue 'by Bob Dylan or the song by Badfinger of the same name - take your pick!

The song was a moderate commercial success, reaching No.25 in the UK Singles Chart and No.23 in the US *Billboard* Chart, but it was a bigger hit in the US *Billboard* Mainstream Rock Chart, where it reached No.2.

Artist - Ringo Starr
Title - King Of Broken Hearts
Year - 1998
Label - Mercury

A latter-day Beatle-esque slow-tempo number from Ringo's critically divisive 1998 *Vertical Man* album featuring George Harrison on lead guitar and background vocals. The title is rather apt, as many hearts were broken when teenage Beatle fangirls found out that Ringo was married (though it was the same with all four Beatles!).

Despite coming from an album that received mixed reviews from critics, it's a stand-out track, which has a latter-day John Lennon-esque vibe, with a musical shout-out to 'Strawberry Fields Forever 'with its use of the Mellotron.

CHAPTER FOURTEEN - PAUL, GEORGE AND RINGO

AKA The Threetles. They returned in 1995 for The Beatles'" reunion" singles 'Free As A Bird 'and 'Real Love'. Believe it or not, they reformed a few times before that, just not under the name of The Beatles. In fact, "The Beatles" (sans John) actually played at Eric Clapton's wedding to Pattie Boyd in 1979 (well, that's a story for another book!).

Artist - Jackie Lomax
Title - Sour Milk Sea
Year - 1968
Label - Apple Records

Have you ever tasted sour milk? Yuck! If you think that's bad, how about a whole sea of it; though in fairness, this isn't what the song is about, thank goodness!

'Sour Milk Sea 'is a song by Jackie Lomax (1944-2013), and it was produced and written by George Harrison. Lomax was an Apple Records artist who initially was part of the Merseybeat scene as a member of the group The Undertakers. They were signed to Brian Epstein's roster, and after his tragic passing in 1967, Apple Records took hold of Lomax's recording career, and with the help of Beatle George promoted him as a solo artist.

The song was originally written during the days in 1968 when our Fabs were in India getting spiritual guidance from the Maharishi Mahesh Yogi. Harrison considered this tune to be something of a follow-up to The Beatles' 'Within You Without You 'from the *Sgt. Pepper* LP released a year previously. Despite the song's rather tasteless title, according to George, it espouses meditation as a means to improve the quality of one's life, not to mention advocating a proactive approach when faced with difficulty. It was initially considered for *The White Album*, as evidenced in their famous Esher demos in May of '68, but the song was eventually given to Lomax; it was the first song George gave away to another artist. It was recorded on the 24th June at EMI (Abbey Road) studios. The song is notable for having every Beatle play on it, except John Lennon (though there is an uncredited Hammond organist, maybe that's John, who knows?), as well as Eric Clapton on lead guitar, and Nicky Hopkins on piano.

Despite the tune having a considerable amount of promotion, being earmarked as a smash, featuring three (maybe four) Beatles and Clapton, the song was surprisingly a flop commercially, and in America only reached a paltry No.117 in *Billboard's* Bubbling Under Chart. The tune did however do well commercially in Canada, reaching a respectful No.29 in the RPM 100.

'Sour Milk Sea' would go on to inspire the name of a hard rock band of the same name featuring Farrokh Bulsara, who would later call himself Freddie Mercury (of Queen fame). The song also contains the line "Get back to where you should be" - sounds a little similar to something I've heard somewhere else!

Artist - Jackie Lomax
Album - Is This What You Want?
Titles - Speak To Me/Is This What You Want?/How Can You Say Goodbye/Sunset/Sour Milk Sea/Fall Inside Your Eyes/Little Yellow Pills/Take My Word/The Eagle Laughs At You/Baby You're A Lover/You've Got Me Thinking/I Just Don't Know
Year - 1969
Label - Apple Records

Is This What You Want? was the debut album from Jackie Lomax, released on the 21st March 1969 on The Beatles 'Apple Records. Just like the single 'Sour Milk Sea 'before it, the album received rave reviews from critics, but sadly had little commercial success.

Recording for the album began at EMI (Abbey Road) Studios in June 1968 around the time The Beatles themselves were recording their *White Album*. The next sessions commenced in Los Angeles from October-November, attended by George, which was also the first time that any Beatles member had recorded in the United States. The final stages of recording took place back at EMI in London between December 1968-January 1969. It was also during this time that George was going to shop his most iconic Beatles song 'Something 'to Lomax, which in hindsight was probably for the best (not because of Lomax's skill as an artist), as it wouldn't have been the massive hit it would end up becoming!

As for the album's personnel, this included George on electric and acoustic guitars, Paul on drums, bass, electric guitar and backing vocals, and Ringo Starr on drums. Many other famous musicians also took part in the recording sessions for this album including Eric Clapton, Leon Russell, Billy Preston (reissue versions only) and even Beatles roadie, Mal Evans.

The album came out in March 1969 to unfortunately little fanfare, reaching a very low No.145 in the *Billboard* Top LPs Chart. This is actually quite sad, as a lot of dedication was put into this release, not to mention the very high quality of the music contained within the album, and of course the involvement of THREE of the four Beatles! "We tried and tried," remembers Apple Records promotions manager, Tony Bramwell." The material was great, but we just couldn't get it to fly... It looked good, sounded good – and didn't work." [28] Not even in Canada, where 'Sour Milk Sea' was a moderate hit, did it take off!

Time thankfully has been kind to this release, as it was popular enough to gain a substantial number of reissues over the years, with a CD release in November 1991 featuring a series of bonus tracks, and a fully remastered edition in 2010, featuring previously unreleased songs recorded during Lomax's time at Apple Records. Interestingly, in the US edition of the album, for unknown reasons, the song 'How Can You Say Goodbye' was substituted for another tune entitled 'New Day'. The latter song was re-included as a bonus track in the 1991 and 2010 editions of the album.

Artist - George Harrison
Title - All Those Years Ago
Year - 1981
Label - Dark Horse Records

George's touching tribute to the then-recently fallen Beatle, John Winston Ono Lennon. Initially, George wrote the song before John's death with different lyrics, as a song for Ringo to record. Ringo rejected it, as he was unsatisfied with the lyrics, and felt it wasn't suited to his vocal range. Harrison took the song back, and after the tragic events of December 8th 1980, the lyrics were altered to be a tribute to Lennon. It makes several references to John compositions such as 'All You Need Is Love' and Lennon's solo hit 'Imagine' with the line "you were the one who imagined it all".

Despite being credited as a George solo single, the song features all three of the living Beatles at the time, and also featured Paul's late wife, Linda McCartney, Denny Laine, Herbie Flowers, Al Kooper and Ray Cooper. It was a commercial success, charting high in America, Canada, Australia, Ireland, Norway, Switzerland, Sweden and the United Kingdom. The three remaining Beatles, with the help of Yoko contributing some unfinished Lennon demos, would reunite again in 1995 for The Beatles'" reunion" singles, 'Free As A Bird' and 'Real Love'. Despite gaining a mixed reception from critics, both singles were huge commercial successes.

CHAPTER FIFTEEN - JOHN, PAUL, GEORGE AND PETE

Before The Beatles were famous outside of Liverpool and Hamburg, they had actually recorded several tunes with an artist named Tony Sheridan, who often shared the bill with our Fabs during their residency in Hamburg. This was the genius of German promoter Bert Kaempfert, who put them together, and got them their first recording contract, before the days of Brian Epstein and Parlophone. They may not have been the best things The Beatles recorded but hey, everyone has to start somewhere...

Artist - Tony Sheridan And The Beat Brothers
Title - My Bonnie
Year - 1961
Label - Polydor

The first ever Beatles recording professionally released and, technically, their debut single, preceding 'Love Me Do 'by a whole year! In their early Hamburg days, John, Paul, George, Pete and Stu befriended a rock 'n' roll guitarist named Tony Sheridan, who they often shared the bill with during their residency at the Top Ten Club in Hamburg, Germany. Real name, Anthony Esmond Sheridan McGinnity, he obviously had to change his name to sound cooler and to save time, as his birth name would have filled up half the concert posters! Hailing from Norwich, the artist formally known as Anthony Esmond Sheridan McGinnity had originally been considered to be the guitarist for Cliff Richard's backing band, The Shadows, but failing to make contact with him, the role went to Hank Marvin and the rest, as they say, is history!

Sheridan, like the Fabs, ended up performing in Hamburg's "red light" district, and German music producer Bert Kaempfert was one of the Top Ten Club's frequenters; he put the two acts together and signed them for their first recording contract with his company, Bert Kaempfert Productions.

On the 22nd June 1961, they recorded five tunes at Hamburg's Friedrich-Ebert-Halle recording studios, with the engineer for the session being Karl Hinze. As well as tunes with Sheridan, The Beatles recorded two songs on their own: a cover of the 1927 Tin Pan Alley standard 'Ain't She Sweet', and an original instrumental piece entitled 'Cry For A Shadow '(also known as 'Beatle Bop') - as you would guess from the title, a pastiche of fellow beat group The Shadows.

'My Bonnie Lies Over The Ocean' is a traditional Scottish folk song, whose origins to this day remain a mystery. Other versions of the song over the years have been recorded by the likes of The Watersons, Peter Kennedy, Duane Eddy, Bing Crosby, Ray Charles... and Woody Woodpecker! The song also inspired the title of the classic 1948 Bugs Bunny cartoon *My Bunny Lies Over The Sea*. The Beatles and Tony Sheridan's version, as you would expect, was done in an early-1960s rock 'n' roll style, but with the song starting off being played traditionally, before going all RnR!

It was released on the 23rd October 1961 and despite the song's mediocre quality, it was a moderate hit in Germany, reaching No.32 in the German singles chart, and it even went to No.4 in a local Hamburg chart. It's probably not the greatest thing that The Beatles have ever recorded. Interestingly, there were two versions, one with Tony's introduction bit being sung in English, and another in German.

One common misconception is that The Beatles had to rename themselves to The Beat Brothers as Beatles sounded too similar to Peedles, which is German slang for a very intimate part of the male anatomy. This is in fact not true, as The Beat Brothers was an umbrella title that Sheridan used for all his backing bands.

Artist - Tony Sheridan And The Beat Brothers
Title - The Saints
Year - 1961
Label - Polydor

AKA the song Homer Simpson calls 'When The Saints Go Over There', this was the second Beatles/Sheridan collabo, and was the B-side to 'My Bonnie'. Not much to say, as it is basically the same format as 'Bonnie': take a traditional song, and "modernise" it with a rock 'n' roll twist. Not exactly *Sgt. Pepper* and it isn't even exactly 'Love Me Do'.

'The Saints'(or 'When The Saints Go Marching In'), like 'My Bonnie', has origins that are to this day unclear, though it is said to have originated around the late 19th century. The first known recorded version was made in 1923 by the Paramount Jubilee Singers, and it became a gospel standard. Other notable versions over the years have included Elvis Presley, Louis Armstrong, Bing Crosby, Judy Garland and Etta James. It is probably best known in the UK as being sung by fans at football (soccer) matches.

Artist - Tony Sheridan And The Beat Brothers
Title - Why (Can't You Love Me Again)
Year - 1961
Label - Polydor

The Beatles backed Tony with a Sheridan self-penned number that was recorded on the 22nd and 23rd June 1961, but didn't get released until July 1963 on a Tony Sheridan with The Beatles EP to cash in on the success of Beatlemania. It's far superior to the two remakes of the traditional tracks, and not a bad one, in my opinion, with a nice 'Please Please Me 'era feel to it. It was produced by Bert Kaempfert and the engineer for the session was Karl Hinze.

Artist - Tony Sheridan And The Beat Brothers
Title - Take Out Some Insurance On Me, Baby
Year - 1961
Label - Polydor

Tony Sheridan mimics Elvis Presley with this Jimmy Reed cover. If only The Beatles 'session with the actual Elvis in 1965 was recorded, that would have been awesome... or maybe not?

This song is notable for containing some mild profanity, which is unusual for a Beatles song (and for something recorded in the early 60s), as Tony sings "some goddamn insurance on me, baby", pretty shocking for 1961 standards!

The song was originally released by Jimmy Reed in 1959, and despite The Beatles/Sheridan version being recorded on the 24th June 1961, it didn't see a commercial release until 29th May 1964, as the B-side to The Beatles 'rendition of 'Ain't She Sweet', which was released on Polydor Records in an attempt to cash-in on the success of Beatlemania.

Artist - Tony Sheridan And The Beat Brothers
Title - Nobody's Child
Year - 1961
Label - Polydor

Another tune recorded in the Hamburg sessions of 1961. This is a cover of a song by Hank Snow, and was eventually released in 1964 on Polydor Records to capitalise on the success of Beatlemania. Alongside this track, there was a recording of a cover of 'Ain't She Sweet 'with John on vocals on the flip-side, which was recorded in the same session. 'Nobody's Child' has been covered by many other artists over the years, such as Lonnie Donegan, Hank Williams Jr, Billy Fury, Max Romeo, and most famously Karen Young, who had a No.6 hit with it in 1969.

George revisited the song in 1990 with The Travelling Wilburys, as a charity single to assist Romanian orphans during the downfall of communism. Despite being made for a fantastic cause, it was a commercial failure, and the only chart position it reached was a modest No.43 in New Zealand.

>
> Artist - Tony Sheridan And The Beat Brothers
> Title - Sweet Georgia Brown
> Year - 1962
> Label - Polydor

A contractual obligation during the transition from Bert Kaempfert to Brian Epstein becoming the band's manager. To make sure the transition was a smooth one, The Fabs were obliged to do one final session with Tony Sheridan, which was recorded on May 24th 1962 at Studio Rahlstedt in Hamburg. Ironically, Sheridan was absent during the recording session, and his vocals were later overdubbed. Also joining The Beatles was pianist Roy Young, who had been occasionally accompanying the boys during their Star Club residency. It was released later in 1962 on Sheridan's EP, 'Ya Ya'.

Following on from the format of 'My Bonnie' and 'The Saints', 'Sweet Georgia Brown' is a rock cover of an old 1925 jazz-pop standard, which was originally written by Ben Bernie, Maceo Pinkard and Kenneth Casey, and has been covered many times over the years. In January 1964, Sheridan rerecorded the lyrics to capitalise on the early stages of Beatlemania, with the words "Fellas that she can't get are fellas she can't get/Georgia claimed her, Georgia named her Sweet Georgia Brown" being altered to "In Liverpool she even dared to criticise The Beatles' hair/With their whole fan club standing there ah, meet Sweet Georgia Brown" in an obvious attempt to cash in on their popularity.

>
> Artist - Tony Sheridan And The Beat Brothers
> Title - Swanee River
> Year - 1962
> Label - Unreleased

Another tune recorded during the same sessions as 'Sweet Georgia Brown'. This was a cover of an 1851 minstrel song written by Stephen Foster, which also goes by the name of 'Old Folks At Home'. It is also the official anthem of the American state of Florida.

Sadly, The Beatles 'recording of this song became lost, but Sheridan recorded another version with another set of musicians.

After The Beatles, Sheridan's musical style went through a drastic metamorphosis, going for a more blues and jazz-orientated sound, which alienated his earlier fanbase. In 1967, Sheridan would serve in Vietnam, and he became an honorary Captain of the United States Army. He would later rejoin the music industry in the early 1970s, achieving some minor success, and he even recorded an album with Elvis Presley's TCB Band, after an American producer was impressed with his early works with The Beatles. Sheridan died on February 16th 2013 in Hamburg after undergoing heart surgery. He will always remain an important figure in the formative years of our fabulous foursome.

CHAPTER SIXTEEN - JOHN, PAUL, GEORGE AND RINGO

Legend, Legend, Legend and Legend.

> Artist - Lu Walters
> Title - Summertime
> Year - 1960
> Label - White Label Acetate

Arranged by their first manager, Allan Williams, this is the very first recording to feature the classic Beatles line-up of John Lennon, Paul McCartney, George Harrison and Ringo Starr. This was a version of the often-covered George Gershwin classic 'Summertime 'and on this recording, they were backing Lu Walters (real name Walter Eymond), who was the bassist for Ringo's previous band, Rory Storm and The Hurricanes. It was recorded in 1960 in Hamburg in a modest studio called Akustik, located in a railway station. It was a drop-in studio open to members of the public, and as well as bands, and people were able to record messages for family and friends. This studio in Hamburg is comparable to the Percy Phillips Recording Studio, where the Proto-Beatles, The Quarrymen, recorded 'That'll Be The Day 'and 'In Spite of All The Danger 'back in the summer of 1958.

Despite the fact that Pete Best was the drummer for The Beatles at the time, he was absent, as he was in town on an errand, and Starr filled in for him (something that would become a regular occurrence, until Ringo eventually joined for real in 1962) and while the late Stuart Sutcliffe was present in the recording session, he didn't play on it.

Six copies of this session were pressed, but none have yet surfaced. Other tunes recorded during this session included covers of Peggy Lee's 'Fever 'and Kurt Weill's 'September Song '(later covered by Jeff Lynne with George Harrison). Like 'Summertime', the archival status of these recordings is currently unknown.

> Artist - Horst Fascher feat. The Beatles
> Album - Live! At The Star-Club In Hamburg, Germany; 1962
> Titles - Be-Bop-A-Lula/Hallelujah I Love Her So
> Year - 1962 (Released 1977)
> Label - Lingasong Records

April 8th 1977 saw the release of The Beatles' live album *Live! At The Star-Club In Hamburg, Germany; 1962*, released without the band's permission on a tiny label called Lingasong Records, which was formed with the sole purpose of releasing this. Despite the Fabs trying to withdraw the release, the banning of it proved to be unsuccessful, though in 1998, Lingasong finally agreed to have the release taken off the market!

This "grey market" release is a low-quality recording of The Beatles performing at the Star Club in Hamburg, Germany in late December 1962, in the early stages of Ringo being the drummer of the band. It was recorded by the club's stage manager, Adrian Barber, for Ted "Kingsize" Taylor on a Grundig home reel-to-reel recording device. Despite the dubious origins and quality of this release, it sold well enough to reach the *Billboard* 200 Album Chart in the US, reaching No.111, though by Beatles standards, it's pretty pathetic.

On the songs 'Be-Bop-A-Lula '(originally by Gene Vincent) and 'Hallelujah I Love Her So '(originally by Ray Charles), we have guest vocals from Horst Fascher, who was the manager of the Star Club, proving that he should not quit his day job! Before he was manager of the Star Club, Fascher was a promising amateur boxer, and was going to represent Germany in the 1960 Olympics, but after accidentally murdering a sailor in a street fight, he was given a lifetime ban in boxing, and had to serve six years in prison. After being released, Fred started his work managing the Star Club.

Fascher was still friends with our Fabs when they were proper famous, and his anecdotes of The Beatles 'Hamburg days have made it into several music biographies. His own memoir was published back in 2006.

Artist - Rolf Harris
Title - Tie Me Kangaroo Down Sport
Year - 1963
Label - BBC

Rolf Harris was a once beloved, but now very much disgraced Australian light entertainment former-legend, who was once extremely popular in the UK. He was probably best known for his songs such as 'Sun Arise 'and 'Two Little Boys', inventing musical instruments such as the wobble board, popularising the stylophone, and for presenting *Animal Hospital*, as well as being known for his artwork.

When he was still respected, one his most famous songs would have to be his 1957 novelty hit 'Tie Me Kangaroo Down Sport', which was a No.1

hit in his homeland and also a Top 10 hit in the UK, and when it was re-recorded in 1963, it was produced by George Martin.

On the 18th December 1963, Rolf recorded a version with our fabulous foursome for the BBC Radio programme *From Us To You Say The Beatles*, with altered lyrics mentioning each member of The Beatles - it was broadcast on Boxing Day of that year.

For obvious reasons, this will probably never see an official release anytime soon.

Artist - The Rolling Stones
Title - Shades of Orange
Year - 1972
Label - Decca (Bootleg)
NOTE - This is actually mislabeled as having involvement from The Beatles. The reason for inserting it here is to set the record straight!

An alleged Rolling Stones bootleg, this was released on an unofficial album in Taiwan. Wow - The Beatles and The Rolling Stones doing a tune together, cats and dogs living together, mass hysteria, this is the most amazing thing in music history... sorry to disappoint you folks, it's not a Beatles or a Rolling Stones tune! The reality is that it's actually a track by an obscure psychedelic band from the 1960s called The End. They were managed and produced by Stones member Bill Wyman, and bootleggers often attribute this tune to being outtakes from The Stones 'not-*Sgt. Pepper* album *Their Satanic Majesties Request*.

Artist - The Rolling Stones
Title - Loving Sacred Loving
Year - 1972
Label - Decca (Bootleg)
NOTE - This is actually mislabeled as having involvement from The Beatles. The reason for inserting it here is also to set the record straight!

See 'Shades Of Orange'.

CHAPTER SEVENTEEN - PEOPLE WHO HAVE WORKED WITH THE BEATLES

Sometimes, you need more than four people to make a tune sound epic and grandiose. It wasn't just The Beatles participating on other people's records, here is a list (not exhaustive) of other people participating on Beatles' records (just as a band, not solo releases). Some of these names you may have heard of…

* **Fredrick Alexander** - A session musician who played cello on 'Martha My Dear' on *The White Album*.
* **Jane Asher** - Paul McCartney's girlfriend and later fiancée 1963-1968. A very attractive actress (and still is today), author, entrepreneur, and celebrity cake maker who has starred in many famous films, theatre productions and TV shows, and is married to the popular illustrator, Gerald Scarfe, who designed the cover for Pink Floyd's *The Wall*. Joined in during the chorus of 'All You Need Is Love'.
* **Neil Aspinall** - The Beatle's roadie, business partner and professional autograph forger. Played the guiro in 'Strawberry Fields Forever' and provided backing vocals on 'All You Need Is Love'.
* **Ted Barker** - A trombonist who worked with the likes of Eric Winstone, Ted Heath (not the former UK Prime Minister of the same name) and Ray Davies (not the member of The Kinks). Played trombone on 'Martha My Dear' on *The White Album*.
* **Michael Barnes** - A tuba player who played on 'A Day In The Life' from the *Sgt. Pepper* LP.
* **Ken Barrie** - Probably best known as the narrator of the beloved 1980s children's TV series *Postman Pat*, the late Ken Barrie sang backing vocals on the song 'Goodnight'. Yes, Postman Pat sang with Ringo AKA narrator for Thomas The Tank Engine… twice! Barrie would later sing with Ringo in 2009 for a charity single for Children In Need 'The Official BBC Children In Need Medley', this time, as their respective children's characters.
* **Peter Beavan** - Played cello on 'Within You Without You' on the *Sgt. Pepper* album.
* **Anil Bhagwat** - Played the tabla on the song 'Love You To' from Revolver. He was a member of the AMC (Asian Music Circle).
* **Lionel Bentley** - A member of the BBC Symphony Orchestra and the Amici String Quartet, who played violin on 'A Day In The Life' from *Sgt. Pepper*.

* **Leo Birnbaum** - A viola player, who also worked with The Beatles' good friend, Harry Nilsson, as well as Tony Bennett, Coldstream Guards, Leslie Jones and His Orchestra and more. Played on 'Hello Goodbye' and 'Martha My Dear'.
* **Greg Bowen** - A German-based trumpet player who played on 'Strawberry Fields Forever'.
* **Eric Bowie** - A member of The Alan Tew Orchestra and The London Jazz Chamber Group. He played violin on 'All Your Need Is Love', 'Glass Onion' and 'Piggies'.
* **Pattie Boyd** - AKA Layla. A model and photographer, who was married to George Harrison (and later married his buddy, Eric Clapton), and sang backing vocals on 'Yellow Submarine', 'All You Need Is Love' and 'Birthday'.
* **D. Bradley** - It is unknown what the D stands for (David, maybe?), but D played violin on 'A Day In The Life'.
* **Alan Branscombe** - A famous English jazz pianist, vibraphonist and alto saxophonist, who played tenor saxophone on 'Got To Get You Into My Life'.
* **Lizzie Bravo** - An Apple Scruff (a Beatles fangirl, who hung around Apple HQ circa 1968-69) turned backing vocalist, who sang the line "Nothing's gonna change my world" on the World Wildlife Fund version of 'Across The Universe'.
* **Jack Bremner** - A clarinetist who played on 'A Day In The Life'.
* **Sheila Bromberg** - Played the harp on 'She's Leaving Home'. She was the first female musician to play on a Beatles recording.
* **Raymond Brown** - Played the trombone on 'A Day In The Life'.
* **James W. Buck** - Played the French horn on the self-titled opening track on *Sgt. Pepper's Lonely Heart's Club Band*.
* **John Burden** - A British French horn player, who also contributed to playing the instrument on the opening track to *Sgt. Pepper's* .
* **Leon Calvert** - A British jazz trumpeter, who played on 'Penny Lane' and both the trumpet and the flugelhorn on 'Martha My Dear'.
* **Barrie Cameron** - The baritone saxophonist from the group Sounds Incorporated, who often opened for The Beatles back in the day. He played saxophone on 'Good Morning, Good Morning' on *Sgt. Pepper's*.
* **Duncan Campbell** - A Scottish jazz trumpeter who played on 'Penny Lane'. He, like the previously mentioned Ted Barker, was a member of Ted Heath's Orchestra, as well as The Jack Nathan Orchestra.
* **William Shears Campbell** - Apparently filled in for Paul McCartney, and masqueraded as him from around 1966, but nothing has been proven, and it's more than likely not true!

* **Ronald Chamberlain** - Played saxophone on 'Honey Pie' on *The White Album*.
* **Hariprasad Chaurasia** - Popular Indian flautist in the Hindustani tradition, who played on the 1968 B-side to 'Lady Madonna', 'The Inner Light'.
* **Jimmy Chester** - A saxophonist who played on 'Honey Pie' from *The White Album*.
* **Alan Civi CBE** - A British horn payer, who was in the Royal Philharmonic Orchestra and the BBC Symphony Orchestra. He played on 'For No One' from the *Revolver* album and 'A Day In The Life' from *Sgt. Pepper's*. He was one of only five session musicians to actually be credited on the liner notes of a Beatles recording. Let's hope he also got paid a decent fee too!
* **Eric Clapton** - A rock guitarist legend, who was in the band Cream with Jack Bruce and Ginger Baker. He famously played electric guitar on 'While My Guitar Gently Weeps' and sang on the chorus of 'All You Need Is Love'. He also hosted and curated the Concert For George in 2002 at the Royal Albert Hall.
* **Frank Clarke** - British double bass player and composer, who worked with many big names such as Georgie Fame, Sammy Davis Jr, Ella Fitzgerald, Petula Clark, and notably Cliff Richard on his debut single 'Move It/Schoolboy Crush'. He played double bass on 'Penny Lane'.
* **Freddy Clayton** - A trumpeter who is most noted for his work with Barry Gray on the soundtrack to Gerry Anderson's brilliant TV puppet series *Thunderbirds* and more infamously for playing on Rolf Harris' hit record 'Two Little Boys'. He played trumpet on 'Penny Lane' as well as the *White Album* cut 'Revolution 1'.
* **Peter Coe** - A saxophonist who was a member of Georgie Fame & The Blue Flames and the Peter Coe Orchestra among others, not to mention conducting Lionel Bart's *Oliver* - the highly successful musical based on the Oliver Twist story, which still plays today. He played tenor saxophone on 'Got To Get You Into My Life' on the *Revolver* LP.
* **Derek Collins** - A woodwind legend, who played tenor saxophone on 'Savoy Truffle'.
* **Les Condon** - A British jazz trumpeter, who was in many jazz groups back in the day. Played trumpet on 'Got To Get You Into My Life'.
* **Roy Copestake** - A trumpeter who played on the title track of the 'Magical Mystery Tour' EP/LP.
* **Bert Courtley** - Born Herbert Courtley, he was a British jazz trumpeter who played both trumpet and flugelhorn on 'Penny Lane'.
* **Keith Cummings** - A session musician who played cello on 'Glass Onion' and 'Piggies', both from *The White Album*.

* **Alan Dalziel** - A cellist, who was a member of the Alan Tew Orchestra and The Chitinous Ensemble. He played cello on 'She's Leaving Home' and 'A Day In The Life' on the *Sgt. Pepper* LP.

* **Hunter Davis OBE** – An award-winning, world famous author/journalist and broadcaster, probably best known to Beatle fans as their official biographer. He has also ghostwritten the autobiographies of football (soccer) stars Wayne Rooney, Paul Gascoigne and Dwight Yorke. Made a brief side-career in music by providing backing vocals on 'All You Need Is Love'. In 2014, he was appointed Order of the British Empire for his services to literature.

* **Bernard Davis** - Not to be confused with the American funk/disco drummer of the same name. Bernard Davis is a viola player who played on 'A Day In The Life'.

* **Henry Datyner** - A Polish classical violinist and rostra leader, who was leader of both the Royal Philharmonic Orchestra and the Royal Liverpool Philharmonic Orchestra. Played violin on 'A Day In The Life' on *Sgt. Pepper*, as well as on 'Glass Onion' and 'Piggies' on *The White Album*.

* **Rij Ram Desad** - An Indian harmonium player who played on 'The Inner Light'. He would also play on George's debut solo album *Wonderwall Music* as well as the George Harrison-produced Ravi Shankar album *Ravi Shankar's Music Festival from India* in 1976.

* **Donovan** - A popular 1960s singer from Glasgow, who is known for his eclecticism, and who was a good pal of our Fabs. He had a string of hit records worldwide. He sang the chorus on 'Yellow Submarine' (and quite rightly too!). He has released 26 albums as of 2023, and is still singing and performing today.

* **Rose Eccles** - Presumably no relation to Jennifer Eccles (although she was Hollies member Graham Nash's ex-wife and the group had a hit with said song, written by Nash and Hollies member Alan Clarke, so she probably inspired the name!). She sang the chorus of 'All You Need Is Love'.

* **Gwyn Edwards** - A viola player, who was the principal violist with the London Symphony Orchestra and The Sinfonia Of London as well as being the co-principal violist of both the BBC Symphony Orchestra and the Royal Philharmonic Orchestra. His Beatle contribution was playing viola on 'A Day In The Life'. He also played with Harry Nilsson, Des O'Connor, and Barry Gray on the soundtrack to the series *Space: 1999*.

* **Art Ellefson** - A Canadian saxophonist who played the instrument on 'Savoy Truffle' from *The White Album*.

* **Jack Ellory** - A flautist who has worked with the likes of John Williams, Barry Gray and Barbara Dixon. He played the iconic flute solo on 'The Fool On The Hill' from the 'Magical Mystery Tour' EP/LP.

* **Ralph Elman** - Another Barry Gray/Supermarionation veteran, who played the violin on 'Within You Without You' on *Pepper's* and 'I Am The Walrus' on 'Magical Mystery Tour'. He has worked with a diverse array of people over the years including The Seekers, Chas and Dave and Tony Bennett.

* **Jack Emblow** - Probably the most successful accordion player in pop music history not named "Weird Al" Yankovic. He played the accordion on 'All You Need Is Love' and he has also played the instrument on records by Elton John, Donovan, Grace Jones and Max Boyce.

* **Geoff Emerick** - Very well-known figure in Beatles circles, as he was, of course, their sound engineer (if you know your Beatles, you'll know that already!). His only record appearance on a Beatles song was singing along during the chorus of 'Yellow Submarine'.

* **Kenneth Essex** - A celebrated violist, who was a key member of many well-known orchestras. He played viola on 'Yesterday', as well as 'Hello, Goodbye'.

* **Mal Evans** - A hugely respected person in the Beatles entourage. He was their road manager and, like Neil Aspinall, ghost-signed autographs for them on their behalf, when they were too busy. His musical contributions to the Beatles back catalogue include playing Hammond organ on 'You Won't See Me', bass drum and vocals on 'Yellow Submarine', tambourine on 'Strawberry Fields Forever', harmonica on 'Being For The Benefit Of Mr. Kite!', alarm clock, piano and the guy that counts in the orchestra on 'A Day In The Life', hand claps on 'Dear Prudence' and 'Birthday', trumpet on 'Helter Skelter', anvil on 'Maxwell's Silver Hammer', and most interestingly a pile of gravel dug with a shovel for that bizarre B-side to 'Let It Be', 'You Know My Name (Look Up The Number)'. He also played hand bell in 'What's The New Mary Jane'.

* **Joey "The Lips" Fagan** - A trumpeter who was a member of a short-lived Dublin soul covers band called The Commitments (as covered by Roddy Doyle in his book!). According to himself, he played on 'All Your Need Is Love', but he is known for telling a good tall tale, and whether his claim is true or not is up for debate!

* **Marianne Faithful** - A famous British singer/songwriter/actress, who shot to fame with her hit single 'As Tears Go By', and she partnered Mick Jagger for several years - the track was one of Jagger/Richards' earliest compositions. Unfortunately, her career hit rock bottom during the 70s, but she had a career resurrection in 1979. Marianne wasn't exactly "faithful" to Jagger, as she sang backing vocals on two songs of their friendly rivals - 'Yellow Submarine' and 'All You Need Is Love'.

* **Jack Fallon** - A Canadian double bass player who played violin on 'Don't Pass Me By'.

* **Horst Fascher** - The manager of the Star Club in Hamburg, Germany, who was a friend of The Beatles in their early days, and remained so after the Hamburg era. Would sometimes sing guest "vocals" during their live performances, as evidenced in the grey market live album *Live! At The Star-Club in Hamburg, Germany' 1962*.
* **Tony Fisher** - Played trumpet on 'Strawberry Fields Forever'.
* **Allen Ford** - A cellist who played on 'Within You Without You'.
* **Eldon Fox** - Played cello on three Beatles compositions - 'I Am The Walrus', 'Glass Onion' and 'Piggies'.
* **Tristan Fry** - An English percussionist who has done session work with a who's-who of 20th century popular music including Frank Sinatra, Elton John, Danny Kaye, Olivia Newton-John, David Essex and John Martyn. He provided additional percussion work and played timpani on 'A Day In The Life'.
* **Francesco Gabarró Solé** - Spanish-born British cellist who played on 'Yesterday' and 'A Day In The Life'.
* **Julien Gaillard** - A British violinist, who played with the BBC Symphony Orchestra, The Royal Philharmonic Orchestra, Philharmonia Orchestra and was leader of the BBC Radio Orchestra. He played violin on the *Sgt. Pepper's* track 'Within You Without You'.
* **Jose Luis Garcia** - A Spanish violinist and conductor. Played on 'She's Leaving Home'.
* **Hans Geiger** - A classical violinist, who was the principal violin player with the London Symphony Orchestra. He played the violin on 'A Day In The Life'.
* **Bernard George** - Played baritone saxophone on 'Savoy Truffle'.
* **Sharad Ghosh** - Played the shehnai on 'The Inner Light'. He also played on George's solo debut album *Wonderwall Music*.
* **Tony Gilbert** - A violinist who has worked with people as diverse as Pete Townshend, Tiny Tim, Freddie Cole, Barry Gray, Lee Towers and KPM Library Music. He played violin on 'Yesterday' and 'Eleanor Rigby'.
* **David Glyde** - A saxophonist who played on 'Good Morning, Good Morning'.
* **Phil Goody** - Phil Goody was a member of Geraldo And His Orchestra and the Laurie Johnson Orchestra, plus he played with Barry Gray's Orchestra on the soundtrack to the Gerry Anderson Supermarionation series *Supercar*. He played the flute on 'Penny Lane'.
* **Jack Greene** - Not the American country singer of the same name, Jack Greene was a session musician who played violin on 'Within You Without You' and 'I Am The Walrus'.

* **Erich Gruenberg** - An Austrian-born British violinist and teacher, who was a member of the London Symphony Orchestra, The Royal Philharmonic Orchestra and Stockholms Konsertförenings Orkester (The Royal Philharmonic Orchestra of Stockholm, Sweden). Played violin on 'She's Leaving Home', 'Within You, Without You' and 'A Day In The Life'.
* **Patrick Hailing** - A session violinist who played on 'All You Need Is Love'.
* **John Hall** - Not the songwriter from US rock band Orleans. He played cello on 'Strawberry Fields Forever'.
* **Ian Hamer** - A British jazz trumpeter, who has played with Ella Fitzgerald, Bing Crosby, Dusty Springfield, Tom Jones, Barbra Streisand, Shirley Bassey, Georgie Fame and many more, and he also played trumpet on the theme tune to the famous 1970s British ITV police drama series *The Sweeney*. His contribution to Beatledom was playing on the iconic 'Got To Get You Into My Life' from the *Revolver* LP.
* **Rolf Harris** - Infamous discredited Australian light entertainment figure. Collaborated with The Beatles on a rendition of his hit single 'Tie Me Kangaroo Down Sport' on the BBC Radio programme *From Us To You Say The Beatles*. You will probably never hear this outside of YouTube uploads!
* **Louise Harrison** - George Harrison's mum. She came up with the line: "What they need is a damn good whacking" on the song 'Piggies' from *The White Album*. They sure do!
* **Jurgen Hess** - A classical violinist, who was a member of The London Bach Orchestra. He played violin on 'Eleanor Rigby' and 'A Day In The Life'.
* **Alan Holmes** - A saxophonist/clarinetist/flautist/oboist, who played with bands such as The Kinks, The Bachelors, CWS and Sounds Incorporated. He played sax on 'Good Morning, Good Morning'.
* **Jack Holmes** - Played violin on 'All You Need Is Love'.
* **Don Honeywill** - A session saxophonist with a cool name, who has played with people such as Tom Jones, Benny Goodman, Stan Kenton and Frank Sinatra. He played tenor saxophone on 'All You Need Is Love'.
* **Nicky Hopkins** - A very well-respected and in-demand British pianist and organist, who played with every big beat group from the 1960s - The Rolling Stones, The Who, The Kinks and, of course, our Beatles! He played on their legendary 1968 double A-side single 'Revolution'. He sadly passed away in 1994.
* **Elgary Howarth** - A session musician who paid trumpet on the title track on 'Magical Mystery Tour'.
* **Ronnie Hughes** - A British jazz trumpeter who played on 'Martha My Dear' on *The White Album*.

* **Derek Jacobs** - A session violinist, who worked with Barry Gray on the soundtrack to Gerry Anderson's *Thunderbirds* series, and also collaborated with the Fabs' good friend, Harry Nilsson, a few times. He played violin on the *Sgt. Pepper* cut 'She's Leaving Home'.
* **Bill Jackman** - A British saxophonist and clarinet player, whose contributions to music are as diverse as performing with artists such as Bing Crosby and Betty Boo. He played tenor saxophone on 'Lady Madonna' and played flute, vocals and hand claps on 'Hey Jude'.
* **Harold Jackson** - A Yorkshire based trumpeter, who was a member of future Apple Records signee, The Black Dyke Mills Band, whose single, the theme tune to the obscure ITV series *Thingumybob*, was produced and written by Paul McCartney. He also played trumpet on 'A Day In The Life'.
* **Hanuman Jadev** - Master of the shehnai, who played this instrument on 'The Inner Light'. He also played on George's solo debut LP *Wonderwall Music*.
* **Mick Jagger** - Needs no introduction. Sang along during the chorus of 'All You Need Is Love' and also sang backing vocals on 'Baby You're A Rich Man'. Great singer.
* **John Jezzard** - A violinist who would later work with Jools Holland. Played violin on that trippy tune of awesomeness known as 'I Am The Walrus' go-goo-g-joob!
* **Brian Jones** - Much missed founding member of The Rolling Stones, who departed from us way too soon. He played saxophone on 'You Know My Name (Look Up The Number)', which was recorded in 1967, but wasn't released until 1970, making it a posthumous release for Jones (he died in 1969). He also sang vocals on 'Yellow Submarine'.
* **Granville Jones** - Late violinist, who was leader of the London Symphony Orchestra, founder leader of The Delme String Quartet and a member of the Fleming String Trio. Played violin on 'A Day In The Life'.
* **Norman Jones** - Session cellist who played on 'Eleanor Rigby' and 'Strawberry Fields Forever'.
* **S. R. Kenkari** - An Indian musician who played shehnai on 'The Inner Light'. Also contributed to George's first solo album *Wonderwall Music*.
* **Ashish Khan** - A popular and well-respected Indian classical musician, who plays the sarode. He played on 'The Inner Light' and would team up with George Harrison on a few future projects.
* **Reginald Kilbey** - A cellist who played on a few Beatle recordings. These include 'Within You Without You', 'Glass Onion', 'Martha My Dear', and 'Piggies'.

* **Harry Klein** - A British baritone saxophonist. He played saxophone on 'Lady Madonna' as well as the *White Album* cuts 'Honey Pie' and 'Savoy Truffle'.

* **Bobby Kok** - Also known as Alexander Kok, he played cello, and also contributed to the vocals and hand claps on 'Hey Jude'. He would work with George Harrison again on his 1987 studio album *Cloud Nine*.

* **Eddie Kramer** - A popular South African recording producer and engineer, who has worked with pretty much every big name in the 1960s and also was a photographer for Jimi Hendrix. He played the vibes on 'Baby You're A Rich Man'.

* **Don Lang** - Born Gordon Langhorn, Don was an English trombonist and singer, who led his own group, Don Lang And The Frantic Five. He had a top five hit in the UK hit parade with his rendition of 'Witch Doctor' in 1958. He played trombone on 'Revolution 1' from *The White Album*.

* **John Lee** - A session trombonist who played on 'Good Morning, Good Morning'.

* **Norman Lenderman** - A violinist who played on 'Glass Onion' and 'Piggies'.

* **Gordon Lewins** - A session musician who played clarinet on 'I Am The Walrus'.

* **Jackie Lomax** - As previously covered in this book, he was an artist who was signed to Apple Records. He contributed some hand claps to the tune 'Dear Prudence' from *The White Album*.

* **Roger Lord** - An oboist who, after working with our Fabs, played on the soundtrack to the Indiana Jones movies. He played the oboe on 'A Day In The Life'.

* **Alan Loveday** - A classical violinist born in New Zealand, who became leader of the Royal Philharmonic Orchestra and was a leader with the Academy of St. Martin in the Fields. He played violin on 'Within You Without You'.

* **Cyril MacArthur** - A session musician who played double bass on 'A Day In The Life'.

* **Henry MacKenzie** - A Scottish clarinetist and saxophonist who played clarinet on 'When I'm Sixty-Four'. He would later play on McCartney's solo song 'Ballroom Dancing' on the soundtrack to *Give My Regards To Broad Street* in 1984.

* **Les Maddox** - A violinist who played on 'Martha My Dear'.

* **John Marson** - A harpist who played on 'A Day In The Life'. He would later work with Cat Stevens, Bing Crosby, Andrew Lloyd Webber and most notably John Williams on the soundtrack to *Star Wars* in 1977.

* **Bram Martin** - A British cellist who played on 'I Am The Walrus'.

* **George Martin** - Not sure whether to put him in this list or not, as I feel he was the fifth member of The Beatles, but anyhow, seeing as he produced the majority of the songs that The Beatles recorded, and even played on many of them, it would be easier to list the tracks George Martin DIDN'T contribute to. All you need to know is that George Martin was awesome, he was a lovely chap, and without him, The Beatles wouldn't have been The Beatles we know and love. Big props to George Martin!
* **David Mason** - Not the same David Mason who was a member of Traffic. Mason was an English orchestral solo and session trumpet player, who played the flugelhorn for the premiere of Ralph Vaughan William's Ninth Symphony. He is probably best known for playing the piccolo trumpet solo on 'Penny Lane'. He also played on 'A Day In The Life', 'Magical Mystery Tour', 'All You Need Is Love' and 'It's All Too Much'.
* **David McCallum Sr.** - A Scottish violinist, and father of actor David McCallum, who is best known for playing Russian secret agent Illya Kuryakin in the TV series *The Man From U.N.C.L.E.*, and the voice of Alfred Pennyworth in several animated Batman movies. McCallum Sr. played violin on 'A Day In The Life'.
* **John McCartney** - As you could probably tell from his surname, John is of course the cousin of Paul McCartney. He collaborated on the track 'Dear Prudence' by hand clapping.
* **Linda McCartney** - The much missed late wife of Paul McCartney, who was a photographer, musician, animal rights activist and business entrepreneur. Her musical contribution to the Beatles canon was singing backing vocals on 'Let It Be'. She later went on to be a founder member with her husband of McCartney's other ultra-successful band, Wings, playing keyboards and vocals.
* **Dennis McConnell** - A session violinist who played on 'A Day In The Life'.
* **Mike McGear** - As previously stated in this book, Mike McGear (Peter Michael McCartney) is Paul McCartney's younger brother. He sang during the chorus of 'All You Need Is Love' - thank you very much, thank you very, very much (for fans of Scaffold!).
* **Andrew McGee** - A violinist who played on 'I Am The Walrus'.
* **John Meek** - A session musician who played viola on 'A Day In The Life'.
* **Bernard Miller** - Played violin on 'Martha My Dear'. Not the songwriter of 'I Can't Stand The Rain' fame or the double bassist, who both share the same name.
* **Morris Miller** - A session musician who played French horn on 'I Am The Walrus'.

*   **The Mike Sammes Singers** - A vocal group who were signed to Disneyland Records. They sang on the title themes to three of Gerry Anderson's Supermarionation puppet shows, and they worked with the likes of Ronnie Hilton, Ken Dodd, Tom Jones, Helen Shapiro and Englebert Humperdink. They're the group that chanted "oompah, oompah, stick it up your jumper" at the end of 'I Am The Walrus' from 'Magical Mystery Tour' as well as providing backing vocals for 'Goodnight' on *The White Album*.
*   **Mahapurush Misra** - A master of the talba, hailing "straight outta" Calcutta. Played on 'The Inner Light' as well as contributing to George Harrison's first album *Wonderwall Music*.
*   **Bill Monro** - Sharing the same name as bluegrass pioneer Bill Monroe (without the silent E), this guy was a violist who played on 'A Day In The Life'.
*   **Monty Montgomery** - Not the Jamaican reggae artist/producer of the same name, Monty Montgomery was a session musician who played trumpet on 'A Day In the Life'.
*   **Keith Moon** - The ultimate definition of a bloke who lived the rock 'n' roll lifestyle to the fullest. This wild, textbook example of the hedonist was the outstanding drummer for the legendary band The Who, and he sang on the chorus of 'All You Need Is Love' and also played brushed drums. Sadly passed away in 1978. He was also a great drinking buddy of our Ringo.
*   **T. Moore** - A session trombonist who played on 'A Day In The Life'.
*   **Dick Morgan** - An oboist who played on 'Penny Lane'. He also played cor anglais on the track too.
*   **Rex Morris** - A British saxophonist who played on 'All You Need Is Love' and 'Honey Pie'. He also played trombone on 'Revolution 1'. As well as working in the fields of jazz, he worked with rock artists like Duane Eddy and even novelty acts like The Wombles.
*   **Danny Moss MBE** - A very prolific saxophonist who played tenor saxophone on 'Savoy Truffle'. He played with many of the 20th century's greats such as Bing Crosby, Louis Armstrong, Ella Fitzgerald, Tony Bennett, Sarah Vaughan and Rosemary Clooney.
*   **Henry Myerscough** - A session musician who played viola on 'Martha My Dear'. He also played with the British rock trio Quartermass.
*   **Graham Nash OBE** - A member of highly popular UK pop group, The Hollies, and the legendary folk-rock supergroup, Crosby, Stills, Nash & Young. He sang during the chorus of 'All You Need Is Love'.
*   **Raymond Newman** - A session clarinetist who played on 'Honey Pie'.
*   **Alex Nifosi** - A session cellist who played on 'A Day In The Life'.

* **Yoko Ono** - John Lennon's famous second wife, and a very important figure in The Beatles' circle. Sang the line "not when he looked so fierce" on 'The Continuing Story Of Bungalow Bill', as well as providing backing vocals on 'Birthday' and 'What's The New Mary Jane'. She also contributed to tape loops, sound effects and spoken-word vocals on that weird "experiment" known as 'Revolution 9'.
* **Gordon Pearce** - Session musician who played double bass on 'She's Leaving Home' and 'A Day In The Life'.
* **Gayleen Pease** - An Apple Scruff, who sang vocals on the World Wildlife Fund version of 'Across The Universe'.
* **J. Power** - Session musician who played trombone on 'Revolution 1' from *The White Album*.
* **Bill Povey** - A jazz mastermind who plays trombone, saxophone and clarinet. He played the tenor saxophone on 'Lady Madonna' and trombone on 'Revolution 1'. He was also a member of Reg Owen And His Orchestra.
* **Raymond Premu** - A late American trombonist, composer and music teacher, who played trombone on 'A Day In The Life'. He also played with The Rolling Stones, Frank Sinatra, Oscar Peterson and Ella Fitzgerald.
* **Billy Preston** - After George Martin, Billy Preston is probably the only other person who deserves the title of 'fifth Beatle' (sixth Beatle?). A friend since the Hamburg days, Preston was brought in by George Harrison to soothe tensions during the turbulent *Get Back* sessions, and when he was around, the band were on their best behaviour, and it showed! He played electric piano on 'Dig A Pony', 'Let It Be', 'Don't Let Me Down', 'I've Got A Feeling', 'The Long And Winding Road', 'One After 909', 'Dig It' and 'Get Back'. He was brought back in for the *Abbey Road* sessions for the song of epic-ness 'I Want You (She's So Heavy)'. He also joined them for their final concert in January 1969 at the rooftop of Apple Studios in London.
* **Tony Randall** - Sharing the same name as an American actor, Tony Randall was a session musician who played French Horn on *Sgt. Pepper's Lonely Hearts Club Band*.
* **Alf Reece** - A jazz tuba player who played on 'Martha My Dear'.
* **Frank Reidy** - A session musician who played the clarinet on 'When I'm Sixty Four'. He is also noted for doing a series of library music albums with British percussionist Eric Allen in the 1970s.
* **Stanley Reynolds** - Not to be mistaken for the prolific Californian sound engineer. Stanley Reynolds played trumpet on 'Martha My Dear'.
* **Jack Richards** - A session violinist who played on 'I Am The Walrus'.

* **Keith Richards** (1943-The End Of Time) - A founder member, lead guitarist and songwriter of The Rolling Stones - the man with the iron constitution! He also sang on the chorus of 'All You Need Is Love'.
* **Stanley Roderick** - A very prolific British trumpet player, who was a member of many bands and orchestras. On his ever-so-busy schedule, he was kind enough to lend a hand playing the trumpet on 'Strawberry Fields Forever'.
* **Lionel Ross** - A member of The Kingsway Symphony Orchestra, who played on 'I Am The Walrus'.
* **Ronnie Ross** - A British jazz baritone saxophonist who played on 'Savoy Truffle'. As well as his work with The Beatles, he also played a baritone sax solo on the Lou Reed hit 'Walk On The Wild Side' in 1972 (as famously sampled by hip-hop group A Tribe Called Quest for their 1990 hit 'Can I Kick It?'), plus he was a saxophone tutor for a young David Bowie. What an interesting life, eh?
* **Jack Rothstein** - A Polish-born violinist, conductor, and future member of The Wombles (!). He also recorded background music for British TV shows including *Last Of The Summer Wine* and *Birds Of A Feather*. Beatle-wise, he played violin on 'Within You Without You' and 'I Am The Walrus'.
* **Neil Sanders** - A prolific French horn player and professor, who was in a series of famous orchestras, and was also the founder of the Fontaine Ensemble. He played the instrument on 'Sgt. Pepper's Lonely Hearts Club Band', 'A Day In The Life' and 'I Am The Walrus'.
* **David Sandeman** - A session musician who played flute on 'A Day In The Life'.
* **Sidney Sax** - A well-known violinist, who was a member of the National Philharmonic Orchestra, as well as having his own band, Sidney Sax and the Harlequins. He played on several Beatles recordings such as 'Yesterday', 'Eleanor Rigby', 'A Day In The Life', 'All You Need Is Love' and 'I Am The Walrus'. Outside of the Beatles, he was well-known for his collaborations with film composer Roy Budd.
* **Paul Scherman** - A Canadian session violinist who played on 'Within You Without You'.
* **Francie Schwartz** - An American scriptwriter who was briefly in a relationship with Paul McCartney. Sang backing vocals on 'Revolution 1'.
* **Ernest Scott** - A Yorkshire-based classical violinist, who was a member of the Quartet Pro Musica. He played violin on 'A Day In The Life'.
* **John Scott** - A famous British composer, conductor, flautist, saxophonist, clarinetist, harpist and vibes player - a real jack-of-all-trades. He

played the famous flute solo on 'You've Got To Hide Your Love Away' from the *Help!* album. Outside of The Beatles, he has worked with Tom Jones, Cilla Black, The Hollies, Nelson Riddle, John Barry and Ravi Shankar.

* **Ronnie Scott** - A very well-known British jazz music legend, who co-founded the famous Ronnie Scott's Jazz Club (my dad played there!) in London's famous Soho district. He played saxophone on the Fabs' hit single 'Lady Madonna' in 1968.

* **Clifford Seville** - A session musician who played flute on 'A Day In The Life'.

* **John Sharpe** - A violinist who played on 'Eleanor Rigby'. He would later play with our Fabs' good pal, Harry Nilsson, a few times, as well as providing string work for comedians Morecambe & Wise's archnemesis, Des O' Connor.

* **Tony Sheridan** - A Norwich-based rock 'n' roll artist who The Beatles befriended during the Hamburg Days, and the Fabs' earliest professional recordings were with this guy, which mainly comprised somewhat corny rock 'n' roll re-workings of traditional songs (see earlier in the book).

* **Stephen Shingles** - A well-known and prolific violist who played on 'Eleanor Rigby' and 'She's Leaving Home'.

* **Pete Shotton** - A member of the Proto-Beatles, The Quarrymen, and one of John Lennon's oldest friends. It is allegedly said that he helped Lennon with the lyrics to 'I Am The Walrus' as well as helping out with the lyrics to 'Eleanor Rigby' with Paul McCartney. It is also said he helped out with the lyrics to 'Penny Lane' and 'Being For The Benefit Of Mr. Kite!' and was the one who suggested the "Hey!" to the start of the refrain of 'You've Got To Hide Your Love Away'. However, this fact has never been established.

* **Derek Simpson** - An English cellist who was known primarily for his work with the Aeolian Quartet, as well as being the teacher for many future cellists. He played cello on 'Eleanor Rigby' and 'Strawberry Fields Forever'.

* **David Smith** - A session clarinetist who played on 'Honey Pie' on *The White Album*.

* **Norman Smith** - AKA Hurricane Smith. This late engineer worked with The Beatles from 1963-1965, around the time of the *Rubber Soul* album, as their sound engineer. He would later work with Pink Floyd, and he had a successful recording career himself in the 1970s under the Hurricane Smith moniker, most notably having a No.2 hit in the UK with 'Don't Let It Die' and an international chart topper with 'Oh Babe, What Would You Say?'. He passed away in 2008, aged 85.

* **Lou Sofier** - A violinist who played on 'Martha My Dear'.

* **Harry Spain** - A session musician who played trombone on 'All You Need Is Love'.
* **Victor Spinetti** - A familiar name in the film world, and for those who read my previous book *Acting Naturally*, Victor Spinetti was a famous actor who starred in the first three of the canon Beatles movies. He even made a backing vocal appearance on a Beatles recording, appearing in the 1967 Fan Club flexi-disc single 'Christmas Time (Is Here Again)'. In 2010, he would cover 'Ob-La-Di, Ob-La-Da' as part of *The Beatles Complete On Ukulele* project, previously mentioned in this book.
* **Maureen Starkey** - Ringo Starr's first wife, who sadly passed away in 1994, and the mother of Zak Starkey (drums with The Who, Oasis among others). Sang backing vocals alongside John's future wife, Yoko Ono, on 'The Continuing Story of Bungalow Bill'.
* **Louis Stevens** - A session musician who played violin on 'I Am The Walrus'.
* **Ray Swinfield** - A saxophonist, flautist and wind player, whose career resumé includes names such as Louis Armstrong, Eartha Kitt, and Bjork, playing on her most famous song 'It's Oh So Quiet'. On the Beatle front, he played flute and piccolo on 'Penny Lane'. He also played with McCartney on his solo tune 'Ballroom Dancing' from the *Give My Regards To Broad Street* album.
* **Christopher Taylor** - A jazz flautist and session musician who recorded many soundtracks to film and television. Played the flute solo on 'The Fool On The Hill' from the 'Magical Mystery Tour' EP/LP. He also played with the London Symphony Orchestra, and performed on many famous soundtracks including *Jesus of Nazareth* and *The Dark Crystal*.
* **Richard Taylor** - The aforementioned Christopher Taylor's brother. He also took part in the flute solo of 'The Fool On The Hill'.
* **Chris Thomas** - A very famous and very prolific producer, who was the co-producer of *The White Album* alongside George Martin. Outside of the Fabs, he has produced for Pink Floyd, U2, Badfinger, Procol Harum, Elton John, Roxy Music, Pete Townshend, The Sex Pistols, The Pretenders, Pulp and many, many more. As well as producing for The Beatles, he played the mellotron on 'The Continuing Story of Bungalow Bill', piano on 'Long, Long, Long', harpsichord on 'Piggies' and both the organ and electric piano on 'Savoy Truffle'. He would later play on George's solo LP *All Things Must Pass*, as well as producing McCartney's final Wings album *Back To The Egg*.
* **Ronald Thomas** - An Australian classical violinist and session musician. He played the violin on two *White Album* cuts, 'Glass Onion' and 'Piggies'.

* **Eddie Thornton** - A Jamaican trumpeter, better known by the name of Tan Tan, whose career has been going since the 1950s. He played the trumpet on the *Revolver* track 'Got To Get You Into My Life'. Outside of The Beatles, he has played with the likes of Georgie Fame, Boney M, 23 Skidoo, Mad Professor, Lily Allen and Kitty, Daisy & Lewis.
* **Basil Tschaikov** - A clarinetist, who played the instrument on 'A Day In The Life'.
* **Tony Tunstall** - A session musician who played French horn on 'I Am The Walrus' and 'Martha, My Dear'.
* **John Underwood** - A classical viola player who played on 'Eleanor Rigby', 'She's Leaving Home', 'A Day In The Life', 'Glass Onion' and 'Piggies'. He would later play on two of Paul McCartney's solo albums *Tug Of War* and *Pipes Of Peace*.
* **Jan Vaughan** - The wife of former Quarryman Ivan Vaughan, who was a childhood friend of John Lennon and Paul McCartney. Jan helped John and Paul with the French lyrics to 'Michelle' from 1965's *Rubber Soul* LP.
* **Dennis Vigay** - A prolific classical cellist who played on 'She's Leaving Home' and 'A Day In The Life'. Like John Underwood, he would later play on two of Paul's solo LPs, *Tug Of War* and *Pipes Of Peace*.
* **Gary Walker** - Real name Gary Leeds. He was the drummer and vocalist of the popular 1960s group The Walker Brothers, and, as of 2023, the only surviving member of the band. He joined along in the chorus of 'All You Need Is Love'.
* **Dennis Walton** - A session woodwind player whose credits included playing with Louis Armstrong and also on the soundtrack to the famous BBC sitcom *Dad's Army*. He played flute and piccolo on 'Penny Lane', as well as saxophone on 'Honey Pie'.
* **Alfred Waters** - A session musician who played bassoon on 'A Day In The Life'.
* **Derek Watkins** - A very prolific trumpeter, whose credentials include playing with Georgie Fame, James Last, Jimmy Nail, Robbie Williams, Westlife, Seal, Frank Sinatra, Barbra Streisand, Eric Clapton, Bill Wyman and most famously, the soundtrack to many films including the James Bond movies as well as the Superman films, *Basic Instinct*, *Bridget Jones' Diary*, *Gladiator*, *Johnny English* and more. Beatle-wise, he played the trumpet on 'Strawberry Fields Forever' and 'Revolution 1'. A true legend in the world of session musicians.
* **Evan Watkins** - A session musician who played trombone on 'All You Need Is Love'.
* **Donald Weekes** - A classical violinist. Donald played violin on 'A Day In The Life' from the *Sgt. Pepper's* album.

* **Terence Weil** - A session musician who played cello on 'I Am The Walrus'. He would also play on Mary Hopkin's 1971 LP for Apple Records, *Earth Song/Ocean Song* (not affiliated with Michael Jackson).
* **Andy White** - Technically, a one-time "member" of The Beatles. As stated previously in this book, White was brought in by George Martin to replace Ringo on the album version of 'Love Me Do' and its B-side 'P.S. I Love You'. He was one of the most prolific session musicians from the late-1950s before his professional retirement in the mid-1970s.
* **John Wilbraham** - A well-known trumpeter and professor, who was in many famous orchestras. He played the trumpet on the title track of the EP/LP 'Magical Mystery Tour'.
* **Trevor Williams** - A British violinist, and professor at the Royal Academy Of Music and at North Carolina University. He played violin on 'She's Leaving Home'.
* **Michael Winfield** - A British cor anglais (English horn) and oboe player and teacher. He played oboe and cor anglais on 'Penny Lane'. Outside of The Beatles, he has worked with Cliff Richard, Linda Lewis and Freddy Cole, but you may know him best for playing the oboe on the theme tune to the famous ITV drama series *Rumpole Of The Bailey*, composed by Joseph Horovitz.
* **Manny Winters** - A session flautist who played flute and piccolo on 'Penny Lane'.
* **David Wolfsthal** - A session musician who played violin on 'Within You Without You'. Like many people on this list, he also played with Barry Gray, on the soundtrack to many of Gerry Anderson's Supermarionation puppet shows.
* **Stanley Woods** - Session musician who played trumpet and flugelhorn on 'All You Need Is Love'.
* **You** - You've bought (or streamed, if you're under 30) their records, so it's YOU who have also contributed to The Beatles' story. Isn't it nice to think that, eh?

CHAPTER EIGHTEEN - WHERE ARE THEY NOW?

What are The Beatles doing today? And what's become of all the other members who were in The Beatles, however briefly?

John Lennon - The founder of our beloved Beatles, and without him, there wouldn't have been The Beatles. John was the first Beatle to marry, which was to his long-term girlfriend, Cynthia Powell, in 1962, and they had a son called Julian, who later became a successful musician in his own right. After divorcing Cynthia in 1968 and leaving the band the following year, Lennon went on to have a very successful solo career, and he and his new wife, Yoko Ono, became famous for their peace activism. Lennon took a hiatus in 1975 to raise his infant son, Sean, before making a comeback in 1980. This was sadly cut short on December 8th of that year, as he was shot dead by a crazed fan outside his apartment in New York City. He was only 40 years old.

Paul McCartney - Despite ridiculous rumours about him being killed in a car crash in 1966, and replaced by a double named William Shears Campbell, Paul McCartney is very much alive and well. After the disbandment of the Fabs, he had a massive solo career and also formed his own very successful band, Wings, in 1971, with his first wife, Linda (who he married in 1969). Linda had one child, Heather, from a previous marriage, and she and Paul had three children, Mary (a successful photographer), Stella (a famous fashion designer) and James (a musician). After an almost-decade-lasting mega-successful career as Wings (particularly in the USA), Macca returned to being a huge solo act. Linda sadly passed away from breast cancer in April 1998, and following a short marriage to Heather Mills from 2002-2008, Paul married American Nancy Shevell in 2011. He is still a successful live performer, selling out stadiums around the world, and in 2022, he headlined Glastonbury Festival at age 80, performing to a record breaking 120,000 happy people - he played for nearly three hours, performing 36 songs, and for the finale, brought out friends Dave Grohl and Bruce Springsteen! His records are still strong sellers, plus he is a philanthropist, an animal rights campaigner, and, as I had the good fortune to meet him backstage in 2018 (see my last book, *Acting Naturally*), I can say that he is a thoroughly nice bloke.

George Harrison - During his time with The Beatles, Harrison married model Patti Boyd in 1966, but they divorced in 1977, and he married Olivia

Arias in 1978. Patti famously married Eric Clapton in 1979. After leaving the Fabs, George also had a very successful solo career, with his acclaimed LP *All Things Must Pass* being the most successful of all The Beatles 'solo albums. As well as embracing Hinduism, he also helped stage the first ever all-star benefit rock concert, The Concert For Bangladesh, and of course was a member of that supergroup of pure awesomeness, The Travelling Wilburys, alongside Bob Dylan, Tom Petty, Roy Orbison and Jeff Lynne. He was also the founder of his own film company, Handmade Films, which he established because he wanted to make sure the Monty Python masterpiece *The Life Of Brian* was made! Handmade would later end up becoming one of Britain's most successful independent film companies. He tragically passed away of lung cancer, aged only 58, in Los Angeles, on the 29th November 2001, leaving Olivia, and son, Dhani, also a musician. His final words were "Love one another."

Ringo Starr - Also during his time with The Beatles, Ringo married Maureen Cox in 1965. They had three children: Zak (now a famous drummer in his own right), Jason, and a daughter, Lee. They divorced in 1975. Like the other Fabs, Ringo also had success going solo, starring in many films, and is arguably the Beatle with the best acting skills, having appeared in movies such as *The Magic Christian* and probably more infamously *The Caveman*, which, on a positive note, is where he met his second wife, Bond girl Barbra Bach. They married in 1981, and they are still together after over 40 years. Outside of music, Ringo may be best known to children for being the narrator of the beloved TV series *Thomas The Tank Engine & Friends* from 1984-1986. Like Paul, Ringo is still performing today with his All-Starr band, though most of his gigs seem to be focused on the United States, where he now lives.

George Martin - The producer for most of The Beatles 'songs, and of course, the honorary fifth member of our Fabs. Martin joined EMI in 1950, managing Parlophone Records 'classical catalogue, and also had success in producing comedy records; he went on to establish a working relationship with Brian Epstein and the artists in his fold. After producing John, Paul, George and Ringo, Martin would work with many big names in music, including Cilla Back, Shirley Bassey, Spike Milligan, Jeff Beck, Kate Bush, Cleo Laine, The Bee Gees, America, Peter Frampton, Aerosmith, Elton John, Celine Dion and many more. He would also help contribute to the main themes of three of the James Bond films. Martin sadly passed away on the 8th March 2016 at this home in Wiltshire, leaving his wife, Judy, and four children - he was 90 years old. His son Greg is an actor, writer and producer, and son Giles followed in his father's footsteps, as a successful music producer; he and his father George helped produce the official 2006 Beatles remix album *Love*, made for the Cirque du Solei show of the same name. Giles has also remastered The Beatles 'back catalogue over the years, and was also the music supervisor for the Beatles TV series in 2021 *The Beatles - Get Back*.

***

Eric Griffiths - An original member of The Quarrymen, the band who ended up becoming The Beatles. After leaving the band in 1957, Griffith would later join the Merchant Navy as a cadet navigator officer. He wanted to keep in touch with his old Beatle buddies, but lost touch with them around the time they started to become famous. He would spend the next 30 years working in the prison service in an attempt to modernise working practices. In 1994, he took over his family business of running a chain of dry cleaners, then returned to music in 1997, when The Quarrymen re-formed around the time of the Cavern Club's 40th anniversary. Griffiths would later pass away of pancreatic cancer on the 29th January 2005 in his home in Edinburgh, aged 64.

Rod Davis - Played banjo with The Quarrymen from 1956-1957 before being replaced by Paul McCartney. He rejoined the reformed Quarrymen in 1997, and has released three solo albums - one with Tony Sheridan in 2001, and two on Scorpion Publications in 2009. He is still performing with The Quarrymen today.

Bill Smith - The first tea chest bass member of The Quarrymen. Like Rod Davis, Smith performs with the reformed Quarrymen today. During the long inactive period before the group reformed, Smith became a caterer for many cruise ships, and in 1963, left Liverpool with his wife to live in South Africa for 40 years. The last time Smith saw John Lennon was in January 1962, when they went to the Storyville Jazz Club in Temple Street, Liverpool, for a couple of pints.

Pete Shotton - One of John Lennon's oldest and dearest friends, and a member of The Quarrymen playing washboard. He remained a friend to Lennon even in the days of The Beatles, and regularly used to visit John and his wife at the time, Cynthia, at his house in Kenwood. Allegedly, he also had a secret hand in the lyrics of several Beatles hits including 'Penny Lane', 'Eleanor Rigby 'and 'I Am The Walrus'. He would later become a businessman, founding an American themed restaurant chain which lasted from 1983-2006 called Fatty Arbuckle's, named after the tragic silent movie star of the same name. Shotton passed away of a heart attack on the 24th March 2017 in his home in Knutsford, Cheshire. He was 75 years old.

Ivan Vaughan - Another childhood friend of Lennon and McCartney. He was a tea chest player for The Quarrymen, and after settling down to family life with a son and daughter in the 1960s, became a teacher. In 1977, Vaughan contracted Parkinson's disease, and wrote a book about his condition *Ivan: Living With Parkinson's Disease*, published in 1986, and he appeared in a 1984 documentary by Jonathan Miller. He sadly passed away of pneumonia on August 16th 1993 in Liverpool, aged 75.

Nigel Walley - An original Quarryman who was one of four tea chest bass players for the group. He was also their manager, even if he didn't set them up with any paid engagements! After leaving The Quarrymen, Walley became one of the youngest golf professionals in Britain, working at Borough Green's Worham Heath Golf Club, and then moving to Austria to the town of Semmering in 1961. Walley sometimes appears on stage with The Quarrymen as a tea chest bass player.

Len Garry - A former Quarryman, and tea chest bass player. After leaving the band, he joined a firm of architects in Liverpool, and then got married and settled down. In 1971, he moved to Chard in Somerset, and became lead vocalist in a rock gospel musical entitled *Come Together*, written by Pat Boone, which toured the south west of England. In 1997, Gary rejoined The Quarrymen, and is still a member today.

Colin Hanton - The original drummer before Ringo and even before Pete Best, back when The Beatles were known as The Quarrymen. He was a member until January 1959, and left after having had an argument with the band, following a performance at the Speke Bus Debut Social Club in Wavetree. He retired from the music industry for several years, until returning for The Quarrymen's reunion in 1995. He occasionally plays with the group today.

John Duff Lowe - Pianist for The Quarrymen for one year only - 1958. After leaving the band, he would join a group called Hobo Rick & The City Slickers, which was fronted by Ricky Tomlinson, who is nowadays a famous comedic actor, best known as Jim Royle from *The Royle Family*. Lowe would later became a stockbroker, and spent a lot of his lunch breaks at The Cavern Club, where lunch was sometimes served by future star, Cilla Black. After leaving the stock market, he became a member of the reformed Quarrymen in the mid 1990s and is still a member today.

Ken Brown - A guitarist for The Quarrymen from 1959-1960. After leaving the band, he would form a short-lived group with Pete Best and Chas Newby called The Blackjacks (which was, coincidentally, the first name of The Quarrymen). After The Blackjacks, Brown never established himself professionally as a musician, though in later years, he did release the odd track through his personal website. He wrote an autobiography entitled *My Life* and subsequently retitled *Some Other Guy*, which remains to this day unpublished. He passed away of emphysema in June 2010 aged 69 years old.

Stuart Sutcliffe - John's good friend from art college, and probably the most mysterious of all The Beatles, who was the bass player from 1960-1961, before being replaced by Paul McCartney. While by all accounts, he wasn't much of a musician, Sutcliffe returned to his true talents of being an artist after leaving The Beatles. Stu fell in love with photographer Astrid Kircherr, who The Beatles befriended in Hamburg, and they were even engaged. Tragically, Stu suffered a severe brain haemorrhage, and passed away aged only 21 on the 10th April 1962 in Hamburg - it is a real shame Sutcliffe never got to see The Beatles become the megastars they ended up being. In 1995, recordings of Stu playing the bass would finally be released to the public as part of the *Anthology* compilation series.

Tommy Moore - A short-lived drummer for The Beatles, who was only in the band from May-June 1960 before being replaced by Pete Best. He is the oldest person to perform in The Beatles, as he was 29 when he was briefly a member. He was in the band during their first professional concert tour, backing the singer Johnny Gentle. Moore continued to work in Liverpool, before dying of a brain haemorrhage on the 29th September 1981, aged 50.

Johnny Hutchinson - A drummer from rival Liverpudlian group, The Big Three, who was a temporary drummer for The Beatles in 1960 for their audition for impresario Larry Parnes. In 1962, Hutchinson (or Hutch as he was nicknamed) was offered to replace Pete Best as the drummer after his sacking, but they eventually went for Ringo Starr. Hutchinson wasn't much of a Beatles fan, and even said they "weren't worth a carrot" - harsh. He died on the 12th April 2019 aged 79.

Cliff Roberts - A member of the now obscure band Cliff Roberts and The Rockers. He played drums for The Beatles (or The Silver-Beats, as they were called for that occasion) on the 14th May 1960 at the Lathom Hall in Liverpool. Roberts would later talk about his time in The Beatles in the critically acclaimed 2013 book *The Fab One Hundred And Four* by David Bedford.

Norman Chapman - Another short-lived drummer, who played in June 1960 for only three shows, but was called up for national service after only a few weeks! He would later play in several local Liverpool bands including Ernie Mack and The Saturated Seven. Chapman sadly died of cancer in July 1995, aged only 58.

Pete Best - "Mean, moody and magnificent", Pete Best is easily the most famous and recognisable of the early members of The Beatles. He was their main drummer from 1960-1962, before being replaced by Ringo Starr. The reasons why Best left the group are debated to this day. After leaving The Beatles, Best would join Lee Curtis and the All-Stars, which then evolved into Pete Best & The All-Stars. They were signed to Decca Records, releasing the unsuccessful single 'I'm Gonna Knock On Your Door'. He then formed The Pete Best Combo, whose repertoire was a hybrid of covers and original tunes. They mainly released tunes on small independent labels, including the rather misleading and cheekily titled album *The Best Of The Beatles* on Savage Records. Best then left the music industry to focus on shift work, but he did however become a technical adviser for the 1979 biopic movie *The Birth Of The Beatles*, directed by Richard Maquand of *Return Of The Jedi* fame. In the mid-1990s good luck finally came to Best's life, as his recordings with The Beatles were used in the *Anthology* compilation series in 1995, and he received a substantial windfall in royalties clocking between £1 million and £4 million. He even has a new group called The Pete Best Band, who have been performing since 1988, and are still doing shows today. Best also appears at many Beatles events around the world.

Chas Newby - A musician who was briefly the bassist for The Beatles in December 1960, when Stuart Sutcliffe was focusing on his art career. After leaving The Beatles, Newby became a maths teacher at Droitwich Spa High School in Droitwich Spa. He would later play for a group called The Racketts, who mainly played at charity events, and in 2016, became the bass player for the reformed Quarrymen, which he still does to this day.

Andy White - After he got, in his own words," into the history books", White would carry on his work as a session drummer, after his very brief stint as a temporary drummer for The Beatles. He would end up playing on hit records such as 'Shout 'by Lulu and' It's Not Unusual 'by Tom Jones, and he worked with the likes of Rod Stewart, Herman's Hermits, Bert

Weedon, Anthony Newley, The BBC Scottish Radio Orchestra… and The Wurzels! He died of a stroke in Caldwell, New Jersey on the 9th November 2015. He was 85 years old.

Jimmie Nichol - A temporary drummer for the Beatles, who was briefly a touring member in 1964, while Ringo suffered a bout of tonsillitis. After leaving The Beatles, Nichol rejoined a previous band of his called The Shubadubs, releasing two unsuccessful singles. He then joined the Swedish group The Spotniks, who actually had a few hit records, having a No.1 in Japan with 1966's 'Karelia'. Nichol left the band in 1967, and was making appearances at Beatles conventions before becoming more reclusive in the 1980s, leading to false rumours about his death. Nowadays, Jimmy Nichol is reluctant to conduct any interviews or talk about his time with The Beatles, and is reportedly living in Mexico.

William Shears Campbell - NEVER WAS A MEMBER AND NEVER WILL BE! William Shears Campbell is a figment of the imagination of some rumourmongering idiots - move along people!

Billy Preston - Another person who deserves the title of "fifth Beatle": Preston, who they had known since the Hamburg days, was brought in to soothe tensions during the turbulent *Get Back/Let It Be* sessions, and was also signed to Apple Records. After The Beatles, he would have a successful solo career of his own, which included the hit songs 'That's The Way God Planned It', 'Will It Go Round In Circles 'and 'Nothing From Nothing'. Unfortunately, Preston suffered from legal issues and drug addiction, and struggled with his homosexuality, at a difficult time for LGBTQI+ people. Preston passed away from pericarditis on the 6th June 2006 aged 59, which was potentially a result of a kidney disease brought on by hypertension.

REFERENCES

[1] https://forums.stevehoffman.tv/threads/beatles-connection-to-the-michael-viners-incredible-bongo-band.206298/
[2] https://en.wikipedia.org/wiki/Cold_Turkey
[3] https://www.the-paulmccartney-project.com/song/penina/
[4] https://www.the-paulmccartney-project.com/song/songbird-in-a-cage/
[5] https://en.wikipedia.org/wiki/Leave_a_Light_On_(Belinda_Carlisle_song)
[6] https://en.wikipedia.org/wiki/Grow_Old_with_Me
[7] https://www.bonhams.com/auctions/19801/lot/395/?category=list
[8] https://www.the-paulmccartney-project.com/song/as-it-comes/
[9] https://www.the-paulmccartney-project.com/album/love-faith-inspiration/
[10] https://www.the-paulmccartney-project.com/song/made-for-you/
[11] https://www.the-paulmccartney-project.com/song/shallow-grave/
[12] https://allenginsberg.org
[13] https://en.wikipedia.org/wiki/Goodbye_(Mary_Hopkin_song)
[14] https://www.the-paulmccartney-project.com/song/best-love/
[15] https://www.the-paulmccartney-project.com/song/live-long-rock-roll/
[16] https://www.the-paulmccartney-project.com/song/mellow-yellow/
[17] https://www.the-paulmccartney-project.com/song/im-the-urban-space-man/
[18] https://www.the-paulmccartney-project.com/song/que-sera-sera/
[19] https://www.the-paulmccartney-project.com/song/the-girl-is-mine/
[20] https://www.the-paulmccartney-project.com/song/hurt-myself/
[21] https://www.the-paulmccartney-project.com/song/heal-the-pain/
[22] https://www.the-paulmccartney-project.com/song/my-soul/
[23] https://en.wikipedia.org/wiki/Hollywood_Vampires_(Hollywood_Vampires_album)
[24] https://www.the-paulmccartney-project.com/song/fourfiveseconds/
[25] https://www.songfacts.com/facts/rodney-crowell/only-happy-when-youre-miserable
[26] https://www.the-paulmccartney-project.com/song/love-song-to-the-earth/
[27] https://comunitaqueeniana.weebly.com/more-of-that-jazz/exclusive-interview-with-doug-bogie-third-bass-player-from-queen
[28] https://en.wikipedia.org/wiki/Is_This_What_You_Want%3F
[29] https://www.the-paulmccartney-project.com/song/peace-dream/
[30] https://www.the-paulmccartney-project.com/song/heres-to-the-nights/
[31] http://www.mottarchive.com/covers_ih18.html
[32] https://www.amazon.co.uk/Beatles-Undercover-Kristofer-K-Engelhardt/dp/1896522432
[33] https://forums.stevehoffman.tv/threads/did-paul-mccartney-play-bass-on-any-of-donovans-records.165696/
[34] https://en.wikipedia.org/wiki/David_Bromberg_(album)
[35] https://www.the-paulmccartney-project.com/album/home-2/
[36] https://www.youtube.com/watch?v=8yllXDn88eI

ABOUT THE AUTHOR

Rory Hoy is a multi-award-winning music producer/DJ, author and film maker. He has released nine albums on various worldwide labels and hundreds of singles, EPs, remixes and collaborations.

In 2018, he wrote the guide to the late 1990s dance music movement, big beat, with *The Little Big Beat Book*, published by New Haven Publishing, to critical and commercial acclaim, in which he interviewed 120 artists from the time, including Fatboy Slim and The Prodigy. A bookazine edition called *The Story of Big Beat* followed a year later. His second music book, *The Beatles – Acting Naturally* was released in 2021, also published by New Haven Publishing, which focused on the more obscure and rare Beatles TV and film appearances.

He has DJ-ed at many major festivals in the UK and his tracks have been used as syncs for the likes of Disney, Google, Sony BET TV, ITV, Costco, Buzzfeed Yellow, FOX TV, Audi, Netflix and Apple +.

He is also a film maker, with the multi-award-winning film, *Autism & Me*, about his own personal experiences living on the autistic spectrum, released on DVD by Jessica Kingsley Publishers. He goes into schools and organisations where they show his film and he talks about autism.

He was the winner of the Yorkshire Young Achiever of the Year Award, hosted by ITV, in the Arts category, which he won alongside actor Mikey North from *Coronation Street*. He won a Film 4 Youth Award, presented by film director Guy Ritchie at the showing of his *Autism & Me* film at the Waterfront Hall in Belfast. He was nominated for a Royal Television Society Award, has a UNICEF Award, 4Front Award and Wavemakers Award among others. He's Youth Patron of the London based charity Resources for Autism, and in this capacity was invited to a special reception at the House of Lords. He was a Centenary Ambassador for the national charity UK Youth, and featured in their promotional film. He continues to be an Ambassador for them. He was invited to be a Royal Commonwealth Associate Fellow. He is also an Ambassador for the charity Henshaws, which supports people with sight loss and other disabilities to go beyond expectations - something we should all strive to achieve.

Ingram Content Group UK Ltd.
Milton Keynes UK
UKHW020719050523
421275UK00011B/266